HARVARD STUDIES
IN COMPARATIVE LITERATURE

HARVARD STUDIES
IN COMPARATIVE LITERATURE

VOLUME XI

LONDON : HUMPHREY MILFORD

OXFORD UNIVERSITY PRESS

HARVARD STUDIES IN COMPARATIVE LITERATURE
VOLUME XI

CHAUCER'S USE OF PROVERBS

BY

BARTLETT JERE WHITING

CAMBRIDGE

HARVARD UNIVERSITY PRESS

1934

PRINTED AT THE HARVARD UNIVERSITY PRESS
CAMBRIDGE, MASS., U. S. A.

TO

FRED NORRIS ROBINSON

PREFACE

IN THIS volume Chaucer's proverbs and other proverbial material are studied in relation to their context. Chaucer's usage is compared with that of other writers of his time or before, and appendices contain the proverbial material, or references to it, in the *fabliaux*, the works of Eustache Deschamps, and the French and English works of John Gower. The proverbs from all these writings have been extracted before, but the present collections are fuller than any others, especially in the case of the proverbial phrases. My original plan to furnish a finding-index to Chaucer's proverbs and to give other occurrences of the proverbs was abandoned because these would have more than doubled the length of the volume. Then, too, I am engaged in the preparation of a dictionary of English proverbs recorded before 1550, which will contain copious later examples, and it did not seem wise to duplicate a part of this work. Notes to the various editions of Chaucer, especially those of Skeat and Robinson, in conjunction with G. L. Apperson's *English Proverbs and Proverbial Phrases* (London, 1929), furnish many illustrative examples. Since a finding-index was not feasible, a full table of contents takes the place of an index of Chaucer's works.

A threefold division of proverbial material is followed in this volume: proverbs, sententious remarks, and proverbial phrases. I consider as proverbs sayings which are, or appear to be, popular in origin, or which have become thoroughly popular in use, while sententious remarks show clearly their learned origin. A proverbial phrase is not ordinarily a directly monitory piece of wisdom. I have segregated the comparisons from the other proverbial phrases. For a further discussion of the matter of definition I may refer to my article in *Harvard Studies and Notes in Philology and Literature*, XIV (1932), 273 ff. It is sometimes very hard to distinguish between a proverb and a sententious remark, and I can scarcely hope that all readers will agree with all my decisions. Inevitably, too, some readers will feel, and perhaps rightly, that I have put in things which should have been left out and left out things which should have been put in. Many people, I have discovered, hold very definite views as to what does or does not constitute a proverb in a particular instance. It is especially difficult to feel secure about the identification of proverbs in another language than one's own. In general I have tried to be inclusive rather than exclusive.

All quotations from Chaucer are from the text of
Fred Norris Robinson (Boston, 1933). For the
Canterbury Tales the groups are indicated by letters
as well as numerals, and in the case of group VII
(formerly treated as part of group B) the line num-
berings of Skeat's edition are given in addition to
those of Robinson's. There will be, therefore, no
difficulty in locating a saying in Skeat's edition.
Citations of the collections of Chaucer's proverbs
made by Haeckel (referred to as *H*) and Skeat (referred to as *S*) are given throughout.

My personal acknowledgments are few but
great. This book was a section of my doctoral dis-
sertation written under Professor George Lyman
Kittredge, and Professor Kittredge also has read
the proof. Professor Hyder Edward Rollins was
kind enough to read the manuscript, and Professor
Francis Peabody Magoun, Jr., read both manuscript and proof. The reader should join me in
gratitude to them for numerous corrections and
emendations. The proof-reading staff of the Harvard University Press coöperated freely and effectively. My wife assisted me in many ways.

The dedication of this volume expresses but
poorly the gratitude and affection which I share
with the host of his students for the genial scholar
who introduced us to the study of Chaucer.

Finally I must not fail to acknowledge the encouragement which a Freshman in Harvard College gave me, perhaps unwittingly, in 1927. The young scholar was discussing the modernity of Chaucer:

> In the *Canterbury Tales* we find him frequently using such maxims, which are nowadays common, as "Mordre wol out." In this respect I think he was ahead of his time. Not simply because he was able to state some maxims, but because he knew enough of life *to realize their truth.*

B. J. W.

LOWELL HOUSE,
CAMBRIDGE, MASSACHUSETTS,
January 17, 1934.

CONTENTS

CHAUCER'S USE OF PROVERBS

CHAPTER I

INTRODUCTION

MUCH has been written about Chaucer's style. The keenness of observation, the depth of understanding, the richness of humor, the sensibility to pathos, the skill in delineation, all the things which help to make Chaucer one of the great poets, have been pointed out again and again. His use of the poet's tool, language, has been discussed often enough, and scholars have analyzed his vocabulary, his grammar, his choice of words, and his exquisite command of metre. Even more attention has been paid to his sources, and if it is a boast to say that we can trace Chaucer's reading almost, if not quite, to the day of his death, we do not boast without some good reason. A vast library of writings on Chaucer has grown up within the last eighty years, and yet little or no systematic attention has been paid to the subject which I propose to discuss, namely, Chaucer's use of proverbial material. No other poet of repute has made so considerable a use of proverbial material as Chaucer, and no one else ever used it so skillfully and effectively. He used proverbs to heighten characterization: the wise saws of Pandarus are as much a part of that engaging and abused companion of Troilus as are his courage and unfailing humor. Chaucer used proverbs to cap a climax, to emphasize a situation; he used them seriously and he used them humorously. He made them a part of his style, and his frequent quotations of them tell us as clearly as one of his contemporaries might have done that, just as Chaucer was a man who dreamed much, so, too, he was a man who loved and appreciated the rich pawky wisdom of the folk. Chaucer's usage disproves the appealing but fallacious belief that because proverbs spring from the folk they are common in literature close to the folk and uncommon in more artistic flights.[1] The ballad and the romance, two literary types which appeal strongly to the folk, contain relatively few proverbs, while Gower and Chaucer use many. The mediaeval drama is an apparent exception, since it abounds in proverbs, but this exception is more apparent than real, since the drama has always been universal in its appeal.

Although Chaucer's use of proverbs has never been studied with care, mention of their frequent appearance in his works was made at an early date; they have been collected at least twice, and numerous notes have been written on the meaning and possible source of individual items.

Scarcely twenty years after Chaucer's death, his admirer and self-styled disciple, Lydgate, wrote that Chaucer adorned his works

> With many prouerbe / diuers and vnkouth,
> Be rehersaile / of his Sugrid mouth.[2]

Lydgate may have modeled his own practice on this trait which he observed in his master's writings. Thirty years later the same trait was mentioned again, this time by John Metham of Norwich,

> My mastyr Chauncerys, I mene, that longe dyd endure
> In practyk off rymyng; qwerffore proffoundely
> With many prouerbys, hys bokys be rymyd naturelly.[3]

The first editorial recognition of Chaucer's proverbs was made by Thomas Speght, who put on the title-page of his second edition (1602) of Chaucer's works the statement, "Sentences and Prouerbes noted," and again in his preface to the reader, "Prouerbes and Sentences marked." [4] From this time on references to individual proverbs are relatively frequent.[5] Ann Bowyr brought together a number in her commonplace book in 1653 or thereabouts.[6] Richard Brathwaite, who wrote in 1665 the first detailed criticism of Chaucer,[7] quotes many proverbs from the tales which he is discussing and adds parallels.[8] Incidentally, we may note that Chaucer's most famous work seems to have given rise to a proverbial saying as early as 1549, when the editor of Latimer's sermons wrote, " We might as well spend that time in reading of profane histories, of Cantorburye tales, or a fit of Robyn Hode." [9] The phrase was also used by Cranmer.[10] In these earliest uses the term "a Canterbury Tale" means a profane story, but gradually [11] it took on the sense of "a long roundabout tale," as Francis Grose (1785) defines "Canterbury Story." [12] Another proverbial phrase, of uncertain but probably bawdy significance, which was current in the sixteenth and seventeenth centuries, is "Chaucer's jest." [13]

The first collection of Chaucer's proverbs of any scope was made by Willi Haeckel,[14] but it is without introductory comment on Chaucer's usage, and is incomplete. In *Das Bild bei Chaucer* [15] Friedrich Klaeber deals with many of Chaucer's comparative phrases, but the book, despite its fullness, is somewhat over-arranged and consequently is less useful for ready reference than it otherwise would be. Examples from Chaucer bulk large in W. W. Skeat's *Early English Proverbs*,[16] but the editor was not especially interested in proverbial phrases and sententious remarks, and he omits many of both.

In order to avoid a multiplicity of detail and to escape an apparent over-emphasis on less important aspects of the question, I have limited my discussion to Chaucer's use of proverbs and sententious remarks. The proverbial phrases I shall give, with the comparisons segregated, in alphabetical order.

Since at the outset it will be useful to gain a comprehensive view of the amount of proverbial material in Chaucer's works and its distribution throughout the various pieces, I have drawn up the following table; the length of the various poems in lines is given.

PROVERBIAL MATERIAL IN CHAUCER'S WORKS

	Lines	Proverbs	Proverbial Phrases		Sententious Remarks
			Comp.	Others	
Romaunt of the Rose, A ..	1705		22	2	6
" " " " B ..	4105	13	15	13	37
" " " " C ..	1885	6		8	13
Book of the Duchess	1334		4	9	6
House of Fame	2158	6	22	8	7
Anelida and Arcite	357	1	3	7	3
Parliament of Fowls	699	2	5	6	10
Boece	75 pages			1	7
Troilus and Criseyde	8239	61	32	55	67
Legend of Good Women ..	2723	3	25	6	6
Prol. F & G			2	1	8
Prol. F only			2		2
Prol. G only					3
Astrolabe	22 pages	1	1		
SHORT POEMS					
A.B.C.	184		1		
Pite	119		1	1	
Lady	127			1	
Mars	298		2	3	2
Rosemounde	24		2		

	Lines	Proverbs	Proverbial Phrases		Sententious Remarks
			Comp.	Others	
Womanly Noblesse	32		1		
Adam	7				
Former Age	63				
Fortune	79				1
Truth	28	2	1	1	
Gentilesse	21				1
Lak of Stedfastnesse	28				
Venus	82				
Scogan	49			2	
Bukton	32				3
Empty Purse	26		1		
Women Inconstant	21		1	1	
Amorous Complaint	91				
Merciles Beaute	39			1	
Balade of Complaint	21				
Proverbs	8				2

CANTERBURY TALES

	Lines	Proverbs	Proverbial Phrases		Sententious Remarks
			Comp.	Others	
General Prologue	858	1	31	7	7
Knight's Tale	2250	12	32	6	18
Miller's Prol.	78	2		4	1
Miller's Tale	668	3	23	12	6
Reeve's Prol.	66	1	1	5	4
Reeve's Tale	404	7	12	10	
Cook's Prol.	40	2			
Cook's Tale	58	1	3		1
Man of Law's Prol.	133	1		3	6
Man of Law's Tale	1030		7		8
Shipman's Prol.	28			1	
Wife of Bath's Prol.	856	14	10	19	25
Wife of Bath's Tale	408	2	3	2	7
Friar's Prol.	36				
Friar's Tale	364	1	3	1	2
Summoner's Prol.	44		2		
Summoner's Tale	586	1	10	3	6
Clerk's Prol.	56		1		2

	Lines	Proverbs	Proverbial Phrases		Sententious Remarks
			Comp.	Others	
Clerk's Tale	1156	1	10	3	8
Merchant's Prol.	32				
Merchant's Tale	1174	5	20	16	14
Merchant's Epil.	22		2		
Introduction to Squire's Tale	8				
Squire's Tale	672	4	10	3	9
Words of the Franklin	36			21	
Franklin's Prol.	20				
Franklin's Tale	896	2	3	2	2
Physician's Tale	286	1	2	1	4
Words of the Host	42	1			
Pardoner's Prol.	134		2	1	1
Pardoner's Tale	506	1	1	2	4
Shipman's Tale	434		7	4	2
Words of the Host	18		1	1	
Prioress's Prol.	35				
Prioress's Tale	202				1
Prol. to Sir Thopas	21		1		
Sir Thopas	207		8	1	
Prol. to Melibee	48			1	
Tale of Melibee	24 pages	9		1	46
Monk's Prol.	102	1	1	1	1
Monk's Tale	776		2		6
Nun's Priest's Prol.	54			2	1
Nun's Priest's Tale	626	3	6	3	7
Nun's Priest's Epil.	16	1	1		
Second Nun's Prol.	119				
Second Nun's Tale	434		5		2
Canons Yeoman's Prol. ...	166		2		2
Canons Yeoman's Tale ...	762	6	4	6	3
Manciple's Prol.	104			4	
Manciple's Tale	258	1	1	3	12
Parson's Prol.	74				1
Parson's Tale	42 pages	6	2	3	18
Total	41,987	187	372	258	421

There are, then, in 41,987 lines of verse (plus one hundred sixty-three pages of prose) one hundred eighty-six proverbs, six hundred thirty phrases, three hundred seventy-two of which are comparisons, and four hundred twenty-one sententious remarks. This represents a larger proportion than is found in any other group of Middle-English poems of an equal number of lines.

We may ask ourselves, Was Chaucer original in his generous use of proverbs, or did he find precedent in his sources? It would be invidious to comb all the works which Chaucer read, or may well have read, for proverbs. His favorite Latin poets, Virgil and Ovid, are largely free from proverbs. Dante uses almost no proverbs and Boccaccio relatively few.[17] The French authors, however, teem with proverbs, and I have chosen two groups of French poems, one the work of a single poet and the other the extant examples of a type, to compare with Chaucer. The single author chosen is Deschamps, the type the *fabliau*, and both author and type were well known to Chaucer.[18] I shall also consider the possible influence of the mediaeval rhetoricians on Chaucer's use of proverbs.

Eustace Deschamps was perhaps the most voluminous of the French poets coeval with Chaucer. His extant writings run to over 80,000 lines of

verse, the bulk of which consists of *ballades*. One
of the conventions of the *ballade* was the use of
proverbs, not only because the *ballades* "lent themselves easily to gnomic uses," but because "the
proverb as a line unit frequently offered a quick
solution of what might otherwise have been a difficult rime-problem." [19] We may expect to find
Deschamps rich in proverbial material, nor are we
disappointed.[20] Deschamps uses eighty proverbs,[21]
twenty-three of which occur more than once; fifty-
two appear in refrains. An example or two will
show how the proverb becomes an integral part of
the *ballade*:

QUI VEUT TUER SON CHIEN L'ACCUSE DE LA RAGE

> Qui ayme bien ne croit pas de legier
> Que son ami lui voulsist nul mal faire,
> Ne qu'il vouldroit contre lui pourchacier;
> Mais au jour d'uy sont maint de tel affere,
> Et ont le cuer si lasche et si contraire
> A fermeté de vray et bon amour
> Qu'ilz se glacent et quierent la rumour
> A ce qu'amer deussent, s'ilz fussent saige,
> En diffamant leur ami; c'est folour:
> Qui son chien het, on li met sus la raige.

> Et comment puet un loial cuer cuidier
> Que vray ami se voulsist contrefaire,
> Qui prest ne fust pour son ami aidier?
> Puis qu'amis est, il se lairoit detraire
> A bons chevaulx, ains qu'il voulsist retraire
> De son ami ou blasme ou deshonour;
> Mais cil qui croit pour neant tel errour
> A cuer coulant, et cuide estre volaige,

Comme le sien, cuer d'ami plain d'onnour:
Qui son chien het, on lui met sus la raige.

Las! quel peril de croire losangier
Sur son ami! Cil vault pis que Macaire
Le traitreux, quant il point par derriere;
On le devroit a un gibet deffaire;
A toutes gens doit un menteur desplaire,
Car par son fait vient haine et tristour,
Perte d'amis, tous maulx, toute dolour;
Diable ont menteurs si fort mis en usaige
Qu'om voit par eulx et de nuit et de jour:
Qui son chien het, on lui met sus la raige.

L'Envoy

Prince, bon fait le cuer avoir entier,
Sanz contre ami croire ainsis en derrier;
Du losangier eschivés le langaige
Et en tous temps tenez vostre ami chier,
On ne doit pas encontre lui clochier:
Qui son chien het, on lui met sus la raige.[22]

DEUX CHIENS POUR UN OS, C'EST TROP

N'a gaires que je m'en aloie
Pour querir mon esbatement
O deux levriers que moult amoye,
Nourriz d'un let; mais en alant,
Treuvent un os qu'ilz vont rungant,
Dont entr'eulx mut trop grans rios,
Et se combatent durement:
Deux chiens sont mauvais a un os.

A grant paine l'os leur tolloie
Et les desmeslay en present.
Mais ainsis que je retournoie,
Vy deux gens qui vont riotant:
Pour amours ont trop grant content,
Car, bien l'entendi par leurs mos,
Pour une dame seulement:
Deux chiens sont mauvais a un os.

> Lors dis que je retourneroie.
> Si fis je, mais en retournant
> Viz gens de court, que vous diroye?
> Qui s'aloient fort regrignant,
> Tous d'un estat, chascun contempt
> D'estre seulz et d'avoir le loz.
> Pour ce dit on communement:
> Deux chiens sont mauvais a un os.[23]

Of proverbial comparisons we find in Deschamps eighty-six, thirty-two of which occur more than once; only two appear in refrains; the comparisons are poetical rather than popular. The absence of these decorative phrases in the refrains is striking. There are ninety-seven other proverbial phrases, fifteen of which occur more than once; twenty-two appear in refrains. Some *ballades* are especially rich in proverbial phrases. In fact, when Deschamps wrote a "proverbial" *ballade* he filled it not so much with proverbs as with proverbial phrases:

VANITÉ DES REMONTRANCES

> Ie ne finay depuis longtemps
> De ramentevoir les vertus,
> Des vices blamer, et les sens
> De mon pouoir remettre sus:
> Et lors vint a moy un bossus
> Qui me dit: "Dieu gart le varlet
> Qui prant les asnes a la glus!
> Tu bas bien l'eaue d'un pilet.
>
> "Veulz tu du doy arer les champs?
> Veulz tu planter bois de festus?

Au cul de l'asne fais tes chans;
Tu bas froit fer, tu es deçus;
Tu chantes comme li cucus
Qui s'estonne et gaste son plet;
Tais toy, des or ne chante plus:
Tu bas bien l'eaue d'un pilet.

"Veulz tu faire loups innocens
Et que les eufs soient velus?
Veulz tu les petis faire grans
Et les saiges des malostrus?
Parle, tes parlers est perdus,
Autant vault le vent d'un souflet;
L'en t'oit bien, c'est tout; si conclus:
Tu bas bien l'eaue d'un pilet."

L'Envoy

Princes, quant cilz la se fut teus,
Et j'oy bien pensé a mon fet,
Vray il me dist, et bien congnus:
Tu bas bien l'eaue d'un pilet.[24]

INUTILITÉ DE SERMONNER LES MÉCHANTS

Trop me merveil de rude entendement
Qui oit et voit, et si ne veult entendre
Ce que je di et pour son sauvement.
— Vous estes sot qui le cuidez aprandre;
Congnoissance l'a de tous fait le mendre;
Il vous oit bien, mais il ne lui en chaut,
Autant vaudroit batre son cul au chaut.
Ou enseignier a harper dix mulès
Que de parler a lui ne bas ne hault:
Chantez a l'asne, il voud fera des pès.

— Que dictes vous? Vous parlez folement;
Ne doit pas homs a toutes vertus tendre
Et eschiver les vices telement
Que de nul mal ne se face reprandre?

Esperit a de raison; si doit tendre
Aux biens de Dieu; la retarder le fault;
Beste bruthe sanz esperit default
De ce regart, en terre est touz ses fès.
— C'est bien romflé; vostre preschier n'y vault.
Chantez a l'asne, il vous fera des pès.

Pourrez vous bien le cours du firmament
Faire muer? eaue devenir cendre,
Et d'un pourcel creer une jument,
Et faire Dieu en la terre descendre?
— Certes nenil. — Neant plus entreprandre
Ne devez vous a rude cuer l'assaut;
Par l'une entre, par l'autre oreille sault
Ce qu'on lui dit, n'est que riote et plès;
Depportez vous d'enseignier tel vassaut:
Chantez a l'asne, il vous fera des pès.

L'Envoy

Princes, cil pert les biens qui veult comprandre
A homme sourt d'enseigner loing ne prés;
A rude engin ne doit son sens estandre:
Chantez a l'asne, il vous fera des pès.[25]

Deschamps uses one hundred sententious remarks, thirty-three of which occur more than once; sixty-one appear in refrains. The sententious remarks, for the most part, are thoroughly mediaeval in their gloom. One of his favorite themes is the instability of human affairs. This forms the refrain of four ballads, expressed in various ways: "C'est tout noient en la conclusion," [26] "Riens estable ne say dessoubz la nue," [27] "Ainsis va chascuns a sa fin," [28] "C'est tout neant des choses de

ce monde." [29] He finds a sad joy in reiterating the
inevitability of death, the theme of four refrains:
"Advise qu'il te fault mourir," [30] "Que chascun
muert et ne puet sçavoir quant," [31] "Tuit y mourront, et li fol et li saige," [32] "Car homme n'est qui
ait point de demain." [33]

That Deschamps had a great interest in proverbial material is unquestioned, but we cannot help
wondering if he would have used so many proverbs
had his verse form been different. There are one
hundred eighty-two expressions of wisdom, proverbs, and sententious remarks, but one hundred
twelve of these are structural parts of the poems in
which they appear, and their use is dictated by con-
vention. Even if we include Chaucer's prose, two
considerable sections of which are almost free from
proverbs,[34] the bulk of his writing is only three-
quarters of that of Deschamps; and yet Chaucer
used almost five hundred expressions of wisdom,
very few of which can be called structural.

The general influence of Deschamps on Chaucer
was considerable, though no more, certainly, than
that of the *fabliaux*.[35] These poems, few of them
seemly and many quite shocking, were the models
which Chaucer used in the years of his artistic maturity. His own *fabliaux*, such as the tales of the
Miller and the Reeve, are unquestionably based on
French poems similar in every way to those in

Montaiglon's collection. Montaiglon brought together one hundred fifty-seven poems (a few of them variants of the same story), aggregating over forty-three thousand lines. We have here, then, a body of verse roughly comparable in bulk to the poetry of Chaucer. Proverbial material is frequent in the *fabliaux*, and much of it has a structural use. There are seventy-three proverbs,[36] of which twelve appear more than once. Sixteen of these appear in the last line or lines of *fabliaux*, and fifteen others within the last ten or fifteen lines. In two cases proverbs appear in the first line, and in three others they appear near the beginning. There are fifty-nine proverbial comparisons, ten of which are repeated, and fifty other proverbial phrases, six of which are repeated; in the nature of things some of these inevitably appear either at the beginning or the end of a poem, but there is nothing to indicate design. When we come to the sententious remarks, we find a usage similar to that noticed in the case of the proverbs. There are seventy-seven such remarks; of these fifteen constitute the endings of *fabliaux* and seven others appear near the end. In other words, about fifty *fabliaux* conclude with a more or less crystallized expression of wisdom. This cannot be accidental and, indeed, to begin or end a poem with a proverb is one of the methods recognized and approved

by the mediaeval rhetoricians.[37] Matthieu de Ven-
dôme [38] and Geoffroi de Vinsauf [39] recommend the
proverb highly as a fitting and artistic beginning
or end for a literary work. To find that the *fabliaux* observe the rules of the rhetoricians is no
small surprise to the average reader, but in reality
these stories of low life were often written by men
of learning, if not taste, and are among the most
highly sophisticated of mediaeval literary types.
In this rhetorical fondness for ending poems with
proverbs we have a link between the *fabliaux* and
Chaucer. Chaucer was interested in rhetoric, or,
at all events, some of his characters were,[40] and
this aspect of Chaucer scholarship has received
considerable attention of late.[41] Chaucer used
proverbs or sententious remarks at the beginning
of literary units four times,[42] and at the end in the
case of six pieces.[43] A single proverb is used in most
cases, but there are four in the prologue to Book II
of *Troilus and Criseyde*, and the *Manciple's Tale*
ends with a stream of proverbs, poured out pell-
mell. Manly and Naunin [44] argue, or assume, that
this use of proverbs to open or conclude a story is
taken by Chaucer from the precepts of the rhetoricians. To deny these assumptions would be
futile, but one cannot help thinking that Chaucer
was more likely to be influenced by Deschamps —
whose use of proverbs as refrains amounted to

ending a poem with them — and the writers,
anonymous or known, of the *fabliaux*. That Deschamps and the *fabliau* writers were somewhat influenced by the rhetoricians is not to be denied.
Deschamps is far more technically rhetorical than
Chaucer, and he does not display Chaucer's tend-
ency to make fun of rhetoric. Chaucer knew about
the rhetoricians and schools of rhetoric, just as the
Franklin knew that colors of rhetoric somehow were
supposed to improve a story. But Chaucer also
knew that he could get a better effect, as in the
Nun's Priest's Tale,[45] by burlesquing the methods
of the rhetoricians than by following them in all
seriousness. The Franklin, too, knew that after
disclaiming knowledge of "colours of rethoryk,"
his use of them, as in the famous lines on the coming of night,[46] would fetch a laugh, or an appreciative smile at least, from half his fellow-pilgrims.
To say that the Franklin employed these figures in
all simplicity, or better, in all artificiality, and only
afterwards bethought himself, is to do both him
and Chaucer a grave injustice. It is this ever present jocularity that makes one doubt any very real
influence of the rhetoricians on Chaucer. Much
that is called rhetorical in Chaucer [47] and other
writers of his time is really one manifestation or
another of the spirit of the age. The mediaeval
fondness for sententiousness is no more dependent

on textbooks than the equally common predilection
for citing authorities. Matthieu and Geoffroi and
John of Garland and the rest were in part holding
to the traditions of the classical rhetoricians, and
in part formulating the literary manners and
customs of their contemporaries. The mediaeval
rhetoricians did not create or direct — they
codified.[48]

CHAPTER II

WORKS OTHER THAN *TROILUS AND CRISEYDE* AND THE *CANTERBURY TALES*

(1) *Romaunt of the Rose*

THERE are no proverbs in the A-fragment of the *Romaunt of the Rose*,[1] but we do find six sententious remarks all matched in the French source.[2] The poem opens with the famous rationalization about dreams, quoted later in Cato's version by Pertelote:

Many men sayn that in sweveninges
Ther nys but fables and lesynges.   (A 1 f. [*H* 129])

> Maintes genz dient que en songes
> N'a se fables non e mençonges.   (II, 1, ll. 1 f.)

When the Lover beholds the sad pictures on the outside of the walls surrounding the garden of Love, he sees among other personified misfortunes Time, and the sight calls forth the following passages:

The tyme, that passeth nyght and day,
And resteles travayleth ay,
And steleth from us so prively
That to us semeth sykerly
That it in oon poynt dwelleth ever,
And certes, it ne resteth never,

But goth so faste, and passeth ay,
That ther nys man that thynke may
What tyme that now present is.   (A 369 ff. [S 240])

> Li Tens qui s'en vait nuit e jor,
> Senz repos prendre e senz sejor,
> E qui de nos se part e emble
> Si celeement qu'il nos semble
> Qu'il s'arest adès en un point,
> Et il ne s'i areste point,
> Ainz ne fine de trespasser,
> Que l'en ne puet neïs penser
> Queus tens ce est qui est presenz.   (II, 20, ll. 361 ff.)

The tyme, that may not sojourne,
But goth, and may never retourne,
As watir that doun renneth ay,
But never drope retourne may.   (A 381 ff.)

> Li Tens qui ne puet sejorner,
> Ainz vait toz jorz senz retorner,
> Con l'eve qui s'avale toute,
> N'il n'en retorne arriere goute.   (II, 20, ll. 373 ff.)

We shall see later how part of this same concept of Time is to haunt the energetic Host.[3]

Poverty, too, last but far from least among the enemies of Youth and Joy and Love, is to be dreaded:

For pover thing, whereso it be,
Is shamefast and dispised ay.   (A 466 f.)

> Car povre chose, ou qu'ele soit,
> Est toz jorz honteuse e despite.   (II, 24, ll. 456 f.)

Inside the garden the Lover sees Liberality, and says of her:

Not Avarice, the foule caytyf,
Was half to gripe so ententyf,
As Largesse is to yeve and spende;
And God ynough alwey hir sende,
So that the more she yaf awey
The more, ywys, she hadde alwey.   (A 1155 ff.)

Nes Avarice la chaitive
N'iert pas si a prendre ententive
Con Largece estoit de doner;
E Deus li faisoit foisoner
Toz ses biens, qu'ele ne savoit
Tant doner come el plus avoit.   (II, 58 f., ll. 1133 ff.)

In *Romaunt* B and C there are nineteen proverbs and fifty sententious remarks, but as these
fragments are certainly not Chaucer's work I shall
do no more than list the sayings.

PROVERBS

"For evermore gladly," as I rede,
"Brent child of fir hath myche drede."
                   (B 1819 f. [*H* 68; *S* 286])

E me doit bien espoenter,
Qu'eschaudez doit eve doter.   (II, 92, ll. 1783 f.)

For men that yift holde more dere,
That yeven is with gladsom chere.
That yift nought to preisen is,
That man yeveth maugre his.   (B 2383 ff.)

Car l'en doit chose avoir mout chiere
Qui est donee a bele chiere,
E je ne pris le don un pois
Que l'en done desus son pois.   (II, 116, ll. 2261 ff.)

Whereso [thou] comest in ony coost,
Who is next fyr, he brenneth moost.   (B 2477 f. [*H* 56b])

Ce sevent tuit sage e musart:
Qui plus est près dou feu plus art.   (II, 121, ll. 2357 f.)

Who serveth a feloun is yvel quit.   (B 3146 [*H* 139])
Qui felon sert itant en a.   (II, 148, l. 2932)

The see may never be so stille
That with a litel wynde it nille
Overwhelme and turne also,
As it were wood, in wawis goo.
Aftir the calm the trouble sone
Mot folowe and chaunge as the moone.   (B 3773 ff.)

La mer n'iert ja si apaisiee
Qu'el ne soit troble a poi de vent.   (II, 175, ll. 3494 f.)

For he may best, in every cost,
Disceyve, that men tristen most.   (B 3931 f.)

Car je voi bien e sai de fi
Que en meillor garde pert l'en.   (II, 180 f., ll. 3614 f.)

This have I herd ofte in seiyng,
That man[ne] may, for no dauntyng,
Make a sperhauk of a bosard.   (B 4031 ff. [*H* 117])

Ce oï dire en reprovier,
Ne l'en ne puet faire esprevier
En nule guise de busart.   (II, 185, ll. 3701 ff.)

Thy tyme thou shalt biwepe sore,
The whiche never thou maist restore;
For tyme lost, as men may see,
For nothyng may recovered be.   (B 5121 ff. [*H* 144b])

Le tens qu'avras perdu plourras,
Mais recouvrer ne le pourras.   (II, 225, ll. 4623 f.)

For whanne he woot his secre thought,
The thridde shal knowe therof right nought;
For tweyne of noumbre is bet than thre
In every counsell and secre.   (B 5257 ff. [*H* p. 69])

Quant son secré dit li avra,
Jamais li tierz ne le savra.   (II, 229 f., ll. 4729 f.)

For every wis man, out of drede,
Can kepe his tunge til he se nede;
And fooles can not holde her tunge;
A fooles belle is soone runge.   (B 5263 ff. [*H* 61; *S* 139])

Car sages on sa langue garde;
Ce ne savrait mie fos faire:
Nus fos ne set sa langue taire.   (II, 230, ll. 4732 ff.)

For freend in court ay better is
Than peny in purs, certis.   (B 5541 f. [*H* 15])

Qu'adès vaut meauz amis en veie
Que ne font denier en courreie.   (II, 238, ll. 4947 f.)

He undirfongith a gret peyne,
That undirtakith to drynke up Seyne.   (B 5709 f. [*H* 58])

Emprise a merveilleuse peine:
Il bee a beivre toute Seine.   (II, 243, ll. 5081 f.)

Bigiled is the giler than.   (B 5759 [*S* 237])
Deceüz est teus decevierres.   (II, 244, l. 5109)

Abit ne makith neithir monk ne frere.   (C 6192 [*H* 133])
La robe ne fait pas le moine.   (III, 185, l. 11058)

What shulde he yeve that likketh his knyf?
It is but foly to entremete,
To seke in houndes nest fat mete.   (C 6502 ff.)

Que donra qui son coutel leche?   (III, 193, l. 11254)

But I, that were my symple cloth,
Robbe bothe robbed and robbours
And gile giled and gilours.   (C 6822 ff.)

Mais je, qui vest ma simple robe,
Lobant lobez e lobeeurs,
Robe robez e robeeurs.   (III, 205, ll. 11550 ff.)

I take youresilf to recorde heere,
That men ne may in no manere
Teren the wolf out of his hide,
Til he be flayn, bak and side,
Though men hym bete and al defile.   (C 7311 ff. [*H* p. 70])

> Car, a tesmoing vous en apel,
> L'en ne peut oster de sa pel
> Le lou tant qu'il seit escorchiez,
> Ja tant n'iert batuz ne torchiez.   (III, 224, ll. 11995 ff.)

It is nat al soth thyng that semeth.   (C 7544 [*H* 132])

> Dire vous os tout en apert
> Qu'il n'est pas veirs quanqu'il apert.   (III, 233, ll. 12217 f.)

All is not gospel, out of doute,
That men seyn in the town aboute.   (C 7607 f. [*H* 134])

> Sire, tout n'est pas evangile
> Quanque l'en dit aval la vile.   (III, 235, ll. 12277 f.)

SENTENTIOUS REMARKS

Be meke, where thou must nedis bow.   (B 1939)

> Il est fos qui moine dangier
> Vers celui qu'il doit losengier
> E qu'il covient a soupleier.   (II, 98, ll. 1889 ff.)

The helthe of love mot be founde
Where as they token first her wounde.   (B 1965 f.)

> J'atent par vos joie e santé,
> Que ja par autre ne l'avrai;
> Se vostre main, qui m'a navré,
> Ne me done la guerison.   (II, 99, ll. 1910 ff.)

For of the body he is full lord
That hath the herte in his tresor.   (B 2084 f.)

> Il est assez sires dou cors
> Qui a le cuer en sa comande.   (II, 103, ll. 1996 f.)

The maister lesith his tyme to lere,
Whanne the disciple wol not here.
It is but veyn on hym to swynke,
That on his lernyng wol not thinke.　(B 2149 ff.)

　Li maistres pert sa poine tute
　Quant li deciples qui escoute
　Ne met son cuer au retenir
　Si qu'il l'en puisse sovenir.　(II, 106, ll. 2053 ff.)

For a reder that poyntith ille
A good sentence, may ofte spille.　(B 2161 f.)

For vilanye makith vilayn,
And by his dedis a cherl is seyn.　(B 2181 f.)

　Vilanie fait les vilains,
　Por ce n'est pas droiz que je l'ains.　(II, 107, ll. 2083 f.)

Mayntene thysilf aftir thi rent,
Of robe and eke of garnement;
For many sithe fair clothyng
A man amendith in myche thyng.　(B 2255 ff.)

　Moine toi bel, selonc ta rente,
　E de robe e de chaucemente:
　Bele robe e bel garnement
　Amendent ome durement.　(II, 110, ll. 2141 ff.)

And if thou have nought, spende the lesse.　(B 2274)

　E se tu n'es de la richece
　Quel puisses faire, si t'estrece.　(II, 111, ll. 2157 f.)

For they in herte cunne thenke o thyng,
And seyn another in her spekyng.　(B 2541 f.)

　Il dient un e pensent el
　Li traîtor felon mortel.　(II, 123, ll. 2409 f.)

A man loveth more tendirly
The thyng that he hath bought most dere.　(B 2738 f.)

Si aime l'en miauz le cheté
Quant l'en l'a plus chier acheté.   (II, 132, ll. 2599 f.)

For wel wot ye that love is free.   (B 3432)

Si ne me poez destorber,
Ja ne vos quier de ce lober,
Car j'aimerai puis qu'il me siet,
Cui qu'il soit bel ne cui qu'il griet.   (II, 160, ll. 3183 ff.)

By sufferaunce and wordis softe
A man may overcome ofte
Hym that aforn he hadde in drede,
In bookis sothly as I rede.   (B 3463 ff.)

Or devez sofrir e atendre
Tant qu'en bon point le puissiez prendre;
J'ai bien esprové que l'en vaint
Par sofrir felon e refraint.   (II, 161, ll. 3213 ff.)

For whoso kyssynge may attayne,
Of loves payne hath (soth to sayne)
The beste and most avenaunt,
And ernest of the remenaunt.   (B 3677 ff.)

E sachiez bien cui l'en otroie
Le baisier il a de la proie
Le miauz e le plus avenant,
Si a erres dou remenant.   (II, 170 f., ll. 3405 ff.)

For no man at the firste strok
Ne may nat felle down an ok;
Nor of the reysyns have the wyn,
Tyl grapes be rype, and wel afyn
Be sore empressid, I you ensure,
And drawen out of the pressure.   (B 3687 ff. [H 44])

Vous savez bien qu'au premier cop
Ne cope l'en mie le chesne,
Ne l'en n'a pas le vin de l'aisne
Tant que li pressoirs soit estroiz.   (II, 171, ll. 3414 ff.)

For Wikkid-Tunge seith never well.   (B 3802)

A fool is eythe to bigyle.   (B 3955)

   Trop l'ont trové icil truant
   Fol e bergier a decevoir.   (II, 181, ll. 3634 f.)

It is of Love, as of Fortune,
That chaungeth ofte, and nyl contune;
Which whilom wol on folk smyle,
And glowmbe on hem another while;
Now freend, now foo, [thow] shalt hir feel.
                          (B 4353 ff. [*H* p. 66])

   Ce est ausi con de Fortune,
   Qui met ou cuer des genz rancune,
   Autre eure les aplaigne e chue.
   E poi d'eure son semblant mue:
   Une eure rit, autre eure est morne.   (II, 199, ll. 3981 ff.)

Hir faire biheeste disceyveth feele;
For she wole byhote, sikirly,
And failen aftir outrely.   (B 4446 ff. [*H* p. 67])

   Maint en deceit par sa promesse,
   Qu'el promet tel chose souvent
   Don el ne tendra ja couvent.   (II, 203, ll. 4074 ff.)

For many tymes, whanne she wole make
A full good silogisme, I dreede
That aftirward ther shal in deede
Folwe an evell conclusioun.   (B 4456 ff.)

   Pour c'est fos qui trop s'en aprime,
   Car, quant el fait bon sillogime,
   Si deit l'en aveir grant peeur
   Qu'el ne conclue le peeur.   (II, 204, ll. 4083 ff.)

And heeste certeyn, in no wise,
Withoute yift, is not to prise.   (B 4475 f. [*H* p. 68])

   Promesse senz don ne vaut gaires.   (II, 204, l. 4097)

A foolis word is nought to trowe,
Ne worth an appel for to lowe.   (B 4531 f. [*H* p. 62])

L'en ne deit pas creire fol ome
De la value d'une pome.   (II, 206, ll. 4139 f.)

For trewe Love ne failide never man.   (B 4587)

Ou deu d'Amours pas ne defaut,
Par fei, que deus ne failli onques.   (II, 208, ll. 4190 f.)

If thou fle it, it shal flee thee;
Folowe it, and folowen shal it thee.   (B 4783 f. [*H* 12])

Se tu le suiz, il te suira,
Se tu t'en fuiz, il s'en fuira.   (II, 215, ll. 4357 f.)

But men this thenken evermore,
That lasse harm is, so mote I the,
Deceyve them than deceyved be.   (B 4840 ff. [*H* p. 54])

Mais cil sont li meins deceü,
Car adès vient il meauz, beau maistre,
Deceveir que deceüz estre.   (II, 217, ll. 4398 ff.)

For bycause al is corrumpable.   (B 4856 [*H* 146])
Pour ce qu'il sont tuit corrompable.   (II, 217, l. 4408)

Youthe gynneth ofte sich bargeyn,
That may not eende withouten peyn.   (B 4929 f.)

E fait comencier teus mellees
Qui puis sont enviz desmellees.   (II, 219, ll. 4467 f.)

For no man wolde bicomen old,
Ne dye, whanne he is yong and bold.   (B 4965 f.)

Car nus ne veaut veauz devenir
Ne jennes sa vie fenir.   (II, 221, ll. 4495 f.)

For present tyme abidith nought;
It is more swift than any thought.
So litel while it doth endure
That ther nys compte ne mesure.   (B 5023 ff.)

Car li presenz si po li dure
Qu'il n' i a conte ne mesure. (II, 222, ll. 4543 f.)

As they shal aftirwardes se,
Whanne they arn falle in poverte,
And ben of good and catell bare;
Thanne shulde they sen who freendis ware.
For of an hundred, certeynly,
Nor of a thousand full scarsly,
Ne shal they fynde unnethis oon,
Whanne poverte is comen upon. (B 5455 ff.)

Si con cil après le savraient
Se touz leur biens perduz avaient,
Qu'il n'eüssent ou recouvrer:
Lors verraient amis ouvrer,
Car de cent amis aparanz,
Seient compaignons ou parenz,
S'uns leur en poait demourer,
Deu en devraient aourer. (II, 236, ll. 4881 ff.)

For who is freend, loveth evermore. (B 5520 [H 13])
Toujourz aime qui est amis. (II, 237, l. 4930)

Frendshipp is more than is catell. (B 5540)

E pour ce que nule richece
A valeur d'ami ne s'adrece. (II, 238, ll. 4943 f.)

For Ynfortune makith anoon
To know thy freendis fro thy foon,
By experience, right as it is. (B 5551 ff.)

E li povres, qui par tel preuve
Les fins amis des faus espreuve. (II, 239, ll. 4961 f.)

For suffisaunce all oonly
Makith men to lyve richely. (B 5583 f. [H 36])

Car soufisance seulement
Fait ome vivre richement. (II, 239, ll. 4977 f.)

Such gredynesse hym assaylith
That whanne he most hath, most he failith.   (B 5719 f.)

> E le destrient en tel defaut:
> Quant plus aquiert, plus li defaut.   (II, 244, ll. 5089 f.)

Phisiciens and advocates
Gon right by the same yates;
They selle hir science for wynnyng,
And haunte her crafte for gret getyng.   (B 5721 ff.)

> Avocat e fisicien
> Sont tuit lié de cet lien;
> S'il pour deniers science vendent,
> Trestuit a cete hart se pendent.   (II, 244, ll. 5091 ff.)

For ofte good predicacioun
Cometh of evel entencioun.   (B 5763 f.)

> Car bone predicacion
> Vient bien de male entencion.   (II, 245, ll. 5113 f.)

For love is overall vendable.   (B 5804 [H p. 53])

> Mais tant est li mondes endables
> Qu'il ont faites amours vendables.   (II, 246, ll. 5149 f.)

For who that dredith sire ne dame,
Shal it abye in body or name.   (C 5887 f.)

> Qu'enfes qui ne craint pere e mere
> Ne peut estre qu'il nou compere.   (III, 173, ll. 10759 f.)

But natheles, though thou beten be,
Thou shalt not be the first that so
Hath for sothsawe suffred woo.   (C 6128 ff.)

> E se pour veir dire iés batuz,
> Si n'en iés tu pas coustumiers;
> Tu ne seras pas li prumiers.   (III, 182, ll. 10996 ff.)

And certeynly, sikerest hidyng
Is undirnethe humblest clothing.   (C 6147 f.)

S'est la celee plus seüre
Souz la plus umble vesteüre.   (III, 183, ll. 11013 f.)

Whoso took a wethers skyn,
And wrapped a gredy wolf theryn,
For he shulde go with lambis whyte,
Wenest thou not he wolde hem bite?   (C 6259 ff.)

Qui de la toison dam Belin,
En leu de mantel sebelin,
Sire Isengrin afublerait,
Li lous, qui mouton semblerait,
Pour qu'o les berbiz demourast,
Cuidiez vous qu'il nes devourast?   (III, 188, ll. 11123 ff.)

But to what ordre that I am sworn,
I take the strawe, and lete the corn.   (C 6353 f.)

Mais de religion, senz faille,
J'en lais le grain e preing la paille.   (III, 191, ll. 11215 f.)

The mene is cleped suffisaunce;
Ther lyth of vertu the aboundaunce.   (C 6527 f.)

Li meiens a non soufisance:
La gist des vertuz l'abondance.   (III, 194, ll. 11275 f.)

For sothfastnesse wole none hidyngis.   (C 6712 [*H* 119])
Car veritez n'a cure d'angles.   (III, 201, l. 11434)

My purchace is bettir than my rente.   (C 6838)
Meauz vaut mes pourchaz que ma rente.
                                    (III, 206, l. 11566)

Outward, lambren semen we,
Fulle of goodnesse and of pitee,
And inward we, withouten fable,
Ben gredy wolves ravysable.   (C 7013 ff.)

Dehors semblons aigneaus pitables,
Dedenz somes lous ravissables.   (III, 212, ll. 11717 f.)

He is the hound, shame is to seyn,
That to his castyng goth ageyn.   (C 7285 f.)

C'est li mastins qui gloutement
Retourne a son vomissement.   (III, 223, ll. 11967 f.)

That hadde of tresoun al his face
Ryght blak withynne and whit withoute.   (C 7332 f.)

Qui de traïson ot la face,
Blanche dehors, dedenz nercie.   (III, 225, ll. 12012 f.)

But shalt thou never of apparence
Sen conclude good consequence
In non argument, ywis,
If existens al fayled is.   (C 7465 ff. [H p. 70])

Mais ja ne verreiz d'aparence
Conclure bone consequence
En nul argument que l'en face,
Se defauz existence efface.   (III, 230, ll. 12139 ff.)

For it is better stylle be
Than for to speken harm, parde!   (C 7511 f. [H 51])

Qu'adès vient il meauz qu'en se taise
Que dire parole mauvaise.   (III, 232, ll. 12185 f.)

(2) Book of the Duchess

The *Book of the Duchess* contains six sententious remarks. The Dreamer, after he has lamented his eight years' lack of sleep, says with philosophical resignation,

That wil not be mot nede be left.   (l. 42)

The Man in Black cries out against Fortune, as well he may, and heaps abuse upon her:

She is the monstres heed ywrien,
As fylthe over-ystrawed with floures.   (ll. 628 f.)

His sorrow cannot be relieved,

For that ys doon ys not to come.   (l. 708)

He became the servant of Love in his youth, and
finds that in maturity he cannot forget it:

I ches love to my firste craft;
Therfore hit ys with me laft.   (ll. 791 f. [*H* p. 65])

His lady, the "goode faire White," knew well what
was the best "mean" for

In all thynges more mesure
Had never, I trowe, creature.   (ll. 881 f.)

So little did she know the sentiment that "out of
sight is out of mind" that she thought no more of a
lover at home than of one in India.   In fact, she
was more than impartial, so that

The formest was alway behynde.   (l. 890)

(3) *House of Fame*

There are six proverbs in the *House of Fame*, of
which two occur in the paraphrase of the love-
story of Æneas.   Women should be careful not to
fall in love with plausible strangers:

Hyt is not al gold that glareth.   (l. 272 [*H* 130; *S* 206])

Dido would have done better to wait before be-
stowing her affections on Æneas:

Therfore I wol seye a proverbe,
That "he that fully knoweth th'erbe
May saufly leye hyt to his yë.   (ll. 289 ff. [*H* 69; *S* 207])

The Eagle tells Chaucer the reasons that impel
Jove to furnish him aërial carriage: the poet has
served Cupid the "reccheles" and now is to hear
news about love; the amours are of various kinds
but the greater number are casual:

That ben betyd, no man wot why,
But as a blynd man stert an hare.   (ll. 680 f. [*H* p. 65; *S* 208])

Chaucer lists many of the musicians whom he sees
about the House of Fame but cannot take time to
enumerate them all,

For tyme ylost, this knowen ye,
Be no way may recovered be.   (ll. 1257 f. [*H* 144a])

The goddess Fame, in her inconsequential way,
denies to the seventh "rout" the petition which
she granted to the sixth, namely, to be renowned
as lovers without having experienced the reality.
She tells the unsuccessful that

    ye be lyke the sweynte cat
That wolde have fissh; but wostow what?
He wolde nothing wete his clowes.   (ll. 1783 ff. [*H* 31; *S* 209])

Chaucer, once admitted to the revolving wicker-
work house finds that it

Was ful of shipmen and pilgrimes,
With scrippes bret-ful of lesinges.   (ll. 2122 f.)

The poem contains seven sententious remarks.
Æneas appears honest enough in Dido's eyes, and
that is the more pity, for

Allas! what harm doth apparence,
Whan hit is fals in existence! (ll. 265 f. [*H* p. 70])

When Æneas departs, Dido bewails her trust,
Æneas's inconstancy, and her own shame:

O, soth ys, every thing ys wyst,
Though hit be kevered with the myst. (ll. 351 f. [*H* 142])

This common belief that truth will be finally clear
is repeated by Chaucer toward the end of the
poem:

For al mot out, other late or rathe,
Alle the sheves in the lathe. (ll. 2139 f.)

Dido's complaint is of no avail, however, since

that is don, is not to done. (l. 361 [*H* 103b])

The Eagle discourses to Chaucer about the air-
marks which they pass, and tells the story of
Phaëthon, over whom he moralizes:

Loo, ys it not a gret myschaunce
To lete a fool han governaunce
Of thing that he can not demeyne? (ll. 957 ff.)

When Chaucer sees that many of the names upon
the hill of ice are partly melted, he remembers that

men seyn, "What may ever laste?"
(l. 1147 [*H* 149; *S* 208, 224])

Once a rumor is started in the revolving house it
goes from mouth to mouth:

And that encresing ever moo,
As fyr ys wont to quyke and goo
From a sparke spronge amys,
Til al a citee brent up ys. (ll. 2077 ff.)

(4) *Anelida and Arcite*

Anelida and Arcite contains one proverb and three sententious remarks. The proverb alluded to in the following lines is one of the relatively few weather sayings in Middle English:

I myghte as wel holde Aperill fro reyn,
As holde yow, to make yow be stidfast.   (ll. 309 f.)

The wicked falseness of Arcite, who seemed so genuinely in love, calls forth the remark:

But nothing thinketh the fals as doth the trewe.
(l. 105 [*H* 125a; *S* 142])

His actions illustrate the common failing of man,

For what he may not gete, that wolde he have.   (l. 203)

Anelida's doctrine of love is like that of the turtle dove in the *Parliament of Fowls*, for she, too, is one of those who

doth her observaunce
Alwey til oon, and chaungeth for no newe.   (ll. 218 f.)

(5) *Parliament of Fowls*

There are two proverbs and ten sententious remarks in the *Parliament of Fowls*. The sparrow-hawk's reproof to the cackling of the goose ends with a blow to the body:

But soth is seyd, "a fol can not be stille.   (l. 574 [*H* 62; *S* 139])

The courtly fowls have no monopoly of proverbs, however, and the duck responds "ful wel and fayre" to what he considers the nonsense of the turtle:

There been mo sterres, God wot, than a payre!
(l. 595 [*H* 37; *S* 140])

Chaucer, or the Dreamer, at the beginning of the poem, applies to Love the adage of Hippocrates:

The lyf so short, the craft so long to lerne.   (l. 1 [*S* 135])

He tells us how avid a reader he is, and excuses himself with a saying which ought to be as well known to the creative writer of to-day as it is to most scholars:

For out of olde feldes, as men seyth,
Cometh al this newe corn from yer to yere.   (ll. 22 f.)

In his adaptation of Dante's famous inscription over the gate of Hell, Chaucer warns those who find themselves in Love's bad books that

Th'eschewing is only the remedye!   (l. 140 [*H* 77; *S* 136])

This inscription dismays the Dreamer little less than the more awful one that had troubled Dante, but Scipio reminds him that he has lost his taste for love, and bids him take heart of grace — and curiosity — in words which explain all too well our love of the prizefight and football game:

For many a man that may nat stonde a pul,
It lyketh hym at the wrastlyng for to be,
And demeth yit wher he do bet or he.   (ll. 164 ff.)

In the inevitable garden the Dreamer finds Venus, and with her Bacchus and Ceres (ll. 275–277), whose presence involves an allusion to the Latin proverb "Sine Cerere et Libero friget Venus." The turtle, more modest than his companions, neatly expresses his sense of unworthiness in two sayings:

But bet is that a wyghtes tonge reste
Than entermeten hym of such doinge,
Of which he neyther rede can ne synge.   (ll. 514 ff.)

For office uncommytted ofte anoyeth.   (l. 518 [*H* 162; *S* 138])

The sparrow hawk assails the goose for exposing his own folly:

  Yit were it bet for the
Han holde thy pes than shewed thy nycete.   (ll. 571 f.)

The duck has nothing but contempt for the turtle's doctrine of endless love:

Daunseth he murye that is myrtheles?
Who shulde recche of that is recheles?   (ll. 592 f.)

Several manuscripts introduce the roundel at the end of the poem with a French proverb, which may possibly give the name of the tune:

Qui bien aime a tard oublie.
                              Between ll. 679 *and* 680 [*H* 10; *S* 141])

(6) *Boece*

The *Boece* contains seven sententious remarks, which I list in the order of their occurrence:

fortune, that is uncerteyn to alle mortel folk.
                              (I, pr. iv, ll. 255 f.)

but wisdom loketh and mesureth the ende of thynges.

(II, pr. i, ll. 94 f.)

As who seith, a pore man that bereth no rychesse on hym by the weie may boldely synge byforn theves, for he hath nat whereof to be robbed.   (II, pr. v, ll. 202 ff.)

And what pestilence is more myghty for to anoye a wyght than a famylier enemy?   (III, pr. v, ll. 78 f. [*S* 20])

the sentence of Plato that nedes the wordis moot be cosynes to the thinges of whiche thei speken.

(III, pr. xii, ll. 225 ff. [*S* 212])

For this sentence is verray and soth, that "no thing hath his beynge of naught," to the whiche sentence noon of thise oolde folk ne withseide nevere.   (V, pr. i, ll. 46 ff.)

   As who seith, nay ; for no man ne travaileth for to witen thingis that he wot.   (V, m. iii, ll. 26 ff.)

(7) *Astrolabe*

The one proverb in the *Astrolabe* occurs in the Prologue; there are many rules for the science,

right as diverse pathes leden diverse folk the righte way to Rome.   (ll. 45 ff.)

(8) *Complaint of Mars*

There are two sententious remarks in the *Complaint of Mars*. The bird that sings the *aubade*, which serves as a proem, consoles lovers who are banished from their loves by the sun, that candle of jealousy, by reminding them that

The glade nyght ys worth an hevy morowe!   (l. 12 [*H* p. 52])

Mars declares roundly that, what with the tattle of the envious and the fear and unkindness of the ladies,

But he be fals, no lover hath his ese.   (l. 208 [*H* p. 65])

(9) *Fortune*

The only bit of proverbial material in *Fortune* is a sententious remark in the response of the Plaintiff to the careless goddess:

Wikke appetyt comth ay before syknesse.   (l. 55)

(10) *Truth*

The notable "balade de bon conseyl," *Truth*, contains two proverbs in its twenty-eight lines. The first points out the dangers of high rank, and the second the folly of futile struggle against odds.

For hord hath hate, and climbing tikelnesse,
Prees hath envye, and wele blent overal.   (ll. 3 f.)

Stryve not, as doth the crokke with the wal.   (l. 12)

(11) *Gentilesse*

The single sententious remark in *Gentilesse*, later to be the theme of an eloquent monologue by the Loathly Lady in the tale of Alice of Bath, serves admirably to point the moral of the poem:

Vyce may wel be heir to old richesse.   (l. 15)

(12) *Envoy to Bukton*

The *Envoy to Bukton*, as befits its subject, contains three sententious remarks, and the proverbial
quality of the whole piece is indicated in the third.
The first represents the Biblical counsel of desperation in favor of marriage, but the others take the
opposite point of view:

But yet, lest thow do worse, take a wyf;
Bet ys to wedde than brenne in worse wise.   (l. 17 f.)

Experience shal the teche, so may happe,
That the were lever to be take in Frise
Than eft to falle of weddynge in the trappe.   (ll. 22 ff.)

This lytel writ, proverbes, or figure
I sende you, take kepe of yt, I rede;
Unwys is he that kan no wele endure.
If thow be siker, put the nat in drede.

(ll. 25 ff. [*H* 86, 187; *S* 144])

(13) *Proverbs*

The so-called *Proverbs* of Chaucer [4] are far from
popular, and consist, in reality, of two sententious
quatrains:

What shul thise clothes thus manyfold,
   Lo! this hote somers day?
After greet heet cometh cold;
   No man caste his pilche away.

Of al this world the large compas
   Hit wol not in myn armes tweyne, —
Whoso mochel wol embrace,
   Litel therof he shal distreyne.

(p. 639 [*H* 23, 39b; *S* 145, 146])

(14) *Legend of Good Women*

We may well consider the two versions of the Prologue to the *Legend of Good Women* apart from the actual legends. There are no proverbs, but eight sententious remarks are found in both F and G, two in F alone, and three in G alone.

Things may well be true, Chaucer remarks at the beginning of the poem, even if they are not known to all men:

Bernard the monk ne saugh nat all, pardee!   (F 16, G 16)

Chaucer meets the God of Love and finds that a certain common saying is not substantiated by his own experience:

And al be that men seyn that blynd ys he,
Algate me thoghte that he myghte se.
(F 237 f., G 169 f. [H p. 64])

Alcestis asks that Love give the poet a hearing; perhaps people have calumniated him, since

Envie ys lavendere of the court alway.   (F 358, G 333 f.)

To condemn him unheard is wrong, she says:

For syr, yt is no maistrye for a lord
To dampne a man without answere of word.
(F 400 f., G 386 f.)

The God of Love is won over by Alcestis's eloquence and forgives Chaucer without delay:

For whoso yeveth a yifte, or dooth a grace,
Do it by tyme, his thank ys wel the more.
(F 451 f., G 441 f. [H 82; S 210])

Chaucer thanks his fair advocate. He has done no wrong to true lovers in upbraiding those who are false to their vows:

For-why a trewe man, withouten drede,
Hath nat to parten with a theves dede.
                              (F 464 f., G 454 f. [*H* 126])

She tells him to argue no more,

For Love ne wol nat countrepleted be
In ryght ne wrong.   (F 476 f., G 466 f.)

The God of Love congratulates Chaucer on having found a lady who will give him such a light penance, and in his congratulation utters what has been called Chaucer's favorite line:

But pite renneth soone in gentil herte.   (F 503, G 491)

The two sayings which appear in the F Prologue only are found close together. Chaucer is describing the songs of the birds, who made their accord and found that Pity

made Mercy passen Ryght.   (F 162)

It was not false Pity who intervened, however,

for vertu is the mene,
As Etik seith.   (F 165 f.)

The God of Love ends his attack on Chaucer in the G Prologue by asking him what makes him

                  wryte
The draf of storyes, and forgete the corn?   (G 311 f.)

Alcestis in the G Prologue adds to her sententious prayer for mercy:

He shal nat ryghtfully his yre wreke,
Or he have herd the tother partye speke. (G 324 f.)

She also reminds Love that

Al ne is nat gospel that is to yow pleyned. (G 326)

The legends themselves contain three proverbs. The battle of Actium must be lost and won at last,

as every thyng hath ende. (l. 651 [*H* 148b])

The fact that the parents of Pyramus and Thisbe disapprove of their romance has an effect opposite to that desired,

As, wry the glede, and hotter is the fyr;
Forbede a love, and it is ten so wod.
       (ll. 735 f. [*H* p. 64; *S* 162, 210])

Tarquin determines to have Lucretia's favor whether she will or no, and his proverbial expression of this resolve is somewhat like Diomede's remark [5] in slightly similar circumstances:

"Hap helpeth hardy man alday," quod he.
       (l. 1773 [*H* 17a; *S* 189, 210])

We find in the legends six sententious remarks. Chaucer, not unwisely, refuses to tell all the details of the wedding of Cleopatra and Antony:

For men may overlade a ship or barge. (l. 621)

Dido's sudden love for Æneas is explained on the
ground that

To som folk ofte newe thyng is sote.   (l. 1077)

Her sister Anna's warnings are of no avail:

Love wol love, for nothing wol it wonde.   (l. 1187 [*H* 1])

Chaucer, when he reaches the story of Hypsipyle
and Medea, is much disturbed that false lovers,
such as Jason, should be more successful than the
true:

For evere as tendre a capoun et the fox,
Thow he be fals and hath the foul betrayed,
As shal the good-man that therfore hath payed.
Al have he to the capoun skille and ryght,
The false fox wol have his part at nyght.   (ll. 1389 ff.)

The story of Phillys begins sententiously:

By preve as wel as by autorite,
That wiked fruit cometh of a wiked tre,
That may ye fynde, if that it like yow.   (ll. 2394 ff. [*H* 110])

Of the falseness of Demophon, son of Theseus,
Chaucer says:

It com hym of nature,
As doth the fox Renard, the foxes sone;
Of kynde he coude his olde faders wone,
Withoute lore, as can a drake swimme
Whan it is caught and caryed to the brymme.   (ll. 2447 ff.)

CHAPTER III

Troilus and Criseyde

TROILUS AND CRISEYDE is not only the longest of Chaucer's works, it is also the most nearly perfect. The *Canterbury Tales*, to be sure, represents a greater literary conception, but it was left unfinished. Among the pilgrims and the characters in their stories we find a fuller and more varied expression of the innumerable facets of human emotion and experience, but no one of the tales has the fixity of purpose or the intensity of passion which we feel in the *Troilus*. The story of the Trojan lovers is a masterpiece of understanding and delineation. The characters, as they develop before our eyes, are more Chaucer's own than Palamon, Arcite and Emily, or Walter and Griselda. They live apart from the frame of the story, as well as in it. Pandarus, despite the infamy that has grown about his name, is one of the great comic characters of all time, and unlike his fellows, such as Don Quixote, Parson Adams, and Mr. Pickwick, his humor never approaches caricature. Cressida is flesh and blood, a lady full of charm, and feeling, and discretion, to say nothing of a humor of

her own, albeit she is "slydynge of corage." Of
Troilus less can be said — after all, he is a lover.

Chaucer uses a greater proportion of proverbs
and sententious remarks in the *Troilus* than in
anything else he wrote. He introduces one hundred twenty-eight sayings, of which sixty-one are
proverbs and only eighty-seven proverbial phrases,
of which thirty-two are comparisons. The number
of comparisons is in striking contrast to some of
Chaucer's other poems: there are thirty-two comparisons in the *Knight's Tale* and twenty or more in
the *House of Fame*, the *Legend of Good Women*, the
General Prologue, the *Miller's Tale*, and the *Merchant's Tale*. Chaucer uses proverbs not only in
the narrative portions of the *Troilus*, but also in
the dialogue. They are, then, aids to characterization, both by their presence in the speeches of
Pandarus and Cressida, and by their absence in
those of Troilus. To make clearer this element of
their use I shall take up the proverbial material
spoken by the various characters apart from that
used by the teller of the story, Chaucer himself.

Before considering in detail the proverbs in the
Troilus, we may profit by commenting on the
proverbial material in the *Filostrato*.[1] Boccaccio's
poem contains five proverbs, four of which are
spoken by Pandaro,[2] while the fifth is by the author.[3] There are twenty-one sententious remarks.

Pandaro[4] and Criseis[5] use four each, Troilo three,[6] and ten[7] appear in the text.

There are fourteen comparisons[8] in the poem and six other proverbial phrases.[9] We observe, then, that Boccaccio had made relatively little use of proverbs, and that he certainly did not use them as a means of characterization.

To return to the *Troilus*, Pandarus makes use of twenty proverbs, the first of which is spoken soon after he appears on the scene. He tries to win the confidence of Troilus in order to aid him in his love-affair, and his reply to Troilus's remonstrance that he himself has been unsuccessful is:

A fool may ek a wis-man ofte gide.   (i, 630 [*H* 63; *S* 150])

He proceeds to strengthen his point with the allied saying that one should try to profit by the mistakes of others:

Thus often wise men ben war by foolys.   (i, 635)

Pandarus thinks well enough of the advice to use a form of it again in the third book, when he is fulminating against "avantours," not because he distrusts Troilus, but,

Wyse ben by foles harm chastised.   (iii, 329 [*S* 176])

Another of his arguments to make Troilus tell him of his love is that

Men seyn, "to wrecche is consolacioun
To have another felawe in hys peyne."   (i. 708 f. [*S* 152])

He upbraids him for never having spoken to his lady, for if a woman does not know about a man's love he is unlikely to get much pleasure from her, since

Unknowe, unkist, and lost, that is unsought.   (i, 809 [*H* 33])

This saying gains added fame from its use at the beginning of E. K.'s letter to Master Gabriel Harvey, concerning *The Shepheardes Calender*: "Uncouthe, unkiste, sayde the olde famous Poete Chaucer." [10]

Pandarus continues to urge Troilus to tell him the lady's name,

For whoso list have helyng of his leche,
To hym byhoveth first unwre his wownde.   (i, 857 f.)

When he at last extracts the information that his friend's "swete fo" is none other than his own niece Cressida, he overwhelms him with advice. Above all Troilus should be moderate, he must not try to rush things:

He hasteth wel that wisely kan abyde.
                    (i, 956 [*H* 83b; *S* 155])

When in Book II Pandarus makes his call upon Cressida, he pours forth a stream of proverbs. He delays communicating the object of his visit, indulges in mysterious hints, and declares that he must be brief and come to the point,

sithen th'ende is every tales strengthe.   (ii, 260)

And this before he has so much as started! He
finally tells her of Troilus's love, and warns her
that Priam's son in desperation will seek his own
death unless she has some pity on him. She will do
well to think a bit before hardening her heart:

Avysement is good byfore the nede.   (ii, 343)

There are personal reasons why she should not re-
ject love. She is not likely to grow younger, and

Lat this proverbe a loore unto yow be:
"'To late ywar,' quod beaute, whan it paste";
And elde daunteth daunger at the laste.
                                    (ii, 397 ff. [*H* 185; *S* 160])

This is parallel to the saying which he casts at her
in his righteous indignation in Book III when she
offers to send Troilus a blue ring:

O tyme ilost, wel maistow corsen slouthe!   (iii, 896)

Unless the ring has a virtue that will raise the dead
she had better do more than that!

   The artful Pandarus leaves Cressida to her
scarcely less artful thoughts and returns to his
moping friend. He assures him of that which he
himself can only guess, and asks permission to sleep
after his labor. Poor Troilus wishes his reward at
once, but Pandarus says that

every thing hath tyme.   (ii, 989 [*H* 145d])

This is the very remark which he makes to Cressida
in the next book, with a wholly different implica-
tion:

Nece, alle thyng hath tyme, I dar avowe.   (iii, 855)

For Troilus it meant "Wait a while "; to Cressida
it said, "Do it now."

To return to Book II, Pandarus makes another
visit to his kinswoman and urges her to write a
letter to Troilus. Cressida finds letter-writing difficult, but her uncle reminds her blithely that perhaps it's a good sign:

God woot, of thyng ful often looth bygonne
Comth ende good.   (ii, 1234 f.)

Pandarus sets the stage for the meeting at the
home of Deiphobus. He tells Troilus to pretend
that his fever is on him. Troilus replies that he
doesn't need to counterfeit since he's sick enough
in all conscience. "So much the better," says
Pandarus in effect,

For hym men demen hoot that men seen swete.   (ii, 1533)

Some time elapses before Pandarus uses another
proverb, but that one, being heeded, was of great
importance for the story. Pandarus has brought
Troilus into Cressida's room, and she, aware only
of her uncle's presence, would call an attendant.
"Not at all," says Pandarus, "they might think
something wrong:"

It is nought good a slepyng hound to wake.
                              (iii, 764 [*H* 72; *S* 178])

The passage that ensues is relatively free from proverbs. The happy Troilus goes in the morning to thank his benefactor, who gives him much good advice, not the least valuable of which is —

For also seur as reed is every fir,
As gret a craft is kepe wel as wynne.   (iii, 1633 f., [S 185])

The story moves on to its inevitable tragedy: Cressida must go, and Pandarus, for all he is "ful ded and pale of hewe," tries to cheer up his friend. He quotes four related proverbs to the effect that Troilus can easily get a new lady who will make him forget Cressida:

And ek, as writ Zanzis, that was ful wys,
"The newe love out chaceth ofte the olde."
                                    (iv, 414 f. [H 9; S 186])

And upon newe case lith newe avys.   (iv, 416)

For also seur as day comth after nyght,
The newe love, labour, or oother wo,
Or elles selde seynge of a wight,
Don olde affecciouns alle over-go.   (iv, 421 ff.)

Absence of hire shal dryve hire out of herte.   (iv, 427)

When he perceives that such easy consolation will be of no avail, he urges Troilus to resist the exchange. Is he nervous about the law? Let Troilus think nothing of it:

Thorugh love is broken al day every lawe.   (IV, 618 [H 5])

"Snatch her away," Pandarus cries, and offers all his aid and friendship. And a friend he was, or tried to be, until the end. His last proverb is a gentle one:

For wel thou woost, my leve brother deere,
That alwey frendes may nat ben yfeere. (v, 342 f.)

Pandarus has not shot his last bolt when his proverbs are used up, for he seeks to educate his companions with no less than twenty-three sententious remarks.[11] In his first conversation with Troilus he supplements his proverbial exhortations to confession with several less popular sayings:

I have myself ek seyn a blynd man goo
Ther as he fel that couthe loken wide. (i, 628 f.)

A wheston is no kervyng instrument,
And yet it maketh sharppe kervyng tolis. (i, 631 f.)

By his contrarie is every thyng declared. (i, 637 [H 118])

For how myghte evere swetnesse han ben knowe
To him that nevere tasted bitternesse? (i, 638 f.)

Sith thus of two contraries is o lore. (i, 645)

The wise seith, "Wo hym that is allone,
For, and he falle, he hath non helpe to ryse."
                              (i, 694 f. [S 151])

Once he has wormed out the truth, he begins to console Troilus with hope of happiness. Things are not all unpleasant,

For thilke grownd that bereth the wedes wikke
Bereth ek thise holsom herbes, as ful ofte
Next the foule netle, rough and thikke,
The rose waxeth swoote and smothe and softe;
And next the valeye is the hil o-lofte;
And next the derke nyght the glade morwe;
And also joie is next the fyn of sorwe.
                                        (i, 946 ff. [*H* p. 67; *S* 154])

Throw off this gloomy cheer; be a man, not a
crushed wretch:

    He that parted is in everi place
Is nowher hol, as writen clerkes wyse.   (i, 960 f.)

It may well be that Cressida will yield herself to the
God of Love since she can scarcely be immune,

For this have I herd seyd of wyse lered,
Was nevere man or womman yet bigete
That was unapt to suffren loves hete,
Celestial, or elles love of kynde.   (i, 976 ff.)

He feels sure that Troilus ought to be one of Love's
staunchest pillars, now that he has been converted
from his old heresy:

Ensample why, se now thise wise clerkes,
That erren aldermost ayeyn a lawe,
And ben converted from hire wikked werkes
Thorugh grace of God that list hem to hym drawe,
Thanne arn they folk that han moost God in awe,
And strengest feythed ben, I undirstonde,
And konne an errowr alderbest withstonde.
                                        (i, 1002 ff. [*S* 156])

We move on to Pandarus's first interview with
Cressida on the twin subjects of love and Troilus.

He prepares her for something of moment and
thinks that he must be very plain:

For tendre wittes wenen al be wyle
Thereas thei kan nought pleynly understonde.   (ii, 271 f.)

After another long interval we find Pandarus in-
structing the lover in the art of letter-writing. No
one as yet has accused Chaucer of taking the precepts which Pandarus gives from some rhetorician's
treatise on *dictamen*, and no one is likely to find
them there. Ovid was more to the point, and after
Ovid the occasional common sense of love. One
suggestion he elaborates sententiously:

For though the beste harpour upon lyve
Wolde on the beste sowned joly harpe
That evere was, with alle his fyngres fyve,
Touche ay o streng, or ay o werbul harpe,
Were his nayles poynted nevere so sharpe,
It sholde maken every wight to dulle,
To here his glee, and of his strokes fulle.   (ii, 1030 ff. [*S* 167])

Pandarus finally induces Cressida to reply to
Troilus's letter, and, when she avows the writing
difficult, he remarks that Troilus may be all the
happier to have won her complaisance,

For-whi men seith, "impressiounes lighte
Ful lightly ben ay redy to the flighte.   (ii, 1238 f. [*S* 168])

He later tells Troilus much the same thing in two
related sayings:

Thenk here-ayeins: whan that the stordy ook,
On which men hakketh ofte, for the nones,

Receyved hath the happy fallyng strook,
The greete sweigh doth it come al at ones,
As doon thise rokkes or thise milnestones;
For swifter cours comth thyng that is of wighte,
Whan it descendeth, than don thynges lighte.

(ii, 1380 ff. [S 172])

And reed that boweth down for every blast,
Ful lightly, cesse wynd, it wol aryse;
But so nyl nought an ook, whan it is cast.

(ii, 1387 ff. [S 149])

After the meeting in the house of Deiphobus, Pandarus warns Troilus not to talk much about his love-affair; to this purpose he quotes the *Distichs* of Cato:

For which thise wise clerkes that ben dede
Han evere thus proverbed to us yonge,
That "firste vertu is to kepe tonge."

(iii, 292 ff. [H 52; S 174])

Proverbes kanst thiself ynowe and woost,
Ayeins that vice, for to ben a labbe,
Al seyde men soth as often as thei gabbe.   (iii, 299 ff.)

He ends by summarizing neatly the current feeling in the society of Courtly Love about the man who kisses and tells:

Avauntour and a lyere, al is on.   (iii, 309 [H 106; S 175])

When Pandarus has at last introduced Troilus into Cressida's chamber, he carries on a long preparatory dialogue with the lady, emphasizes Troilus's despair, and urges immediate action:

For, nece myn, thus writen clerkes wise,
That peril is with drecchyng in ydrawe.   (iii, 852 f. [S 179])

He makes a typically sententious excuse for leaving the lovers alone:

This light, nor I, ne serven here of nought.
Light is nought good for sike folkes yën. (iii, 1136 f.)

Once the love of Troilus and Cressida is consummated, Pandarus warns Troilus against losing his fresh-won joy,

For of fortunes sharpe adversitee
The worste kynde of infortune is this,
A man to han ben in prosperitee,
And it remembren, whan it passed is. (iii, 1625 ff.)

And again:

Be naught to rakel, theigh thow sitte warme;
For if thow be, certeyn, it wol the harme. (iii, 1630 f.)

In one of the most pathetic passages in the poem Troilus later asks Pandarus why he ever said

That "hym is wors that is fro wele ythrowe,
Than he hadde erst noon of that wele yknowe?" (iv, 482 f.)

Cressida must leave Troy and her friends are distraught. Pandarus cries out upon the Goddess Fortuna:

Ne truste no wight to fynden in Fortune
Ay propretee; hire yiftes ben comune. (iv, 391 f. [H p. 66])

His inconsistency about the goddess is quite in keeping with that lady's character, for while trying to persuade Troilus to resist the exchange he says:

Thenk ek Fortune, as wel thiselven woost,
Helpeth hardy man to his enprise,
And weyveth wrecches for hire cowardise.

(iv, 600 ff. [*H* 17b; *S* 189])

Let Troilus set his face against the world; let the town cry,

For whan men han wel cryd, than wol they rowne.   (iv, 587)

Let others lament:

Bet is that othere than thiselven wepe.   (iv, 591)

He urges Cressida to keep a stiff upper lip: her weeping will quite overcome Troilus if he sees it:

Bet is a tyme of cure ay than of pleynte.   (iv, 931)

She may be able to find a way out of this trouble if she applies herself:

Women ben wise in short avysement.   (iv, 936)

In the fifth and final book his sole object is to cheer his friend and to postpone the inevitable hour when Troilus will know the truth. He urges Troilus to pay attention to his advice, for

whoso wol nought trowen reed ne loore,
I kan nat sen in hym no remedie.   (v, 327 f.)

Others have borne up under griefs such as this:

As tyme hem hurt, a tyme doth hem cure.   (v, 350 [*H* p. 53])

When Troilus dreams of the boar in Cressida's arms, Pandarus asks, not too consistently,

Have I nat seyd er this,
That dremes many a maner man bigile?   (v, 1276 f. [*H* 128])

Second to Pandarus [12] in the use of proverbial
material is the far from artless Cressida. She quotes
eleven proverbs, eight of which occur in Book iv.
When Pandarus threatens to go on a hunger strike
unless she has pity on Troilus, she says,

Of harmes two, the lesse is for to chese.
                                    (ii, 470 [*H* 73; *S* 161])

Left alone, she reflects on the dangers in which
love involves women, and on the busy care which
she must have in order to keep her honor un-
blemished. At last she decides, typically enough,
that

He which that nothing undertaketh,
Nothyng n'acheveth, be hym looth or deere.
                                    (ii, 807 f. [*H* 30a; *S* 164])

While her love-affair runs smoothly she has no
need of proverbial philosophy; once disaster comes,
she falls back upon it, and when she first finds that
she must go, she doubts if she can live away from
Troilus:

For which ful ofte a by-word here I seye,
That "rooteles moot grene soone deye."
                                    (iv, 769 f. [*H* 186; *S* 192])

During her last night with her lover she uses seven
proverbs. At the beginning she says,

I am a womman, as ful wel ye woot,
And as I am avysed sodeynly,
So wol I telle yow, whil it is hoot.   (iv, 1261 ff.)

Even so, she does not mean to preach a long sermon,

For tyme ylost may nought recovered be.   (iv, 1283)

She thinks that she knows a trick to cajole her father, for he is old and covetous:

Lo, Troilus, men seyn that hard it is
The wolf ful, and the wether hool to have;
This is to seyn, that men ful ofte, iwys,
Mote spenden part the remenant for to save.
                              (iv, 1373 ff. [H p. 54, S 194])

Troilus offers to elope with her, to quit the war, leave his friends, and forsake Troy, but she will hear none of it:

Beth naught to hastif in this hoote fare;
For hastif man ne wanteth nevere care.
                              (iv, 1567 f. [H 85; S 155])

She bids him think of his own honor and hers and to restrain himself:

Ek "whoso wol han lief, he lief moot lete";
Thus maketh vertu of necessite
By pacience.   (iv, 1585 ff. [H 96c; S 199])

She promises to return on the tenth day. Her father may try to stop her, but she has the will, and

who may holde a thing that wol awey?   (iv, 1628 [H 98])

Once in the Greek camp, she does not find escape
as easy as she had expected, and she wishes that
she had heeded Troilus's plea for flight. Her last
proverb is sad indeed:

But al to late comth the letuarie,
Whan men the cors unto the grave carie.   (v, 741 f.)

Cressida, like Pandarus, has her full share of
sententious remarks, using sixteen. She laments
Troilus's lover's malady, and promises to try to
cure him, always saving her honor:

But cesse cause, ay cesseth maladie.   (ii, 483)

In her soliloquizing she argues with herself and is
most persuasive in discussing reasons why she
should see Troilus. She doesn't want to be ex-
treme:

In every thyng, I woot, there lith mesure.
For though a man forbede dronkenesse,
He naught forbet that every creature
Be drynkeles for alwey, as I gesse.   (ii, 715 ff. [*H* 87, 174])

She ends her self-addressed remarks with four sayings:

But harm ydoon is doon, whoso it rewe.   (ii, 789)

Ful sharp bygynnyng breketh ofte at ende.
                              (ii, 791 [*H* p. 52])

That erst was nothing, into nought it torneth.
                              (ii, 798 [*H* 34])

And who may stoppen every wikked tonge,
Or sown of belles whil that thei ben ronge?   (ii, 804 f.)

Small wonder that her thought begins to clear! She is overwhelmed when Pandarus tells her that Troilus has come to his house in all this rain greatly distressed because of her reported love for Horaste:

"O God!" quod she, "so worldly selynesse,
Which clerkes callen fals felicitee,
Imedled is with many a bitternesse!" (iii, 813 ff. [*H* p. 66])

Cressida has no more use for sententious remarks than for proverbs while her love for Troilus is warm and prosperous; when happiness is threatened she returns to them again. "Can I live without Troilus?" she asks herself, and later:

How sholde a fissh withouten water dure? (iv, 765 [*S* 191])

By the time Pandarus arrives, she is sure that her very bliss itself had made the blow inevitable:

Endeth thanne love in wo? Ye, or men lieth!
(iv, 834 [*H* p. 64])

The ende of blisse ay sorwe it occupieth. (iv, 836 [*S* 193])

During her last night with Troilus she uses six sententious remarks, most of them optimistic. She can get out of the Greek camp easily by playing on her father's weakness:

My fader, as ye knowen wel, parde,
Is old, and elde is ful of coveytise. (iv, 1368 f.)

The war may end:

And if so be that pees heere-after take,
As alday happeth, after anger, game. (iv, 1562 f.)

She is sure to win, however, and without the violence which Troilus advocates:

Men seyn, "the suffrant overcomith," parde.
                              (iv, 1584 [*H* 46; *S* 197])

Strategy has its value:

And thynketh wel, that somtyme it is wit
To spende a tyme, a tyme for to wynne.   (iv, 1611 f.)

When she asks Troilus to be true during her absence the irony becomes almost unbearable:

For I am evere agast, forwhy men rede
That love is thyng ay ful of bisy drede.
                              (iv, 1644 f. [*H* p. 64; *S* 200])

Her last sententious remark comes when she determines to go in defiance of gossip from the Greek camp to Troy.   She cannot take everyone's advice:

For whoso wol of every word take hede,
Or reulen hym by every wightes wit,
Ne shal he nevere thryven, out of drede.   (v, 757 ff.)

Cressida uses two comparisons [13] and ten other proverbial phrases.[14]

Troilus is no amateur of proverbs.   When Pandarus tries to cheer him with his steady flow of edifying talk, Troilus bids him be gone:

For thi proverbes may me naught availle.   (i, 756)

He uses but four himself.   One of these, occurring in his formal confession of sin to Love, is reported by Pandarus to Cressida:

And wel the hotter ben the gledes rede,
That men hem wrien with asshen pale and dede.
                                    (ii, 538 f. [*S* 162])

The other three appear within six lines and repre-
sent Troilus's reaction to Cressida's optimism and
use of proverbs. She is certain that she can evade
her father, and bolsters her opinions with numerous
sayings. Troilus is afraid of Calchas, and in three
proverbs expresses his fear, and also, perhaps, his
irritation at people who cannot talk five minutes
without becoming sententious:

For thus men seyth, "that on thenketh the beere,
But al another thenketh his ledere."   (iv, 1453 f.)

Youre syre is wys; and seyd is, out of drede
"Men may the wise atrenne, and naught atrede."
                                    (iv, 1455 f. [*H* 67; *S* 195])

It is ful hard to halten unespied
Byfore a crepel, for he kan the craft.   (iv, 1457 f.)

We are uncommonly close to a desperate parody of
Cressida's conversational style.

Troilus is scarcely more liberal with sententious
remarks and makes use of but six. As he walks
through the temple he uses one in speaking of the
lovers whom he scorns so heartily:

O veray fooles, nyce and blynde be ye!
Ther nys nat oon kan war by other be.   (i, 202 f.)

The next is in his song when he wonders about love
and its effect on himself:

For ay thurst I, the more that ich it drynke.   (i, 406)

Before he has told Pandarus the name of his beloved, he complains of Fortuna:

For wel fynde I that Fortune is my fo;
Ne al the men that riden konne or go
May of hire cruel whiel the harm withstonde;
For, as hire list, she pleyeth with free and bonde.

(i, 837 ff. [H p. 66])

Pandarus urges Troilus to be patient, but he replies that it is all very well to cry "abide";

but he
That hangeth by the nekke, soth to seyne
In gret disese abideth for the peyne.   (ii, 985 ff.)

He is true to the rules of the courtly game of love,
and once Cressida has yielded to him, he says:

Here may men seen that mercy passeth right.

(iii, 1282; [H 159a; S 184])

When Pandarus tries to reconcile him to the im-
pending departure of Cressida, he retorts that that
is as much as to say,

Thynk nat on smert, and thow shalt fele non.   (iv, 466)

He begins his famous adaptation of Boethius on the
eternal theme of God's foreknowledge and man's
free will with a thoroughly sententious statement,

For al that comth, comth by necessitee.   (iv, 958 [H 102])

After he dreams of Cressida in the embrace of the
boar, he feels sure that she has betrayed him and
calls out:

Who may bet bigile, yf hym lyste,
Than he on whom men weneth best to triste?   (v, 1266 f.)

Troilus uses four comparisons [15] and two other proverbial phrases.[16]

Few proverbs are used by the minor characters. Antigone introduces two into her song; people, she says, talk about love who have little knowledge of his weapons:

Thei speken, but thei benten nevere his bowe!

(ii, 861 [*S* 165])

This is the proverb which ordinarily runs, "Many speak of Robin Hood who never shot in his bow." In two manuscripts of the *Troilus*, marginal glosses supply Robin's name.[17] A few lines later Antigone gives the familiar warning:

And forthi, who that hath an hed of verre,
Fro cast of stones war hym in the werre!   (ii, 867 f.)

The "sudden" Diomede uses two proverbs which sum up his character admirably. As he leads Cressida toward the Greek camp, he thinks that there may be some profit for him in the trip after all, and he determines to try for it, since

I have herd seyd ek tymes twyes twelve,
"He is a fool that wole foryete hymselve."

(v, 97 f. [*H* 53; *S* 201])

Later, though he realizes from Cressida's sadness that she must have a lover in Troy, he decides to make an attempt:

For he that naught n'asaieth, naught n'acheveth.

(v, 784 [*H* 30b; *S* 164, 202])

He uses one proverbial phrase,[18] as does another minor figure, Cassandra.[19]

We must now consider the proverbs which occur in the narrative portions of the poem and which we may call Chaucer's own. Here we find seventeen proverbs and, curiously concentrated, twelve are in Books I and II. Chaucer observes Troilus in his pride as he scorns love, and he sees, too, that the God of Love is shooting at him. Troilus is going to be sadly beguiled, thinks the poet, and says, perhaps unkindly:

> Alday faileth thing that fooles wenden.   (i, 217 [S 148])

We are thus prepared at the outset to find our hero brave and courtly enough, but not overburdened with intelligence. Chaucer advises us to be warned by Troilus and to abstain from stubbornness in matters of love:

> The yerde is bet that bowen wole and wynde
> Than that that brest.   (i, 257 f. [H 75; S 149])

Troilus, smitten by Cressida's charms, would see her as often as possible, though his beloved's presence does not cure his pangs, for

> ay the ner he was, the more he brende.
> For ay the ner the fir, the hotter is, —
> This, trowe I, knoweth al this compaignye.
>
> (i, 448 ff. [H 56a])

When Pandarus asks Troilus to confide to him his
trouble, he refuses. He does not wish to tell any-
one, since, as Chaucer reminds us,

it is seyd, "man maketh ofte a yerde
With which the maker is hymself ybeten
In sondry manere," as thise wyse treten.
(i, 740ff. [*H* 21; *S* 153])

Chaucer puts four proverbs into the prologue to
Book II. He seems here to be using them structur-
ally; for he ends stanzas three, four, and six with
proverbs, and begins stanza six with one. Probably
he was influenced by the usage in the *ballades*, so
many of which, as we have seen in the case of Deschamps,[20] have a proverb at the end of each stanza.
Chaucer is not writing a *ballade*, and he does not
repeat the same proverb, but, for all that, the
influence is not only possible but likely. The
proverbs follow:

A blynd man kan nat juggen wel in hewis.
(ii, 21 [*H* 94; *S* 157])

In sondry londes, sondry ben usages.   (ii, 28 [*S* 158])

For every wight which that to Rome went
Halt nat o path, or alwey o manere.   (ii, 36 f.; [*H* p. 69])

Forthi men seyn, ecch contree hath his lawes.
(ii, 42 [*H* 113; *S* 158])

Chaucer fears lest some envious person will say
that Cressida fell in love with Troilus "right for the
firste sighte." It was not so at all, he assures us.
She did not fall, she merely inclined, and anyhow,

Every thyng, a gynnyng hath it nede.   (ii, 671 [*S* 163])

When Cressida sees Troilus riding by with his nine companions, she is visibly impressed, so much so that

Pandare, which that stood hire faste by,
Felte iren hoot, and he bygan to smyte.   (ii, 1275 f. [*S* 169])

When Troilus receives his first letter from Cressida, it makes him take hope, since,

as we may alday oureselven see,
Thorugh more wode or col, the more fir.   (ii, 1331 f. [*S* 170])

On the fateful night Pandarus entertains Cressida to the best of his ability, but at last she must take her leave despite his songs and his "Tale of Wade,"

as every thyng hath ende.   (iii, 615)

When Pandarus, with the deftness of a magician taking a rabbit out of his silk hat, produces Troilus, Cressida protests her faithfulness and begins to weep. The poet hopes that God will quench all this sorrow, and he has no doubt as to the Deity's ability:

For I have seyn, of a ful misty morwe
Folowen ful ofte a myrie someris day;
And after wynter foloweth grene May.
Men sen alday, and reden ek in stories,
That after sharpe shoures ben victories.
                    (iii, 1060 ff. [*H* 24, 25; *S* 182])

Cressida recovers her self-possession, and, woman-
like, begins to ask questions, such as "of what man,
and ek wheer, and also why He jalous was?"
Poor Troilus must say something, else she would
surely suspect a plot; accordingly he tells her an
arrant story of a cock and bull:

for the lasse harm, he moste feyne.   (iii, 1158)

At what has been called the Trojan tea-party
held for the consolation of Cressida, her women
friends talk of this and that — all "nyce vanitee,
she thinks," to keep her mind from her trouble:

Right as a man is esed for to feele,
For ache of hed, to clawen hym on his heele!   (iv, 727 f.)

Cressida yields to Diomede, but is too tender-
hearted to disillusion Troilus. He must find out
her faithlessness, however, for

men seyen that at the laste,
For any thyng, men shal the soothe se.   (v, 1639 f.)

Chaucer uses twelve sententious remarks. At
the outset he invokes Tisiphone's aid:

For wel sit it, the sothe for to seyne,
A woful wight to han a drery feere,
And to a sorwful tale, a sory chere.   (i, 12 ff.)

The pride of Troilus as he prances through the
temple does not amuse the poet, who knows that

This Troilus is clomben on the staire,
And litel weneth that he moot descenden.   (i, 215 f.)

We find three sayings about love in the passages
describing the fall of Troilus:

For evere it was, and evere it shal byfalle,
That love is he that alle thing may bynde,
For may no man fordon the lawe of kynde.
(i, 236 ff. [H p. 64])

Men reden nat that folk han gretter wit
Than they that han be most with love ynome.   (i, 241 f.)

Love to wide yblowe
Yelt bittre fruyt, though swete seed be sowe.
(i, 384 f. [H p. 64])

Pandarus promises to help Troilus "in loving of
Criseyde" and then draws up a plan of action. He
does not rush in blindly, but

caste his werk ful wisely or he wroughte.   (i, 1071)

After Pandarus's first chat with Cressida about
Troilus, Cressida sits by a window and sees the
object of her thoughts ride by, acclaimed by the
shouts of the populace. It was fate that produced
him at the psychological moment:

For which, men seyn, may nought destourbed be
That shal bityden of necessitee.   (ii, 622 f. [H 97])

Cressida's letter relieves Troilus somewhat of his
woe and his hope begins to mount,

As an ook comth of a litel spir.   (ii, 1335)

After Cressida is finally won, Chaucer reminds us
that it was through sorrow that Troilus's joy had
come:

O, sooth is seyd, that heled for to be
As of a fevre, or other gret siknesse,
Men moste drynke, as men may ofte se,
Ful bittre drynke; and for to han gladnesse,
Men drynken ofte peyne and gret distresse.   (iii, 1212 ff.)

When Pandarus appears the next morning, Cressida is at first inclined to upbraid him. She soon
becomes reconciled with her uncle, and Chaucer,
piously, gives us high authority for her act:

God foryaf his deth.   (iii, 1577)

Book iv begins with a complaint against Fortuna,

That semeth trewest whan she wol bygyle.   (iv, 3 [*H* p. 66])

She is cruel as well as fickle;

And whan a wight is from hire whiel ythrowe,
Than laugheth she, and maketh hym the mowe.
                              (iv, 6 f. [*H* p. 66])

Chaucer makes use of sixteen comparisons [21] and
of sixteen other proverbial phrases.[22]

To recapitulate, Chaucer uses proverbs in *Troilus and Criseyde* largely for purposes of characterization. There are some in the narrative, but
less than half as many as occur in the dialogue. The
greatest number of proverbs are put in the mouths

of the most sophisticated and self-possessed characters, Pandarus and Cressida. Troilus uses few,
and three of his few seem to have been evoked in
desperate parody. Even Antigone and Diomede,
who say relatively little, quote two proverbs each
to Troilus's four. Neither here nor elsewhere does
Chaucer regard proverbs as fitting wisdom for
peasants and rustics. He feels that they add *ton*
and a touch of sophistication to the characters who
use them.

CHAPTER IV

THE CANTERBURY TALES

(1) *General Prologue*

THE single reference to a proverb in the General Prologue to the *Canterbury Tales* is part of the description of the Miller:

And yet he hadde a thombe of gold, pardee.
(I [A] 563 [*H* p. 71])

There are, however, seven sententious remarks. Whatever may be the immediate application of the motto on the Prioress's brooch it is thoroughly sententious:

Amor vincit omnia.   (I [A] 162 [*H* 6])

The Friar, that noble pillar of his order, is skillful enough in picking up objects here and there, so much so, indeed, that

His purchas was wel bettre than his rente.   (I [A] 256)

Since the Middle Ages thought to find two atheists among every three medical men, the Doctor is characteristic of his profession, and we learn that

His studie was but litel on the Bible.   (I [A] 438)

Good parsons seem scarce, and without them we
cannot hope to find good parishioners, but our Parson knows the truth and asks:

If gold ruste, what shal iren do?
For if a preest be foul, on whom we truste,
No wonder is a lewed man to ruste;
And shame it is, if a prest take keep,
A shiten shepherde and a clene sheep.   (I [A] 500 ff.)

The Summoner speaks a little Latin, and well he
may, since he hears it daily:

And eek ye knowen wel how that a jay
Kan clepen "Watte" as well as kan the pope.   (I [A] 642 f.)

Chaucer apologizes for repeating all the words of
all his fellow-pilgrims, but he must record the
stories as they come, and

Eek Plato seith, whoso that kan hym rede,
The wordes moote be cosyn to the dede.
                    (I [A] 741 f. [*H* 47a; *S* 212])

The pilgrims were eager enough to accede to
Harry Bailey's plans, but next morning he wonders

If even-song and morwe-song accorde.   (I [A] 830)

Thus, with a sentiment not unlike Lady Mac-
beth's "Was the hope drunk Wherin you dress'd
yourself," the pilgrimage gets under way.

(2) *Knight's Tale*

Chaucer introduces twelve proverbs into the
Knight's Tale. Three of these are spoken by Arcite
and two by Theseus; the rest are in the narrative.
Arcite will not yield priority in love of Emily to
Palamon, and asks him,

Wostow nat wel the olde clerkes sawe,
That "who shal yeve a lovere any lawe?"
Love is a gretter lawe, by my pan,
Than may be yeve to any erthely man.

(I [A] 1163 ff. [*H* p. 64])

He strengthens this with even more worldly philosophy:

And therfore, at the kynges court, my brother,
Ech man for hymself, ther is noon oother.

(I [A] 1181 f. [*S* 213])

Palamon and Arcite meet in the woods, and Arcite
once more enunciates his doctrine of self-deter-
mination in love:

What, verray fool, thynk wel that love is free.

(I [A] 1606 [*H* 4])

Theseus uses his two proverbs in his speech at the
end of the poem; he is speaking of the inevitability
of change and decay:

Thanne may ye se that al this thyng hath ende.

(I [A] 3026 [*H* 148a])

Thanne is it wysdom, as it thynketh me,
To maken vertu of necessitee

(I [A] 3041 f. [*H* 96a; *S* 199])

The Knight had used the first proverb earlier in
describing the tournament:

Som tyme an ende ther is of every dede.
(I [A] 2636 [*H* 147; *S* 224])

The Knight prepares us for the meeting of Palamon and Arcite in the forest by means of two proverbs, which indicate that one may expect almost
anything in the woods:

But sooth is seyd, go sithen many yeres,
That "feeld hath eyen and the wode hath eres."
(I [A] 1521 f. [*H* 71; *S* 216])

It is ful fair a man to bere hym evene,
For al day meeteth men at unset stevene.
(I [A] 1523 f. [*cf.* I (A) 4383] [*S* 217])

Arcite is riding along lover-like, now happy, now
depressed, as changeable as Friday's weather, for

Selde is the Friday al the wowke ylike.
(I [A] 1539 [*H* 115; *S* 219])

The sworn brothers meet, but not in friendship,
parting only to come together in warlike array on
the following day. This draws an apostrophe from
the Knight:

O Cupide, out of alle charitee!
O regne, that wolt no felawe have with thee!
Ful sooth is seyd that love ne lordshipe
Wol noght, his thankes, have no felaweshipe.
(I [A] 1623 ff. [*H* 7; *S* 220])

The reader may think it an undue coincidence that
Theseus should have come riding along as Palamon and Arcite engage in mortal combat:

Yet somtyme it shal fallen on a day
That falleth nat eft withinne a thousand yeer.

(I [A] 1668 f. [S 221])

Old Saturn settles the strife on Olympus, and the
Knight's remark about his wisdom reminds us of
Troilus's mournful prophecy as to Cressida's pros-
pects of deceiving Calchas: [1]

Men may the olde atrenne, and noght atrede.

(I [A] 2449 [H 66; S 195])

Of the eighteen sententious remarks in the
Knight's Tale, Theseus speaks seven, Arcite three,
and Palamon and an anonymous Theban lady one
each. Theseus wonders at the madness of Palamon
and Arcite, who might have escaped clear and free,
and blames it to love, and asks:

Who may been a fool, but if he love?   (I [A] 1799)

The two youngsters are fighting over a lady who
has no notion of their love for her:

But all moot ben assayed, hoot and coold;
A man moot ben a fool, or yong or oold.   (I [A] 1811 f.)

Theseus regrets Arcite's untimely death, but rec-
ognizes in it the common fate of humanity:

He moot be deed, the kyng as shal a page.   (I [A] 3030)

Thanne may I seyn that al this thyng moot deye.

(I [A] 3034 [H 150])

Still there is no need to be always mourning for the
unrecallable dead:

But after wo I rede us to be merye.   (I [A] 3068 [H 22b])

He suggests that Emily show compassion to Palamon,

For gentil mercy oghte to passen right.

(I [A] 3089 [H 159b])

Arcite, while maintaining his right to love Emily
if he wishes, points out the futility of his present
disagreement with Palamon:

We stryve as dide the houndes for the boon;
They foughte al day, and yet hir part was noon.
Ther cam a kyte, whil that they were so wrothe,
And baar awey the boon bitwixe hem bothe.

(I [A] 1177 ff.)

Freedom, when it comes to Arcite unasked, is no
undiluted pleasure. He must leave Athens and is
sore afraid lest Palamon should in his absence gain
Emily's love,

syn Fortune is chaungeable.   (I [A] 1242 [H 16])

He wants happiness but has little notion how to
attain it. He is, he feels, like one under the influence of strong waters:

A dronke man woot wel he hath an hous,
But he noot which the righte wey is thider,
And to a dronke man the wey is slider.   (I [A] 1262 ff.)

The anonymous Theban lady blames Fortuna for her unhappy plight:

Thanked be Fortune and hire false wheel,
That noon estaat assureth to be weel.   (I [A] 925 f. [*H* p. 65])

Palamon's single expression of wisdom in the poem comes when he learns that Arcite is at large:

Allas, I se a serpent or a theef,
That many a trewe man hath doon mescheef,
Goon at his large.   (I [A] 1325 ff. [*S* 281])

We may note that the stronger characters in the *Knight's Tale*, Arcite and Theseus, use proverbs as the stronger characters do in *Troilus and Criseyde*.

The remaining sententious remarks are scattered through the narrative portions of the text. Palamon escaped from prison on the third day of May in the seventh year of his incarceration. Whether this was by "aventure or destynee" the Knight does not profess to know, but

whan a thyng is shapen, it shal be.   (I [A] 1466)

The erstwhile friends meet and fight. Theseus finds them, orders their death, but is assuaged by the entreaties of the ladies,

For pitee renneth soone in gentil herte.   (I [A] 1761)

The tournament is arranged, and the preparations are made. The arms are elaborate. After mention

of the Prussian shield we are quite ready to believe
that

Ther is no newe gyse that it nas old.   (I [A] 2125 [S 222])

In the best Homeric manner the contest eventually
spreads to the gods, and Saturn, old and wise, suggests a compromise:

As sooth is seyd, elde hath greet avantage;
In elde is bothe wysdom and usage.   (I [A] 2447 f. [H p. 68])

Arcite wins on the field, and Emily looks down upon
him in friendly fashion:

For wommen, as to speken in comune,
Thei folwen alle the favour of Fortune.   (I [A] 2681 f.)

But he, alas, is not to enjoy the fruits of his victory;
Pluto's fury frightens his horse, which throws him;
no medicine, "vomyt upward, ne dounward laxa-
tif," will avail:

And certeinly, ther Nature wol nat wirche,
Fare wel phisik! go ber the man to chirche!   (I [A] 2759 f.)

He dies, and all are saddened, especially Theseus,
who can be consoled only by Ægeus, his father,
who has lived long enough to expect

Joye after wo, and wo after gladnesse.
                    (I [A] 2841 [H 22a; S 225])

(3) Miller's Prologue and Tale

The Miller's Prologue contains two proverbs and
a sententious remark. The Miller himself advises

the angry Reeve not to put on the cap unless it
fits him. If he is not married, there can be no
slur, for

Who hath no wyf, he is no cokewold.   (I [A] 3152)

No man ought to look for trouble:

An housbonde shal nat been inquisityf
Of Goddes pryvetee, nor of his wyf.   (I [A] 3163 f.)

Chaucer apologizes again for the nature of some of
the tales. Here is a warning: let those who do not
wish to hear turn over the leaf and choose another
tale. Those who do read may well remember that

men shal nat maken ernest of game.   (I [A] 3186 [H 122])

There are three proverbs in the Miller's tale of a
carpenter and his wife. The wanton Alison prefers
the ever present Nicholas to the usually absent
Absalom, and proverbial authority is given to
justify her choice:

Ful sooth is this proverbe, it is no lye,
Men seyn right thus, "Alwey the nye slye
Maketh the ferre leeve to be looth."
                    (I [A] 3391 ff. [H 166; S 226])

Nicholas forms his elaborate plan to cornute the
"sely carpenter," and sends that worthy off with a
word of praise:

Men seyn thus, "sende the wise, and sey no thyng.
                    (I [A] 3598 [H 172])

Absalom calls at an inopportune time and receives
an unexpected greeting with the result that

His hoote love was coold and al yqueynt.   (I [A] 3754)

The sententious remarks number six. It would
have been well for the carpenter's brows and for his
arm had he been a student of sententious literature
before he married, but

He knew nat Catoun, for his wit was rude,
That bad man sholde wedde his simylitude.   (I [A] 3227 f.)

Men sholde wedden after hire estaat,
For youthe and elde is often at debaat.   (I [A] 3229 f.)

While Absalom's wooing, so melodious and so
foully repaid, proceeds swimmingly, the Miller
asks:

What wol ye bet than weel?   (I [A] 3370)

Nicholas goes into retirement to aid his plot; the
carpenter fears lest his lodger's studies in astron-
omy have made him mad. If so, it is no more
than he has expected all along, for such studies are
not fit for honest Christian men who

sholde nat knowe of Goddes pryvetee.   (I [A] 3454)

The clerk appears at last and tells his specious tale.
His host can save himself and wife by heeding good
advice:

For thus seith Salomon, that was ful trewe,
"Werk al by conseil, and thou shalt nat rewe."
                              (I [A] 3529 f. [H 90a])

No time is to be lost:

This asketh haste, and of an hastif thyng
Men may nat preche or maken tariyng.   (I [A] 3545 f.)

(4) *Reeve's Prologue* and *Tale*

The Reeve is heavily sententious in the Prologue to his tale. He could tell a story about a miller if he chose, but he "list not pley for age." A discourse on age follows:

We olde men, I drede, so fare we:
Til we be roten, kan we nat be rype.   (I [A] 3874 f.)

The Reeve has much more to say in like vein, but his audience is not wholly sympathetic, and the comparison of human life to a tun with the tap running is too much for the Host. Perhaps the thought of wasted liquor is a blow to his professional sensibility, but, at all events, he bursts out:

The devel made a reve for to preche,
Or of a soutere a shipman or a leche.   (I [A] 3903 f.)

Harry's remarks do not perturb the Reeve, who apologizes a little for his tale, but

leveful is with force force of-showve.   (I [A] 3912)

The Miller is to blame, the Reeve declares, for

He kan wel in myn eye seen a stalke,
But in his owene he kan nat seen a balke.   (I [A] 3919 f.)

The *Reeve's Tale* contains seven proverbs, five of which are spoken by John and one by the miller.

John greets Simkin with two proverbs when the
miller asks the reason for their visit:

"Symond," quod John, "by God, nede has na peer."

(I [A] 4026 [H 95; S 231])

Hym boes serve hymself that has na swayn,
Or elles he is a fool, as clerkes sayn.

(I [A] 4027 f. [H p. 53; S 232])

Simkin, true to his calling, determines to cheat
Aleyn and John, and anticipates little difficulty:

"The gretteste clerkes been noght wisest men,"
As whilom to the wolf thus spak the mare.

(I [A] 4054 f. [H 64; S 233])

The students are forced to ask "herberwe and ese"
of Simkin, who says he hasn't much room but does
not doubt their ability to make more space by
"argumentes."   John replies:

I have herd seyd, "man sal taa of twa thynges
Slyk as he fyndes, or taa slyk as he brynges."

(I [A] 4129 f. [H p. 53; S 234])

He also offers to pay, and shows his understanding
of the miller's character by remarking:

With empty hand men may na haukes tulle.

(I[A] 4134 [H 32a; S 235])

In the night John finds that he is alone and urges
himself to seek adventure and solace:

"Unhardy is unseely," thus men sayth.

(I [A] 4210 [H 18; S 189])

The Reeve ends his tale with an appropriate proverb:

And therfore this proverbe is seyd ful sooth,
"Him thar nat wene wel that yvele dooth";
A gylour shal hymself bigyled be.
                    (I [A] 4319 ff. [*H* 137; *S* 236, 237])

(5) *Cook's Prologue* and *Tale*

In the *Cook's Prologue* Harry Bailey reminds Roger of his fly-blown parsley, and adds:

But yet I pray thee, be nat wroth for game;
A man may seye ful sooth in game and pley.
                    (I [A] 4354 f. [*H* 120])

Roger agrees to the sentiment and caps Harry's proverb with another:

But "sooth pley, quaad pley" as the Flemyng seith.
                    (I [A] 4357 [*H* 123; *S* 238])

The Cook's tale did not get very far, but Roger had time, none the less, to introduce a proverb and a sententious remark. Perkin's master sends him packing on the authority

Of a proverbe that seith this same word,
"Wel bet is roten appul out of hoord
Than that it rotie al the remenaunt."
                    (I [A] 4405 ff. [*H* 74; *S* 239])

The outcast apprentice then goes to his inevitable accomplice,

for ther is no theef withoute a lowke,
That helpeth hym to wasten and to sowke
Of that he brybe kan or borwe may.

(I [A] 4415 ff. [H 105])

(6) *Man of Law's Introduction, Prologue,* and *Tale*

The Man of Law uses a single proverb in his head-link, and that a legal one. When the Host reminds him of the agreement, he replies:

Biheste is dette.   (II [B] 41 [*H* 48; *S* 241])

This he substantiates at once with a sententious remark:

For swich lawe as a man yeveth another wight,
He sholde hymselven usen it, by right;
Thus wole oure text.   (II [B] 43 ff. [*H* 78; *S* 242])

Two of the remaining five sententious remarks are spoken by the Host, who seems to have taken over the Reeve's trick of preaching:

Leseth no tyme, as ferforth as ye may.
Lordynges, the tyme wasteth nyght and day,
And steleth from us, what pryvely slepynge,
And what thurgh necligence in oure wakynge,
As dooth the streem that turneth nevere agayn,
Descendynge fro the montaigne into playn.

(II [B] 19 ff. [*H* p. 70])

Wel kan Senec and many a philosophre
Biwaillen tyme moore than gold in cofre;
For "los of catel may recovered be,
But los of tyme shendeth us," quod he.

It wol nat come agayn, withouten drede,
Namoore than wole Malkynes maydenhede,
Whan she hath lost it in hir wantownesse.

(II [B] 25 ff. [H p. 71; S 104])

In his Prologue proper the lawyer furnishes us with three sayings on the woes of poverty:

Herkne what is the sentence of the wise:
"Bet is to dyen than have indigence."

(II [B] 113 f. [H 151a])

Yet of the wise man take this sentence:
"Alle the dayes of povre men been wikke." (II [B] 117 f.)

If thou be povre, thy brother hateth thee,
And alle thy freendes fleen from thee, allas!

(II [B] 120 f. [H 27; S 243])

The *Man of Law's Tale* is innocent of proverbs, but contains eight sententious remarks. We hear of the arguments in the sowdan's privy council concerning Constance, and

Diverse men diverse thynges seyden.   (II [B] 211)

The mutability of human fortunes, changing usually for the worse, is the subject of three sayings. Two of these occur in the passage telling of the murder of the sowdan at his mother's instigation:

O sodeyn wo, that evere art successour
To worldly blisse, spreynd with bitternesse!
The ende of the joye of oure worldly labour!
Wo occupieth the fyn of oure gladnesse.

(II [B] 421 ff. [S 193])

Upon thy glade day have in thy mynde
The unwar wo or harm that comth bihynde.

> (II [B] 426 f. [H p. 67])

The third passage reminds us that even after their
reunion Ælla and Constance cannot be happy
long:

Joye of this world, for tyme wol nat abyde;
Fro day to nyght it changeth as the tyde.   (II [B] 1133 f.)

Ælla first meets Constance when she is accused of
killing her benefactor's daughter. The king feels
compassion for her,

As gentil herte is fulfild of pitee.   (II [B] 660)

Her innocence established, Ælla marries Constance, to the joy of all save Donegild. The Man
of Law will not tell all the details of the royal
wedding, for

Me list nat of the chaf, ne of the stree,
Maken so long a tale as of the corn.   (II [B] 701 f.)

When Donegild succeeds in getting the messenger
drunk the lawyer has a saying ready:

Ther dronkenesse regneth in any route,
Ther is no conseil hyd, withouten doute.

> (II [B] 776 f. [S 244])

King Ælla dies, despite his rank,

For deeth, that taketh of heigh and logh his rente,
Whan passed was a yeer, evene as I gesse,
Out of this world this kyng Alla he hente.

> (II [B] 1142 ff. [H 155])

(7) *Wife of Bath's Prologue* and *Tale*

No other of the pilgrims cares for proverbs so much as the Wife of Bath. She values experience above authority, and, despite their frequent dogmatism, proverbs are close enough to experience to appeal to her. Of all philosophical, or semi-philosophical, statements proverbs are the most realistic and Dame Alice is above all a realist. When we remember in addition that one of her husbands, that lusty clerk who gave her a deaf ear,[2] was addicted to proverbs of a certain sort, we need not be surprised to find fourteen proverbs and twenty-five sententious remarks in her *Prologue*.

Virginity is for those who want it — a prize is offered:

Cacche whoso may, who renneth best lat see.   (III [D] 76)

If chastity is to be observed, men and women must be kept apart:

For peril is bothe fyr and tow t'assemble.
(III [D] 89 [*H* 57; *S* 262])

Husbands are full of lies, old dotard shrews that they are, and say that the plainest wife can find another mate in time:

Ne noon so grey goos gooth ther in the lake
As, seistow, wol been withoute make.
(III [D] 269 f. [*H* 104; *S* 264])

Jealous husbands are unreasonable. Why should
they care for that which they cannot use?

He is to greet a nygard that wolde werne
A man to lighte a candle at his lanterne.   (III [D] 333 f.)

Dame Alice gave her earlier husbands grounds for
complaint, but she stifled their remonstrances by
crying "thief" first:

Whoso that first to mille comth, first grynt.
                    (III [D] 389 [H 79; S 266])

They were no match for her in subterfuge:

Deceite, wepyng, spynnyng God hath yive
To wommen kyndely, whil that they may lyve.
                    (III [D] 401 f. [S 267])

Whosoever the fault, no peace was made until
"our dame" received some reward. Her husbands
found

2. With empty hand men may none haukes lure.
                    (III [D] 415 [H 32b; S 235])

She is free to confess that she loves wine, nor does
she shame to recount its effect upon her:

And after wyn on Venus moste I thynke,
For al so siker as cold engendreth hayl,
A likerous mouth moste han a likerous tayl.
In wommen vinolent is no defence, —
This knowen lecchours by experience.
                    (III [D] 464 ff. [H 177])

Her fourth husband was a "revelour," who seems
to have been untrue to her, a reversal of the cus-

tomary procedure in her marriages which she did
not accept meekly:

For, God it woot, he sat ful ofte and song,
Whan that his shoo ful bitterly hym wrong.
(III [D] 491 f. [S 277])

As fifth husband she selected an educated man,
a clerk of Oxford, and she loved him best, perhaps
because he was "dangerous" of his love to her:

With daunger oute we al oure chaffare;
Greet prees at market maketh deere ware,
And to greet cheep is holde at litel prys.
(III [D] 521 ff. [H 109])

She had known Jenkin the clerk before her fourth
spouse died. He was in her mind as a next husband,
for she always had a runner-up on hand:

I holde a mouses herte nat worth a leek
That hath but oon hole for to sterte to,
And if that faille, thanne is al ydo.   (III [D] 572 ff. [S 270])

Jenkin turned out to be less amenable than the
earlier husbands. He told her stories of other
wives who had had her failings and had received
punishment for them. He also quoted proverbs at
her, and she was annoyed to be attacked with her
own weapons:

Thanne wolde he seye right thus, withouten doute:
"Whoso that buyldeth his hous al of salwes,
And priketh his blynde hors over the falwes,

And suffreth his wyf to go seken halwes,
Is worthy to been hanged on the galwes!"

(III [D] 654 ff. [*H* 171; *S* 271])

But all went for nothing, she "sette noght an hawe Of his proverbes n'of his olde sawe." He told her the sad adventure which befell Socrates on his own doorstep and of the sage's comment:

Er that thonder stynte, comth a reyn!   (III [D] 732 [*H* 26])

In the interlude furnished by the exchange of incivilities between the Friar and the Summoner, the latter uses a pointed proverb:

A frere wol entremette hym everemo.
Lo, goode men, a flye and eek a frere
Wol falle in every dyssh and eek mateere.

(III [D] 834 ff. [*H* 176])

There are twenty-five sententious remarks in Dame Alice's self-portrait. A majority of these are common mediaeval generalizations about the fair sex, which the Wife ascribes to her various husbands. She has been married five times and thinks that she ought to know enough about marriage:

Diverse scoles maken parfyt clerkes,
And diverse practyk in many sondry werkes
Maketh the werkman parfyt sekirly.   (III [D] 44c, d, e)

She quotes St. Paul with approval:

3 Bet is to be wedded than to brynne.   (III [D] 52 [*H* p. 52])

Virginity may be preferable in the sight of God, but he has use for the less perfect:

⊸| .conseillyng is no comandement.   (III [D] 67)

For wel ye knowe, a lord in his houshold,
He nath nat every vessel al of gold;
Somme been of tree, and doon hir lord servyse.
God clepeth folk to hym in sondry wyse.   (III [D] 99 ff.)

The Pardoner interrupts and is advised not to jump to conclusions but to wait and hear her stories, then model his own conduct accordingly:

Whoso that nyl be war by othere men,
By hym shul othere men corrected be.   (III [D] 180 f.)

She tells us altogether too much about her life with her old husbands. We could hardly condemn them if they had actually said the things which she accused them of saying:

She may no while in chastitee abyde,
That is assailled upon ech a syde.   (III [D] 255 f.)

Thou seyst men may nat kepe a castel wal,
It may so longe assailled been over al.   (III [D] 263 f.)

And seyst it is a hard thyng for to welde
A thyng that no man wole, his thankes, helde.
                                        (III [D] 271 f.)

Thow seyst that droppyng houses, and eek smoke,
And chidyng wyves maken men to flee
Out of hir owene hous.   (III [D] 278 ff. [H 158a; S 249])

Thou seyst we wyves wol oure vices hide
Til we be fast, and thanne we wol hem shewe, —
Wel may that be a proverbe of a shrewe!
                            (III [D] 282 ff. [H 182])

Thou seydest this, that I was lyk a cat;
For whoso wolde senge a cattes skyn,
Thanne wolde the cat wel dwellen in his in;
And if the cattes skyn be slyk and gay,
She wol nat dwelle in house half a day,
But forth she wole, er any day be dawed,
To shewe hir skyn, and goon a-caterwawed.

(III [D] 348 ff.)

Thou seydest eek that ther been thynges thre,
The whiche thynges troublen al this erthe,
And that no wight may endure the ferthe.
O leeve sire shrewe, Jhesu shorte thy lyf!
Yet prechestow and seyst an hateful wyf
Yrekened is for oon of thise meschances.   (III [D] 362 ff.)

Thou liknest it [*woman's love*] also to wilde fyr;
The moore it brenneth, the moore it hath desir
To consume every thyng that brent wole be.   (III [D] 373 ff.)

Thou seyest, right as wormes shende a tree,
Right so a wyf destroyeth hire housbonde.   (III [D] 376 f.)

She replies to their supposed accusations as cogently as if they had been authentic:

The wise astrologien Daun Ptholome,
That seith this proverbe in his Almageste:
"Of alle men his wysdom is the hyeste
That rekketh nevere who hath the world in honde."

(III [D] 324 ff. [*H* 65; *S* 265])

Thogh thou preye Argus with his hundred yen
To be my warde-cors, as he kan best,
In feith, he shal nat kepe me but me lest.

(III [D] 358 ff. [*H* p. 71])

They paid, too, for any fault that they might find:

Wynne whoso may, for al is for to selle.

(III [D] 414 [*H* 168; *S* 268])

Her beauty, if not her strength and love of life, is fading, and she bids "the devel go therwith":

The flour is goon, ther is namoore to telle;
The bren, as I best kan, now moste I selle.   (III [D] 477 f.)

She tells the Pardoner and other young men the secret of success with her sex:

Wayte what thyng we may nat lightly have,
Therafter wol we crie al day and crave.
Forbede us thyng, and that desiren we;
Preesse on us faste, and thanne wol we fle. (III [D] 517 ff.)

Her fifth husband was almost more than a match for her. The things which she put into the mouths of her first three husbands he actually said, and more thereto:

And thanne wolde he upon his Bible seke
That ilke proverbe of Ecclesiaste
Where he comandeth, and forbedeth faste,
Man shal nat suffre his wyf go roule aboute.
                        (III [D] 650 ff. [*H* 170])

"Bet is," quod he, "thyn habitacioun
Be with a leon or a foul dragoun,
Than with a womman usynge for to chyde."
                        (III [D] 775 ff. [*H* 183])

"Bet is," quod he, "hye in the roof abyde,
Than with an angry wyf doun in the hous."
                        (III [D] 778 f. [*H* 184])

They haten that hir housbondes loven ay.   (III [D] 781)

He seyde, a "womman cast hir shame away,
Whan she cast of hir smok." (III [D] 782 f. [*H* 156])

A fair womman, but she be chaast also,   •
Is lyk a gold ryng in a sowes nose.   (III [D] 784 f. [H 157a])

There are two proverbs in the Wife's Tale. The first of these is used rather as a supplement to the Prologue than as an organic part of the tale proper:

For trewely ther is noon of us alle,
If any wight wol clawe us on the galle,
That we nel kike, for he seith us sooth.

(III [D] 939 ff. [S 297])

The old lady reminds the lusty bachelor of Arthur's house that her very age is a warrant for the soundness of her opinion:

"Thise olde folk kan muchel thyng," quod she.

(III [D] 1004)

The seven sententious remarks all appear in the curtain lecture of the Loathly Lady. Six of them deal with true gentility and the nobility of the poor.

For vileyns synful dedes make a cherl.   (III [D] 1158])

Reedeth Senek, and redeth eek Boece;
Ther shul ye seen expres that it no drede is
That he is gentil that dooth gentil dedis.   (III [D] 1168 ff.)

Glad poverte is an honest thyng, certeyn;
This wole Senec and othere clerkes seyn.
Whoso that halt hym payd of his poverte,
I holde hym riche, al hadde he nat a sherte.

(III [D] 1183 ff. [H 28])

He that coveiteth is a povre wight,
For he wolde han that is nat in his myght;

But he that noght hath, ne coveiteth have,
Is riche, although ye holde hym but a knave.

(III [D] 1187 ff.)

Verray poverte, it syngeth proprely;
Juvenal seith of poverte myrily:
"The povre man, whan he goth by the weye,
Bifore the theves he may synge and pleye."

(III [D] 1191 ff.)

Poverte a spectacle is, as thynketh me,
Thurgh which he may his verray freendes see.

(III [D] 1203 f.)

For filthe and eelde, also mote I thee,
Been grete wardeyns upon chastitee.   (III [D] 1215 f.)

(8) *Friar's Tale*

The *Friar's Tale* contains a single proverb. The summoner tells the yeoman from the North the principle on which he operates:

I spare nat to taken, God it woot,
But if it be to hevy or to hoot.   (III [D] 1435 f. [*S* 273])

The first of the two sententious remarks echoes a saying of Chaucer's about the Friar in the General Prologue:

My purchas is th'effect of al my rente.   (III [D] 1451)

The fiend uses the second:

Alle thyng hath tyme.   (III [D] 1475 [*H* 145a])

(9) *Summoner's Tale*

The Summoner uses no more proverbs than the Friar. His hero reminds Thomas that anger is a sin, and prays:

An irous man, God sende hym litel myght!　(III [D] 2014)

The greater part of the Summoner's story consists of the friar's very real sermon, which loses nothing of point even if it is the Summoner who is preaching for one of his rival's colleagues. We may expect to find the preachment sententious, and it is: it contains six sententious remarks. The friar defends his interpretation of Scripture:

Glosynge is a glorious thyng, certeyn,
For lettre sleeth, so as we clerkes seyn.
                    (III [D] 1793 f. [*H* p. 68])

He shows clearly that a man should give to the friars, or better to a particular friar, namely himself:

Therfore, right as an hauk up at a sours
Up springeth into th'eir, right so prayeres
Of charitable and chaste bisy freres
Maken hir sours to Goddes eres two.　(III [D] 1938 ff.)

What is a ferthyng worth parted in twelve?
Lo, ech thyng that is oned in himselve
Is moore strong than whan it is toscatered. (III [D] 1967 ff.)

The hye God, that al this world hath wroght,
Seith that the werkman worthy is his hyre.
                    (III [D] 1972 f. [*H* 43])

He comes easily to reproof of Thomas for abusing his wife lest he sour her naturally sweet disposition:

War fro the serpent that so slily crepeth
Under the gras, and styngeth subtilly.   (III [D] 1994 f.)

Ther nys, ywys, no serpent so cruel,
Whan man tret on his tayl, ne half so fel,
As womman is, whan she hath caught an ire. (III [D] 2001 ff.)

(10) *Clerk's Prologue* and *Tale*

The Host flings two sentientious remarks at the Clerk while demanding that he cease his introspection and tell a story:

But Salomon seith, "every thyng hath tyme."
(IV [E] 6 [*H* 145e])

For what man that is entred in a pley,
He nedes moot unto the pley assente. (IV [E] 10 f. [*S* 275])

One proverb occurs in the *Clerk's Tale*. Griselda is taking her leave of Walter:

But sooth is seyd — algate I fynde it trewe,
For in effect it preeved is on me —
Love is noght oold as whan that it is newe.
(IV [E] 855 ff. [*H* 8])

There are eight sentientious remarks. Walter's subjects urge him to marry before it is too late:

For though we slepe, or wake, or rome, or ryde,
Ay fleeth the tyme; it nyl no man abyde.
(IV [E] 118 f. [*S* 240])

He stipulates that he shall be free to choose a wife without regard for rank. Birth does not always count:

For God it woot, that children ofte been
Unlyk hir worthy eldres hem bifore.   (IV [E] 155 f.)

And the Clerk points out that

> hye God somtyme senden kan
> His grace into a litel oxes stalle.   (IV [E] 206 f.)

Walter's wisdom won him the admiration of his people:

> And for he saugh that under low degree
> Was ofte vertu hid, the peple hym heelde
> A prudent man, and that is seyn ful seelde.   (IV [E] 425 ff.)

Griselda turns out to be a good wife, but Walter is impelled to test her again and again. It was all unnecessary, the Clerk says:

> But wedded men ne knowe no mesure,
> Whan that they fynde a pacient creature.   (IV [E] 622 f.)

When Walter discards Griselda, he does so with words that ring familiar to-day:

> No man may alwey han prosperitee.   (IV [E] 810 [*H* p. 65])

The new wife appears, and the people hail her joy-fully, forgetful of Griselda. This calls forth from the "Auctor" an outburst which is sufficiently in character for the Clerk himself:

> O stormy peple! unsad and evere untrewe!
> Ay undiscreet and chaungynge as a fane!
> Delitynge evere in rumbul that is newe,
> For lyk the moone ay wexe ye and wane!
> Ay ful of clappyng, deere ynogh a jane!
> Youre doom is fals, youre constance yvele preeveth;
> A ful greet fool is he that on yow leeveth.
>
> (IV [E] 995 ff. [*S* 147])

The Clerk tells us at the end that there are no wives like Griselda nowadays. The mints no longer function properly:

The gold of hem hath now so badde alayes
With bras, that thogh the coyne be fair at ye,
It wolde rather breste a-two than plye.   (IV [E] 1167 ff.)

The curious stanza which seems to have been intended to bring the tale to an end after either l. 1162 or l. 1169 contains a sententious remark by the Host:

But thyng that wol nat be, lat it be stille.   (IV [E] 1212g)

(11) *Merchant's Tale*

The *Merchant's Tale* includes five proverbs, three of which are spoken by January. He wants a young wife:

"Oold fissh and yong flessh wolde I have ful fayn.
Bet is," quod he, "a pyk than a pykerel,
And bet than old boef is the tendre veel."
                              (IV [E] 1418 ff. [H 116])

Justinus tries to warn him by saying that he has had trouble himself, however meek his wife may appear:

But I woot best where wryngeth me my sho.
                              (IV [E] 1553 [H 20; S 277])

This does not please January, who replies, "Straw for thy Senec, and for thy proverbes!" On his wedding night he waxes proverbial:

Ther nys no werkman, whatsoevere he be,
That may bothe werke wel and hastily;
This wol be doon at leyser parfitly.

(IV [E] 1832 ff. [H p. 67])

A man may do no synne with his wyf,
Ne hurte hymselven with his owene knyf.   (IV [E] 1839 f.)

January becomes blind in the midst of his lust and good fortune. May loves Damyan. The "Auctor" remarks that she could have deceived her husband even if he had his sight, and returns to the story thus:

Passe over is an ese, I sey namoore.   (IV [E] 2115)

There are fourteen sententious remarks. January thinks of the pain and woe of bachelors:

On brotel ground they buylde, and brotelnesse
They fynde, whan they wene sikernesse.   (IV [E] 1279 f.)

A wife, says the Merchant (sarcastically, I fear), is an insurance against adversity; to follow her advice is all man needs to do:

For which, if thou wolt werken as the wyse,
Do alwey so as wommen wol thee rede.   (IV [E] 1360 f.)

January will not marry a widow. Widows know too much:

For sondry scoles maken sotile clerkis;
Womman of manye scoles half a clerk is.   (IV [E] 1427 f.)

His friends give him various counsel:

Diverse men diversely hym tolde.   (IV [E] 1469)

Placebo does not hesitate to flatter his brother.
You are too wise, he says,

To weyven fro the word of Salomon.
This word seyde he unto us everychon:
"Wirk alle thyng by conseil," thus seyde he,
"And thanne shaltow nat repente thee."
                              (IV [E] 1483 ff. [*H* 90c])

At last January picks out a wife, and the Merchant
remarks slyly:

Love is blynd alday, and may nat see.
                    (IV [E] 1598 [*H* 2; *S* 278])

At the wedding Damyan, the squire, falls in love
with May. He is likely to be a menace to January:

For in this world nys worse pestilence
Than hoomly foo al day in thy presence.   (IV [E] 1793 f.)

The next day January arises at prime or a little
later, but May keeps her chamber until the fourth
day:

For every labour somtyme moot han reste,
Or elles longe may he nat endure.   (IV [E] 1862 f. [*H* 42a])

Poor Damyan succumbs to lovesickness. May
visits the sick-room and is favorably impressed by
the squire. The Merchant does not know why she
fell in love at that particular time: perhaps the
constellations were just right,

For alle thyng hath tyme, as seyn thise clerkes.
                              (IV [E] 1972 [*H* 145b])

She would love him if he had no more than his shirt. This is saying a good deal for May, who seems to have had an eye to the main chance, but

Lo, pitee renneth soone in gentil herte!   (IV [E] 1986)

She writes a letter of love to Damyan, who recovers at once and is more attentive to January than ever,

For craft is al, whoso that do it kan.   (IV [E] 2016)

January and May live together happily enough,

But worldly joye may nat alwey dure.   (IV [E] 2055)

I need not recount the sorry tale of the adventure in the garden, and how Proserpina wins a wager from Pluto. May's last words, however, uttered as she leapt down from the tree, were:

He that mysconceyveth, he mysdemeth.

(IV [E] 2410 [*H* 91])

(12) *Squire's Tale*

There are four proverbs in the *Squire's Tale*. The populace examine the brazen horse and express their opinions:

Diverse folk diversely they demed;
As many heddes, as manye wittes ther been.

(V [F] 202 f. [*H* 114; *S* 279])

The peregrine falcon introduces three proverbs into her complaint:

But sooth is seyd, goon sithen many a day,
"A trewe wight and a theef thenken nat oon."

> (V [F] 536 f. [H 125b; S 142, 281])

That I made vertu of necessitee.

> (V [F] 593 [H 96b; S 199])

"Therfore bihoveth hire a ful long spoon
That shal ete with a feend," thus herde I seye.

> (V [F] 602 f. [H 70; S 282])

There are nine sententious remarks. The Squire is not surprised that the people think the horse a potential source of trouble:

As lewed peple demeth comunly
Of thynges that been maad moore subtilly
Than they kan in hir lewednesse comprehende;
They demen gladly to the badder ende.   (V [F] 221 ff.)

After the banquet the people troop off to bed by twos and threes:

The norice of digestioun, the sleep,
Gan on hem wynke and bad hem taken keep
That muchel drynke and labour wolde han reste.

> (V [F] 347 ff. [H 42b])

The remaining seven sayings are used by the falcon. She begins by complimenting Canace in familiar words:

Pitee renneth soone in gentil herte.   (V [F] 479)

For gentil herte kitheth gentillesse.   (V [F] 483])

She will tell her story because Canace has asked for it:

And for to maken othere be war by me,
As by the whelp chastised is the leon. (V [F] 490 f. [S 280])

Her other remarks all deal with the falsity and fickleness of her lover:

Right as a serpent hit hym under floures
Til he may seen his tyme for to byte.   (V [F] 512 f.)

Who kan sey bet than he, who kan do werse?   (V [F] 600)

I trowe he hadde thilke text in mynde,
That "alle thyng, repeirynge to his kynde,
Gladeth hymself," thus seyn men, as I gesse.
                        (V [F] 607 ff. [H p. 69])

Men loven of propre kynde newefangelnesse,
As briddes doon that men in cages fede. (V [F] 610 f.)

We observe in the falcon another obvious effort to use proverbs and sententious remarks as an aid to characterization.

(13) *Franklin's Tale*

The Franklin introduces two proverbs and two sententious remarks into his tale. In his resolution of the marriage question he says:

Love wol nat been constreyned by maistrye.
Whan maistrie comth, the God of Love anon
Beteth his wynges, and farewel, he is gon!
Love is a thyng as any spirit free. (V [F] 764 ff. [H 3])

When Dorigen tells her husband of her foolish promise, he replies:

"Ye, wyf," quod he, "lat slepen that is stille." (V [F] 1472)

The Franklin believes in "pacience" and "suffraunce" in love:

Pacience is a heigh vertu, certeyn,
For it venquysseth, as thise clerkes seyn,
Thynges that rigour sholde nevere atteyne.

(V [F] 773 ff. [S 197])

Greatly as Dorigen mourns her husband's absence, she is at last somewhat consoled:

By proces, as ye knowen everichoon,
Men may so longe graven in a stoon
Til som figure therinne emprented be.   (V [F] 829 ff.)

(14) *Physician's Tale*

The *Physician's Tale* contains one proverb and four sententious remarks. In the curious passage on governesses, which, if it refers to John of Gaunt's household, and particularly to Katherine Swynford, does not suggest too friendly a family spirit on Chaucer's part, we find the proverb:

A theef of venysoun, that hath forlaft
His likerousnesse and al his olde craft,
Kan kepe a forest best of any man.   (VI [C] 83 ff. [S 259])

The fourteen-year-old Virginia does not worship Bacchus; her abstinence speaks well for her morals:

For wyn and youthe dooth Venus encresse,
As men in fyr wol casten oille or greesse.   (VI [C] 59 f.)

Children should be brought up sternly and not given their own way:

Under a shepherde softe and necligent
The wolf hath many a sheep and lamb torent.
                    (VI [C] 101 f. [*H* 165; *S* 260])

Appius receives due reward for his misdeeds:

Heere may men seen how synne hath his merite.
                    (VI [C] 277 [*H* 141])

The poem ends sententiously:

Forsaketh synne, er synne yow forsake.   (VI [C] 286)

(15) *Pardoner's Prologue* and *Tale*

The Pardoner's desire for a drink and a cake (VI [C] 321 f.) before he can begin his tale may well refer to the proverb that "A story needs a drink." In his Prologue the Pardoner announces as the text of his sermon:

Radix malorum est Cupiditas.   (VI [C] 334, 426 [*H* 38a])

There is one proverb in his tale. The three rioters determine not to let their new-found treasure burn holes in their pockets:

And lightly as it comth, so wol we spende.
                    (VI [C] 781 [*S* 261])

Two of the Pardoner's three sententious remarks show him to be a man of strong principles:

For dronkenesse is verray sepulture
Of mannes wit and his discrecioun.

In whom that drynke hath dominacioun
He kan no conseil kepe, it is no drede.

                                        (VI [C] 558 ff. [S 244])

Hasard is verray mooder of lesynges.   (VI [C] 591)

The third scoundrel goes off for provender, and the
others plot his destruction, thinking it should not
be difficult to dispose of him, since

two of us shul strenger be than oon.   (VI [C] 825)

The Host does not recognize the Pardoner's revul-
sion of feeling at the end of his tale, or at least fails
to give him credit for it.   When he sees that the
Pardoner is too angry to speak, Harry says:

  I wol no lenger pleye
With thee, ne with noon oother angry man.   (VI [C] 958 f.)

(16) *Shipman's Tale*

The *Shipman's Tale* was evidently intended for
a woman, but if Chaucer wrote it for Dame Alice of
Bath he had not yet decided to make her a pur-
veyor of proverbs.   The tale contains no proverbs
and only two sententious remarks.   Women love
to be well dressed and their appearance wins them
many compliments,

But wo is hym that payen moot for al!   (VII, 10 [B 1200])

The merchant, at the end of the story, finds that
he is not likely to get the money which Dan John
repaid to his wife.   He takes it philosophically:

This marchant saugh ther was no remedie,
And for to chide it nere but folie,
Sith that the thyng may nat amended be.

(VII, 427 ff. [B 1617 ff.])

(17) *Prioress's Tale*

The Prioress makes use of two proverbs and one sententious remark in her short tale. Of the "litel clergeon" she says:

Sely child wol alday soone leere.

(VII, 512 [B 1702] [*H* 173; *S* 245])

His murder cannot be hidden:

Mordre wol out, certeyn, it wol nat faille.

(VII, 576 [B 1766] [*S* 246])

The Jews who knew of the murder are all killed by the provost on the principle that

Yvele shal have that yvele wol deserve.

(VII, 632 [B 1822] [*H* 138; *S* 247])

(18) *Tale of Melibee*

Chaucer does not use any proverbs in his own first tale, that of Thopas, but in his account of Melibee and Prudence, not to mention Sophie, he brings forward many. In his curious apology lest his account differ from some others which the pilgrims may know he speaks specifically of proverbs:

As thus, though that I telle somwhat moore
Of proverbes than ye han herd bifoore
Comprehended in this litel tretys heere.

(VII, 955 ff. [B 2145 ff.])

Chaucer seems to be trying to avert the suspicion that, although the story ought to have been translated directly from the Latin of Albertano of Brescia, he was perhaps using a French intermediary. As a matter of fact the *Tale of Melibee* is a very close translation of the French version,[3] marked only by frequent verbal expansion.[4] Chaucer used two proverbs not in the French, of which the most striking is: "The proverbe seith: 'He hasteth wel that wisely kan abyde,'" (VII, 1054 [B 2244]);[5] and the other: "He that is irous and wrooth, he ne may nat wel deme" (VII, 1125 [B 2315]). The sententious "Bettre holde thy tonge stille than for to speke" (VII, 1219 [B 2409]) does little more than paraphrase the French. The sole proverbial phrase in the *Tale*, "Be they nat worth a stree" (VII, 1336 [B 2526]) is translated from "Elles ne vallent riens" (I, 209). Chaucer also, as Tatlock points out,[6] took pains to omit a passage on the theme "De quoy Salemon dit: dolente est la terre qui a enfant à seigneur" (I, 202). With these exceptions the proverbial and sententious matter in the French is reproduced literally enough by Chaucer. I shall not try to discuss the fifty-six sayings in relation to their immediate context, but simply list them in order of occurrence, and give in each instance the French original.

PROVERBS

For the commune proverbe seith thus: "He that soone
deemeth, soone shal repente."

(VII, 1030 [B 2220] [*H* 92a; *S* 248])

car l'on dit communément: qui tost juge, tost se repent.

(I, 190)

right so as, whil that iren is hoot, men sholden smyte.

(VII, 1036 [B 2226] [*H* 80; *S* 169])

et dirent que tout ainsi comme l'en doit batre le fer tant
comme il est chault.   (I, 191)

"I see wel," quod this wise man, "that the commune proverbe
is sooth, that 'good conseil wanteth whan it is moost nede.'"

(VII, 1048 [B 2238] [*H* 89])

je vois bien maintenant que le proverbe commun est
vray: lors fault le bon conseil, quant le grant besoing est.

(I, 192)

and "he that al despiseth, al displeseth," as seith the book.

(VII, 1070 [B 2260])

car il est escript: qui tout desprise, à tout desplait.

(I, 194)

And as to youre fourthe resoun, ther ye seyn that the jang-
lerie of wommen kan hyde thynges that they wot noght, as
who seith that a womman kan nat hyde that she woot.

(VII, 1084 [B 2274])

Quant à la quarte raison, où tu dis que la jenglerie des
femmes ne puet céler fors ce qu'elles ne scevent pas.

(I, 195)

he that is irous and wrooth, he ne may nat wel deme.

(VII, 1125 [B 2315])   [*not in French*]

For, as ye herde her biforn, the commune proverbe is this,
that "he that soone deemeth, soone repenteth."

(VII, 1135 [B 2325] [*H* 92b; *S* 248])

car, selon ce que tu as oy dessus, l'en dist communément:
qui tost juge, tost se repent.   (I, 198)

For the proverbe seith: "He that to muche embraceth, dis-
treyneth litel."   (VII, 1215 [B 2405] [*H* 39a; *S* 146])

L'en dit en un proverbe: qui trop embrasse, pou estraint.
(I, 203)

Sententious Remarks

Salomon seith: "Werk alle thy thynges by conseil, and thou
shalt never repente."   (VII, 1003 [B 2193] [*H* 90b])

car Salemon dit: tous tes fais par conseil feras, ainsi ne
t'en repentiras.   (I, 189)

And eek men seyn that thilke juge is wys that soone under-
stondeth a matiere and juggeth by leyser.
(VII, 1031 [B 2221] [*H* 93])

et dit-on aussi que le juge est bon qui tost entent et tart
juge.   (I, 190)

ther is ful many a man that crieth "Werre! werre!" that woot
ful litel what werre amounteth.   (VII, 1038 [B 2228])

moult de gens crient *guerre*! haultement, qui ne scevent
que guerre se monte.   (I, 191)

For soothly, he that precheth to hem that listen nat heeren
his wordes, his sermon hem anoieth.   (VII, 1044 [B 2234])

car la narration de cellui qui presche à ceulx qui ne le
veulent oïr, est ennuyeuse.   (I, 192)

For I seye that it is no folie to chaunge conseil whan the thyng
is chaunged.   (VII, 1065 [B 2255])

car je dy qu'il n'est pas folie de changer son conseil quant
la chose se change.   (I, 193)

For the book seith that "the wise man maketh no lesyng whan he turneth his corage to the bettre."

> VII, 1067 [B 2257])

car il est escript: le sage ne ment mie quant il mue son courage en mieulx.   (I, 193-194)

of whiche wommen men seyn that thre thynges dryven a man out of his hous, that is to seyn, smoke, droppyng of reyn, and wikked wyves.   (VII, 1086 [B 2276] [H 158b; S 249])

on dit: trois choses sont qui gettent homme hors de sa maison, c'est assavoir la fumée, la goutière et la femme mauvaise.   (I, 195)

where as ye seyn that in wikked conseil wommen venquisshe men.   (VII, 1090 [B 2280])

où tu dit que en mauvais conseil les femmes vainquent les hommes.   (I, 195)

the philosophre that seith, "In wikked conseil wommen venquisshen hir housbondes."   (VII, 1094 [B 2284])

le dit du philosophe: en mauvais conseil vainquent les femmes les hommes.   (I, 196)

Eek som men han seyd that the conseillynge of wommen is outher to deere, or elles to litel of pris.

> (VII, 1096 [B 2286] [S 257])

l'en a acoustumé de dire: conseil de femme, ou il est très chier, ou il est très vil.   (I, 196)

Heere may ye se that if that wommen were nat goode, and hir conseils goode and profitable,/oure Lord God of hevene wolde nevere han wroght hem, ne called hem help of man, but rather confusioun of man.   (VII, 1105 f. [B 2295 f.] [S 256])

Se elles doncques n'estoient bonnes et leur conseil [bon], nostre Seigneur ne les eust pas appellées adjutoires de hommes, car elles ne fussent adjutoires de l'homme, mais en dommage et en nuisance.   (I, 196)

And thanne shul ye dryve fro youre herte thre thynges that been contrariouse to good conseil; / that is to seyn, ire, coveitise, and hastifnesse.   (VII, 1121 f. [B 2311 f.] [*H* 88a])

Et lors dois-tu oster trois choses de toy qui sont contrarieuses à conseil, c'est assavoir: ire, convoitise et hastiveté.   (I, 197)

For the Apostle seith that coveitise is roote of alle harmes.
(VII, 1130 [B 2320] [*H* 38b])

selon ce que dit l'apostre, convoitise est racine de tous maulx.   (I, 198)

For Seneca seith: "If so be that thou ne mayst nat thyn owene conseil hyde, how darstou prayen any oother wight thy conseil secrely to kepe?"   (VII, 1147 [B 2337])

car Sénèque dit: se tu ne te pues taire et ton secret céler, comment ose-tu prier un autre qu'il le vueille céler?
(I, 199)

men seyn that the riche man hath seeld good conseil, but if he have it of hymself.   (VII, 1153 [B 2343])

riche homme n'aura jà bon conseil se il ne l'a de soy mesmes.   (I, 199)

For the book seith that "in olde men is the sapience, and in longe tyme the prudence."   (VII, 1164 [B 2354] [*H* p. 69])

car il est escript en Job: ès anciens est la sapience, et en moult de temps est prudence.   (I, 200)

The book seith that "no wight retourneth saufly into the grace of his olde enemy."   (VII, 1183 [B 2373])

car il est escript: nul ne retourne seurement en la grâce de son ennemy.   (I, 201)

Thou shalt also eschue the conseiling of folk that been dronke-
lewe, for they ne kan no conseil hyde. / For Salomon seith,
"Ther is no privetee ther as regneth dronkenesse."
(VII, 1193 f. [B 2383 f.] [S 244])

> Après, tu dois fuir le conseil de ceulx qui sont souvent
> yvres, car ils ne scevent riens céler, et dit Salemon: nul
> secret n'est là où règne yvresse.　(I, 202)

And in alle thise thynges thou shalt chese the beste, and
weyve alle othere thynges.　(VII, 1208 [B 2398])

> et en toutes ces choses tu dois tousjours eslire ce qui est
> ton prouffit, toutes autres choses reffusées et rabatues.
> (I, 203)

bettre holde thy tonge stille than for to speke.
VII, 1219 [B 2409] [H 49]) [not in French]

For the lawe seith that "upon thynges that newely bityden
bihoveth newe conseil."　(VII, 1225 [B 2415])

> Car la loy dit: les choses qui de nouvel surviennent ont
> mestier de nouvel conseil.　(I, 204)

for ye han broght with yow to youre conseil ire, coveitise, and
hastifnesse, / the whiche thre thinges been contrariouse to
every conseil honest and profitable.
VII, 1246 f. [B 2436 f.] [H 88b])

> Après tu as erré quant tu es venu à conseil, car tu avoies
> avec toy ensemble ire, convoitise et hastiveté, lesquelles
> trois choses sont contraires à conseil, et ne les as pas
> abaissées en toy ne en ton conseil ainsi comme tu deusses.
> (I, 205)

The proverbe seith that "for to do synne is mannyssh, but
certes for to persevere longe in synne is werk of the devel."
(VII, 1264 [B 2454] [H 140])

> car péchier est euvre d'omme, mais persévérer en péchié
> est euvre de déable.　(I, 206)

For Catoun seith: "If thou hast nede of help, axe it of thy freendes; / for ther nys noon so good a phisicien as thy trewe freend." (VII, 1306 f. [B 2496 f.] [*H* 14])

> car Caton dit: se tu as besoing d'aide, demande-le à tes amis, car il n'est si bon phisicien comme le loyal amy.
>
> (I, 207)

for every wys man dredeth his enemy. (VII, 1316 [B 2506])

> car sage homme doit tousjours doubter, espécialment ses ennemis. (I, 208)

The book seith that "somme folk han greet lust to deceyve, but yet they dreden hem to be deceyved."

(VII, 1328 [B 2518])

> car il est escript: aucunes gens ont enseignié leur décevoir mais ils ont trop doubté que l'en les déceust.
>
> (I, 209)

the Book of Decrees seith, "Seelden, or with greet peyne, been causes ybroght to good ende whanne they been baddely bigonne." (VII, 1404 [B 2594])

> la raison du Décret qui dit: à grant peine sont menées à bonne fin les choses qui sont mal commencées. (I, 213)

and Salomon seith, "If thou hast founden hony, ete of it that suffiseth; / for if thou ete of it out of mesure, thou shalt spewe." (VII, 1416 f. [B 2606 f.] [*S* 250])

> Et Salemon dit: se tu as trouvé le miel, si en mengue à souffisance, car se tu en mengues oultre mesure, il te convendra vomir. (I, 213)

Forthermoore, ye knowen wel that after the comune sawe, "it is a woodnesse a man to stryve with a strenger or a moore myghty man than he is hymself; / and for to stryve with a man of evene strengthe, that is to seyn, with as strong a man as he is, it is peril; / and for to stryve with a weyker man, it is folie." (VII, 1481 ff. [B 2671 ff.])

Après, tu scez que l'en dit communément que contendre
à plus fort, c'est enragerie: contendre à esgal, c'est péril:
contendre à moindre, c'est honte.   (I, 217)

And therfore me thynketh men oghten nat repreve me, though
I putte me in a litel peril for to venge me, / and though I do a
greet excesse, that is to seyn, that I venge oon outrage by
another. /   (VII, 1524 f. [B 2714 f.])

et pour ce il me semble que l'en ne me doit pas reprendre
se je me met en un pou de péril pour moy vengier et se je
fais un grant excès, car on dit que excès n'est corrigé que
par excès, c'est à dire que oultrage ne se corrige fors que
par oultrage.   (I, 219)

For right as he that taketh a straunge hound by the eris is
outherwhile biten with the hound.   (VII, 1543 [B 2733])

Et aussi comme cellui qui tient le chien estrange qu'il ne
congnoist est aucune fois mors du chien.   (I, 220)

and Salomon seith that "alle thynges obeyen to moneye."
(VII, 1550 [B 2740] [H 35])

et Salemon dit que toutes choses obéissent à pécune.
(I, 221)

And if thy fortune change that thou wexe povre, farewel
freendshipe and felaweshipe; / for thou shalt be alloone
withouten any compaignye, but if it be the compaignye of
povre folk.   (VII, 1559 f. [B 2749 f.] [H p. 67; S 243])

et se ta fortune se change et que tu soies povre, tu de-
moureras tout seul.   (I, 221)

And therfore seith Salomon that "bet it is to dye than for to
have swich poverte."   (VII, 1571 [B 2761] [H 151b])

Et pour ce dit Salemon que mieulx vault mourir que avoir
telle povreté.   (I, 222)

And as the same Salomon seith, "Bettre it is to dye of bitter
deeth than for to lyven in swich wise (*poor*)."

(VII, 1572 [B 2762] [*H* 152])

> selon ce qu'il dit autre part, mieulx vault la mort amère
> que telle vie.   (I, 222)

For Salomon seith that "ydelnesse techeth a man to do manye
yveles."   (VII, 1589 [B 2779] [*H* 40])

> car Salemon dit que oisiveté enseigne moult de maulx à
> faire.   (I, 222–223)

For ther is a versifiour seith that "the ydel man excuseth hym
in wynter by cause of the grete coold, and in somer by enche-
soun of the greete heete."   (VII, 1593 [B 2783])

> car, selon ce que dit un versifieur, il s'excuse en yver de
> ce qu'il fait trop froit, et en esté de ce qu'il fait trop
> chault.   (I, 223)

And therfore seith a philosophre, "That man that desireth
and wole algates han werre, shal nevere have suffisaunce; /
for the richer that he is, the gretter despenses moste he make,
if he wole have worshipe and victorie."

(VII, 1651 f. [B 2841 f.])

> Pour ce dit un philosophe: homme qui guerre vuelt avoir,
> n'aura jà à souffisance avoir, car de tant comme l'omme
> est plus riche, de tant lui convient faire plus grans mises
> se il veut avoir honneur et victoire.   (I, 225)

And by cause that in batailles fallen manye perils, / and
happeth outher while that as soone is the grete man slayn as
the litel man.   (VII, 1666 f. [B 2856 f.])

> et pour ce que ès batailles a moult de périls, et advient
> aucunes fois que aussi tost occist-l'en le grant comme le
> petit.   (I, 226)

For Salomon seith, "He that loveth peril shal falle in peril."

(VII, 1671 [B 2861] [*H* 55])

car Salemon dit: qui aime le péril, il cherra en péril.
(I, 226)

For right as men seyn that "over-greet hoomlynesse engendreth dispreisynge," so fareth it by to greet humylitee or
mekenesse. (VII, 1686 [B 2876] [S 251])

car ainsi comme l'on dit que trop grant familiarité engendre mesprisement, aussi fait trop grant humilité.
(I, 227)

For the wise man seith "The dissensioun bigynneth by another man, and the reconsilyng bygynneth by thyself.
(VII, 1691 [B 2881])

car un sage dit: la dissension tousjours commence par
autre et la paix par toy. (I, 227)

they that been wrothe witen nat wel what they don, ne what
they seyn. / Therfore the prophete seith that "troubled eyen
han no cleer sighte." (VII, 1700 f. [B 2890 f.] [S 252])

et ceulx qui sont courroucés ne scevent pas bien qu'ils
font ne qu'ils dient; pour ce, dit le philosophe que les
troublés ne sont pas bien cler-voyans. (I, 228)

"Ther is an old proverbe," quod she, "seith that 'the goodnesse that thou mayst do this day, do it, / and abide nat ne
delaye it nat til to-morwe.'"
(VII, 1794 f. [B 2984 f.] [H 81])

L'en dist, fist-elle, ès Proverbes: le bien que tu peus faire
au matin, n'attens pas le soir ne l'endemain. (I, 232)

For after the sawe of the word of the Apostle, "Coveitise is
roote of alle harmes." (VII, 1840 [B 3030] [H 38c])

convoitise . . . est un grant vice et racine de tous maulx.
(I, 234)

(19) *Monk's Prologue* and *Tale*

The Host makes use of a proverb and a sententious remark in the Prologue to the *Monk's Tale*. The proverb is the very one which he had tried on the Cook [7] and which serves to render his insults doubly insulting:

Ful ofte in game a sooth I have herd seye!
(VII, 1964 [B 3154] [H 121; S 253])

He had already said that the monk would make a better provider of posterity than many a layman:

Of fieble trees ther comen wrecched ympes.
(VII, 1956 [B 3146] [H 111])

The Monk uses six sententious remarks in the course of his "tragedies," and naturally enough five of them deal with Fortuna:

For certein, whan that Fortune list to flee,
Ther may no man the cours of hire withholde.
(VII, 1995 f. [B 3185 f.] [H p. 65])

Lo, who may truste on Fortune any throwe?
(VII, 2136 [B 3326] [H p. 66])

For whan Fortune wole a man forsake,
She bereth awey his regne and his richesse,
And eek his freendes, bothe moore and lesse.
For what man that hath freendes thurgh Fortune,
Mishap wol maken hem enemys, I gesse;
This proverbe is ful sooth and ful commune.
(VII, 2241 ff. [B 3431 ff.] [H 19; S 254])

But ay Fortune hath in hire hony galle.
(VII, 2347 [B 3537] [H p. 66; S 255])

Thus kan Fortune hir wheel governe and gye,
And out of joye brynge men to sorwe.

> (VII, 2397 f. [B 3587 f.] [*H* p. 66])

The other occurs in the account of Hercules:

Ful wys is he that kan hymselven knowe!

> (VII, 2139 [B 3329] [*H* p. 52])

(20) *Nun's Priest's Prologue* and *Tale*

The Knight stops the Monk in full career, and then the Host gladly turns on him. He requests Dan Pierce to tell another story, for that one has almost put him to sleep, and with the judge asleep it could hardly profit the Monk to tell his tale:

For certeinly, as that thise clerkes seyn,
Whereas a man may have noon audience,
Noght helpeth it to tellen his sentence.

> (VII, 2800 ff. [B 3990 ff.])

The Nun's Priest uses three proverbs in his tale. The first is not given in full, but "Hunger is the best sauce" must lie behind the description of the widow's appetite:

Of poynaunt sauce hir neded never a deel.

> (VII, 2834 [B 4024])

Chanticleer, in his account of the murder in the inn, falls back on a proverb already used by the Prioress: [8]

Mordre wol out, that se we day by day.

> (VII, 3052, 3057 [B 4242, 4247] [*H* 143a, b; *S* 246])

The Nun's Priest, intimidated perhaps by his mistress and Dame Alice of Bath, accuses Chanticleer, with no apparent basis in fact, of uttering the old proverb:

Wommennes conseils been ful ofte colde.
(VII, 3256 [B 4446] [S 257])

We find seven sententious remarks. Pertelote uses two against dreams:

Nothyng, God woot, but vanitee in sweven is.
(VII, 2922 [B 4112])

Lo Catoun, which that was so wys a man,
Seyde he nat thus, "Ne do no fors of dremes?"
(VII, 2940 f. [B 4130 f.])

Chanticleer closes his argument with his wife by quoting and roguishly translating that old and ignoble ecclesiastical saying:

Mulier est hominis confusio.   (VII, 3164 [B 4354] [*S* 256])

The catastrophe is introduced fittingly with:

Evere the latter ende of joye is wo.
VII, 3205 [B 4395] [S 193])

Once Chanticleer has escaped from the clutches of the fox, he and Dan Russell exchange moralizations:

For he that wynketh, whan he sholde see,
Al wilfully, God lat him nevere thee!
(VII, 3431 f. [B 4621])

God yeve hym meschaunce,
That is so undiscreet of governaunce
That jangleth whan he sholde holde his pees.

(VII, 3433 ff. [B 4623 ff.])

The tale ends with an exhortation to apply the lesson of the story to human life:

Taketh the fruyt, and lat the chaf be stille.

(VII, 3443 [B 4633] [*H* p. 52])

(21) *Second Nun's Prologue* and *Tale*

The Second Nun begins her tale with a sententious remark:

The ministre and the norice unto vices,
Which that men clepe in Englissh ydelnesse,
That porter of the gate is of delices.　(VIII [G] 1 ff.)

One of the typical comments by which Cecilia seeks to endear herself to Almachius is to tell him that his power amounts to nothing:

For every mortal mannes power nys
But lyk a bladdre ful of wynd, ywys.
For with a nedles poynt, whan it is blowe,
May al the boost of it be leyd ful lowe.　(VIII [G] 438 ff.)

(22) *Canon's Yeoman's Prologue* and *Tale*

There are two sententious remarks in the prologue to the *Canon's Yeoman's Tale*. His master, the Yeoman says, is too wise for his own good:

That that is overdoon, it wol nat preeve
Aright, as clerkes seyn; it is a vice.　(VIII [G] 645 f. [*S* 283])

When the Canon sees his servant whispering to
Harry Bailly he becomes suspicious:

For Catoun seith that he that gilty is
Demeth alle thyng be spoke of hym, ywis.   (VIII [G] 688 f.)

Six proverbs in the tale come from the Yeoman
himself. Three suggest, apropos of the wisdom of
alchemists, that things are not always what they
seem:

But al thyng which that shineth as the gold
Nis nat gold, as that I have herd it told.
                        (VIII [G] 962 f. [H 131; S 206])

Ne every appul that is fair at eye
Ne is nat good, what so men clappe or crye.
                        (VIII [G] 964 f. [H 131; S 284])

He that semeth the wiseste, by Jhesus!
Is moost fool, whan it cometh to the preef;
And he that semeth trewest is a theef.
                        (VIII [G] 967 ff. [H p. 70])

The canon offers to teach the gullible priest the
secrets of "philosophy":

Ful sooth it is that swich profred servyse
Stynketh, as witnessen thise olde wyse.
                        (VIII [G] 1066 f. [H 161; S 285])

The Yeoman wonders that people once taken in
permit themselves to be fooled again:

O! fy, for shame! they that han been brent,
Allas! kan they nat flee the fires heete?
                        (VIII [G] 1407 f. [S 286])

He advises gulls to give it up before they lose everything,

For bet than nevere is late.   (VIII [G] 1410 [*H* 76; *S* 287])

The first of the three sententious remarks is used by the Yeoman to explain why one victim of alchemy tries to ensnare others:

Unto shrewes joye it is and ese
To have hir felawes in peyne and disese.
Thus was I ones lerned of a clerk.   (VIII [G] 746 ff. [*S* 152])

The others form part of his warning to adepts or dabblers in the art:

Nevere to thryve were to long a date.
(VIII [G] 1411 [*S* 287])

Withdraweth the fir, lest it to faste brenne;
Medleth namoore with that art, I mene.   (VIII [G] 1423 f.)

(23) *Manciple's Tale*

The *Manciple's Tale* contains one proverb and twelve sententious remarks. The proverb is part of the lore that the Manciple learned from his mother:

The Flemyng seith, and lerne it if thee leste,
That litel janglyng causeth muchel reste.
(IX [H] 349 f. [*S* 290])

Apollo, the Manciple tells us, was jealous of his wife; it is folly to try to guard a woman:

A good wyf, that is clene of werk and thoght,

Sholde nat been kept in noon awayt, certayn;
And trewely, the labour is in vayn
To kepe a shrewe, for it wol nat bee.
This holde I for a verray nycetee,
To spille labour for to kepe wyves:
Thus writen olde clerkes in hir lyves.   (IX [H] 148 ff.)

That constraint can never work against nature is proved by an example from the animal kingdom:

Taak any bryd, and put it in a cage, . . .
His libertee this brid desireth ay.   (IX [H] 163–174)

The Manciple is more prudish than some of his fellow-pilgrims and apologizes for using the word "lemman":

The wise Plato seith, as ye may rede,
The word moot nede accorde with the dede.
If men shal telle proprely a thyng,
The word moot cosyn be to the werkyng.
                        (IX [H] 207 ff. [*H* 47b; *S* 212])

Apollo learns of his wife's infidelity and kills her. He is smitten with remorse, and cries:

Smyt nat to soone, er that ye witen why.   (IX [H] 285)

Anger is a terrible vice:

Allas! a thousand folk hath rakel ire
Fully fordoon, and broght hem in the mire.
                (IX [H] 289 f. [*H* 180b — "Dun hath broght"])

The remaining sayings are warnings given to the Manciple by his mother against too much talking:

A wikked tonge is worse than a feend.
                        (IX [H] 320 [*H* p. 52])

My sone, ful ofte, for to muche speche
Hath many a man been spilt, as clerkes teche;
But for litel speche avysely
Is no man shent, to speke generally.   (IX[H] 325 ff.)

The firste vertu, sone, if thou wolt leere,
Is to restreyne and kepe wel thy tonge.
                              (IX [H] 332 f. [S 174])

My sone, of muchel spekyng yvele avysed,
Ther lasse spekyng hadde ynough suffised,
Comth muchel harm; thus was me toold and taught.
                                      (IX [H] 335 ff.)

In muchel speche synne wanteth naught.   (IX [H] 338)

Right as a swerde forkutteth and forkerveth
An arm a-two, my deere sone, right so
A tonge kutteth freendshipe al a-two.   (IX [H] 340 ff.)

But he that hath mysseyd, I dar wel sayn,
He may by no wey clepe his word agayn.
Thyng that is seyd is seyd, and forth it gooth,
Though hym repente, or be hym leef or looth.
He is his thral to whom that he hath sayd
A tale of which he is now yvele apayd.
                        (IX [H] 353 ff. [H p. 53; S 291])

(24) *Parson's Prologue* and *Tale*

The Parson refuses to tell a "fable," and asks the Host:

Why sholde I sowen draf out of my fest,
Whan I may sowen whete, if that me lest?   (X [I] 35 f.)

The *Parson's Tale* is a disquisition on the Seven Deadly Sins, and it will suffice merely to list the six proverbs and eighteen sententious remarks which it contains:

PROVERBS

For the proverbe seith that "manye smale maken a greet."
(X [I] 361 [*H* 45; *S* 292])

And ofte tyme swich cursynge wrongfully retorneth agayn to
hym that curseth, as a bryd that retorneth agayn to his owene
nest. (X [I] 619 [*S* 293])

as whoso toucheth warm pych, it shent his fyngres.
(X [I] 853 [*S* 294])

Certes, they been lyk to houndes; for an hound, whan he
comth by the roser or by othere [bushes], though he may nat
pisse, yet wole he heve up his leg and make a contenaunce to
pisse. (X [I] 857)

hooly writ may nat been defouled, namoore than the sonne
that shyneth on the mixne. (X [I] 910 [*S* 295])

For certes, whan the pot boyleth strongly, the beste remedie
is to withdrawe the fyr. (X [I] 950)

SENTENTIOUS REMARKS

And therfore repentant folk, that stynte for to synne, and forlete synne er that synne forlete hem, hooly chirche holdeth
hem siker of hire savacioun. (X [I] 93)

And therfore oure Lord Jhesu Crist seith thus: "By the fruyt
of hem shul ye knowen hem." (X [I] 115 [*H* 112])

remembreth yow of the proverbe of Salomon. He seith:/
Likneth a fair womman that is a fool of hire body lyk to a
ryng of gold that were in the groyn of a soughe.
(X [I] 154 f. [*H* 157b])

Certes also, whoso prideth hym in the goddes of fortune, he is
a ful gret fool. (X [I] 470 [*H* p. 66])

Certes, the commendacioun of the peple is somtyme ful fals
and ful brotel for to triste; this day they preyse, tomorwe they
blame. (X [I] 472)

and therfore seith a wys man that Ire is bet than pley.
(X [I] 538)

For after the habundance of the herte speketh the mouth ful ofte.   (X [I] 626 [H 124])

And therfore seith Salomon, "An hous that is uncovered and droppynge, and a chidynge wuf, been lyke."
(X [I] 630 [H 29])

"bettre is a morsel of breed with joye than an hous ful of delices with chidynge," seith Salomon.   (X [I] 632 [H 29])

Thanne comth ydelnesse, that is the yate of alle harmes. An ydel man is lyk to a place that hath no walles; the develes may entre on every syde, or sheten at hym at discovert, by temptacion on every syde.   (X [I] 713]

of which synne seith Seint Paul that "the roote of alle harmes is Coveitise."   (X [I] 738 [H 38d])

Thynk eek that of swich seed as cherles spryngen, of swich seed spryngen lordes. As wel may the cherl be saved as the lord. / The same deeth that taketh the cherl, swich deeth taketh the lord. Wherfore I rede, do right so with thy cherl, as thou woldest that thy lord dide with thee, if thou were in his plit.   (X [I] 760 f. [H 154])

attemperaunce, that holdeth the meene in alle thynges.
(X [I] 833)

mesure also, that restreyneth by resoun.   (X [I] 834)

God woot, a man may sleen hymself with his owene knyf, and make hymselven dronken of his owene tonne.   (X [I] 858)

For certes, namoore may maydenhede be restoored than an arm that is smyten fro the body may retourne agayn to wexe.
(X [I] 870)

Soothly, a whit wal, although it ne brenne noght fully by stikynge of a candele, yet is the wal blak of the leyt.
(X [I] 953)

for wikked haste dooth no profit.   (X [I] 1002 [H 84b])

CHAPTER V

CHAUCER AND GOWER

WE HAVE now completed a detailed survey of Chaucer's use of proverbs and sententious remarks. It remains to summarize the results and to give a general estimate of Chaucer's usage. In order to avoid monotonous restatements of conclusions drawn while discussing the individual works, I am going to arrive at this final estimate by means of a comparison. At the outset I described the characteristic use of proverbs in the works of Deschamps and in the *fabliaux*, literary monuments which exerted some influence on Chaucer. Here at the end it will be enlightening to discuss briefly the use of proverbs in the works of the greatest narrative poet among Chaucer's contemporaries, John Gower.[1] In the interests of brevity I shall consider only the proverbs in the *Confessio Amantis* in relation to their context.[2] Gower's other works, especially the *Mirour de l'Omme*, are also rich in proverbs and sententious remarks.[3]

The table presented on the following page indicates the amount and dispersal of the proverbial matter in the *Confessio*:

	Lines	Proverbs	Proverbial Phrases		Sententious Remarks
			Comp.	Others	
Prologue	1088	8		7	19
I............	3446	15	10	10	14
II............	3530	5	13	6	15
III............	2774	20	9	14	29
IV............	3712	9	8	15	16
V............	7844	22	19	18	27
VI............	2440	4	8	6	17
VII............	5438	6	16	7	15
VIII............	3172	5	7	5	28
Totals	33,444	94	90	88	180

There are eight proverbs in the Prologue to the *Confessio Amantis*. Gower, in the cancelled passage on Richard II, tells how he began the work at the king's command, and sought to make a good beginning, for

in proverbe I have herd seye
That who that wel his werk begynneth
The rather a good ende he wynneth.   (Pr 86*ff. [1a])

Love is generally fallen into discord and the poet calls for confirmation of this unhappy state of affairs from

The comun vois, which mai noght lie.   (Pr 124)

The world's only hope is in its rulers, and they ought to be eager to accept good advice:

Althogh a man be wys himselve,
Yit is the wisdom more of tuelve.   (Pr 157 f.)

The church, too, has come upon evil days. Avignon struggles against Rome, and the Christian world is divided:

Bot it is seid and evere schal,
Betwen tuo Stoles lyth the fal.   (Pr 335 f. [142a])

Nevertheless there is no real need for despair; God is supreme, and in His good time all will be well,

For trowthe mot stonde ate laste.   (Pr 369 [115])

Gower, as a warning, tells the story of Nebuchadnezzar's dream, and argues against precipitousness, since

So mot it nedes faile in haste.   (Pr 650 [7a])

Empires have risen and fallen, man has grown rich and yet suffered woe; for

in proverbe natheles
Men sein, ful selden is that welthe
Can soffre his oghne astat in helthe.   (Pr 786 ff. [268])

Evil is rife in the world, and it would be well if another Arion might arise with a harp to bring back Peace. Talk, however, will never serve:

Whan the scharpnesse of the spore
The horse side smit to sore,
It grieveth ofte.   (Pr 1084 ff.)

As he begins Book i, Gower wisely decides that his is not the hand to put the world back into joint, and sets out upon a discussion of Love, which, he says, no man can control:

For loves lawe is out of reule.   (i, 18 [168b])

Who can hope to master passion, what man is wise enough to rule Love?   There is none such:

It hath and schal ben everemor
That love is maister wher he wile.   (i, 34 f. [166a])

The Confessor describes the sins of Seeing and tells of Acteon, whose sad story conveys an obvious moral:

For ofte, who that hiede toke,
Betre is to winke than to loke.   (i, 383)

The long survey of the Seven Deadly Sins begins with Pride, the first of whose ministers, Hypocrisy, is all too common:

For now aday is manyon
Which spekth of Peter and of John
And thenketh Judas in his herte.   (i, 655 ff.)

Lovers, above all, should refrain from deceiving Love by hypocritical acts; to be sure,

To love is every herte fre,   (i, 752 [167a])

but treachery to Love is always punished. Hypocrisy is illustrated by the story of Mundus, who, with the aid of two priests, impersonated the god Anubis. Taxed with the fraud, the priests tried to place all the blame on Mundus, but the Emperor rejects this excuse,

For he is on and thei ben tuo,
And tuo han more wit then on.   (i, 1020 f.)

The victims of Hypocrisy are often distinguished by an excessive credulity which plays a large part in their misfortunes:

On other half, men scholde noght
To lihtly lieve al that thei hiere.   (i, 1062 f. [59a])

The Confessor goes on in the same vein:

I finde a gret experience,
Wherof to take an evidence
Good is, and to be war also
Of the peril, er him be wo.   (i, 1073 ff.)

From Hypocrisy the priest Genius passes on to Disobedience, and asks the Lover if he has committed this sin. "Only in that I cannot obey my mistress's command not to love her, and that I dare not be still when she bids it,

For specheles may noman spede."   (i, 1293 [44])

Obedience is often helpful to lovers, and this can scarcely be better exemplified than by the story of Florent's adventures. He is loath indeed to wed the old hag who has saved his life, but since his word is passed there is no escape:

Nede he mot that nede schal.   (i, 1714 [132a])

Pride's third minister is Presumption, who will not see the truth until trouble comes upon him, and when

Upon his fortune and his grace
Comth "Hadde I wist" fulofte aplace.   (i, 1887 f.)

Presumption seeks for things beyond his reach:

Fulofte he heweth up so hihe,
That chippes fallen in his yhe.   (i, 1917 f. [65])

The Lover feels that no one is so humble a lover as he; if he is to be blamed for being a lover at all, he can only reply:

I seie in excusinge of me,
To alle men that love is fre.   (i, 1929 f. [167b])

His chief fault, he admits, is that he has sometimes imagined himself loved when the reverse was the case:

Wenyng beguileth many a man.   (i, 1958 [143])

Before embarking on the last story in Book i, that of the "Three Questions," the Confessor says that it will serve to make the Lover eschew Pride, for

It schal doun falle and overthrowe.   (i, 3066)

Book ii deals with Envy, one sign of which is to feel joy for another's woe. The Lover confesses his fault:

It is a confort, as men sein,
To him the which is wo besein
To sen an other in his peine.   (ii, 261 ff. [221])

His lady is surrounded with a crowd of lusty young suitors, but she is wise and keeps herself to herself,

for men sein unknowe unkest.   (ii, 467)

They may make love to her, but

Sche lieveth noght al that sche hiereth,   (ii, 471)

and above all she is

war of "hadde I wist." (ii, 473)

The remaining proverb in Book II appears in the description of the man who practices Supplantation. Such an one seeks ever to get the profits of others,

And takth the bridd to his beyete,
Wher othre men the buisshes bete. (ii, 2355 f. [85a])

Despite the fact that Book III is, with one exception, the shortest, only one other, namely Book V, contains more proverbs. The subject of the book is Wrath, whose first servant is Melancholy. It was Melancholy which afflicted the father of Canace and Machaire on discovery of their incestuous love, and discover it he was bound to do, for

sothe . . . mai noght ben hid. (iii, 205)

The Confessor asserts that the brother and sister must not be blamed too harshly,

For it is seid thus overal,
That nedes mot that nedes schal
Of that a lif doth after kinde. (iii, 351 ff. [132b])

Wrath's second tool is Chest, or Wordy Argument, which can cause enormous trouble,

For men sein that the harde bon,
Althogh himselven have non,
A tunge brekth it al to pieces. (iii, 463 ff. [35a])

The Lover asserts that he has never been guilty of chiding his mistress; indeed he often feels that he has said too little to her, and then he is angry with himself,

For noman mai his time lore
Recovere.   (iii, 577 f. [236a])

Bitter and hasty words are of no avail,

Bot Oule on Stock and Stock on Oule;
The more that a man defoule,
Men witen wel which hath the werse.   (iii, 585 ff. [261])

The Priest, to illustrate Hate, tells how King Namplus wrecked many Greek ships by means of false beacons. Men must be on guard against fraud,

Forthi the wise men ne demen
The thinges after that thei semen,
Bot after that thei knowe and finde.   (iii, 1073 ff.)

The Lover confesses that he has "Conteck" in his being, for Reason and Wit struggle against Will and Hope. The Priest reprimands him, but gently, because

love is of so gret a miht,
His lawe mai noman refuse.   (iii, 1194 f.)

Pyramus and Thisbe found out the reality of this power when Love forced them

To folwe thilke lore and suie
Which nevere man yit miht eschuie;
And that was love.   (iii, 1355 ff.)

Their subsequent tragedy illustrates the evils of foolish haste, and the Priest drives home the point with five proverbs, to say nothing of six sententious remarks and four proverbial phrases. The proverbs are:

Men sen alday that rape reweth.   (iii, 1625 [8])

And who so wicked Ale breweth,
Fulofte he mot the werse drinke.   (iii, 1626 f. [259])

For this thei tellen that ben wise,
Wicke is to stryve and have the werse.   (iii, 1650 f.)

Ne haste noght thin oghne sorwe,
Mi Sone, and tak this in thi witt,
He hath noght lost that wel abitt.   (iii, 1656 ff. [5a])

It mai noght helpe forto rape.   (iii, 1678)

Another story which exemplifies Fool-haste is that of Athemas and Demephon, the two kings who set out to exterminate their rebellious subjects. To carry out this laudable ambition they sought

frendes ate nede,   (iii, 1772)

but, by Nestor's advice, ended by making peace with the rebels.

Homicide is a great crime and always punished. The Confessor sketches the story of Orestes, whose tragedy may be said to have begun when Egistus supplanted the absent Agamemnon in the affections of Clytemnestra:

An olde sawe is, "Who that is slyh
In place where he mai be nyh,

He makth the ferre Lieve loth":
Of love and thus fulofte it goth.   (iii, 1899 ff. [281])

When Agamemnon came home, the guilty lovers put him to death,

Bot moerdre, which mai noght ben hedd,
Sprong out to every mannes Ere.   (iii, 1920 f.)

Egistus did not long enjoy his ill-gotten power; he was blamed on all sides:

Men sein, "Old Senne newe schame."   (iii, 2033 [31a])

After Orestes had slain his mother, in accordance with divine commands Fame carried the story far and wide. Some people believed one thing, some another, but

    comunliche in every nede
The worste speche is rathest herd
And lieved, til it be ansuerd.   (iii, 2120 ff.)

Wrath causes war, the Priest urges, and tells of Alexander and the captured pirate's pert retort, which gained him honor from the king:

Such Capitein such retenue.   (iii, 2421 [249])

Book III ends with the Priest's calling on the Lover to make his shrift, and warning him that confession without reformation is of no value,

For word is wynd.   (iii, 2768 [37])

Book IV carries the Lover through the various categories of Sloth. The Priest advises the Lover to flee laziness and to remember that

many a vice, as seith the clerk,
Ther hongen upon Slowthes lappe
Of suche as make a man mishappe,
To pleigne and telle of hadde I wist.   (iv, 302 ff.)

Pusillanimity, a subdivision of Sloth, is something indeed to beware of,

For who that noght dar undertake,
Be riht he schal no profit take.   (iv, 319 f. [2a])

Forgetfulness is another danger, and here the Lover confesses freely that he is guilty. Whatever fine speeches he may prepare, he forgets everything in the presence of his mistress. Between forgetfulness and dread he is in a maze, and says to himself:

"O fol of alle foles,
Thou farst as he betwen tuo stoles
That wolde sitte and goth to grounde."   (iv, 625 ff. [142b])

Sloth has a secretary, none other than Negligence, whose carelessness is amended too late,

For whan the grete Stiede
Is stole, thanne he taketh hiede,
And makth the stable dore fast.   (iv, 901 ff. [69])

Idleness, too, is to be found in Sloth's company, and an idle lover is

as a cat wolde ete fisshes
Withoute wetinge of his cles,
So wolde he do, bot natheles
He faileth ofte of that he wolde.   (iv, 1108 ff. [80])

The Lover denies that he is in any way idle; whatever his lady demands he is glad to do, and indeed must do,

For as men sein, nede hath no lawe.   (iv, 1167 f. [131a])

The Confessor believes his asseverations, but, nevertheless, tells him stories which indicate Venus's distaste for people who are slow to love. Cultivate honest love without loss of time:

Men mai recovere lost of good,
Bot so wys man yit nevere stod,
Which mai recovere time lore.   (iv, 1485 ff. [236b])

The Lover complains bitterly of his ill success, and the Priest replies that he must be patient and wait for his time:

Betre is to wayte upon the tyde
Than rowe ayein the stremes stronge.   (iv, 1780 f. [61])

Later he urges him to renewed efforts; nothing was ever gained without trying,

For he which dar nothing beginne,
I not what thing he scholde achieve.   (iv, 2694 f. [2b])

Avarice is the theme of Book v, and fittingly enough the first story is that of Midas, who said

that a man mai sothly telle
That al the world to gold obeieth.   (v, 244 f. [124])

Jealousy is a subdivision of Avarice, and is to be avoided; the man who substantiates his suspicions gets more shame than if he had kept still,

For this thou myht wel understonde,
That where a man schal nedes lese,
The leste harme is forto chese.   (v, 714 ff. [54])

The story of Venus and Mars and Vulcan's self-exposed cuckoldom leads to a long disquisition on the religions of the world, ending with remarks on the decay of Christianity. Christ died for the faith, but now our fearful prelate says:

The lif is suete.   (v, 1861)

To illustrate the vice of Covetousness the Priest tells the story of the "Two Coffers," at the beginning of which we learn that

ther is nothing seid so softe,
That it ne comth out ate laste.   (v, 2286 f.)

Lovers are notoriously covetous, desiring for one reason or another almost every woman they see. They are, however, like the blind man:

The blinde man no colour demeth,
But al is on, riht as him semeth.   (v, 2489 f. [72])

The Lover denies that he has ever been guilty of Usury, but, since he has

herd seid that thoght is fre,   (v, 4485 [43])

dares to state that his lady may be justly blamed for that vice. The Confessor warns him against such ideas; he has no right to expect any return in love,

For love is lord in every place.   (v, 4556 [166b])

That pandering receives its due punishment is revealed by the story of Echo, who procured new loves for Jupiter in secret,

Bot so prive mai be nothing,
That it ne comth to knowleching;
Thing don upon the derke nyht
Is after knowe on daies liht.   (v, 4597 ff. [27])

The Lover is told that Parsimony will never advance him in his suit. It is well to bestow gifts,

For thus men sein, in every nede
He was wys that ferst made mede;
For where as mede mai noght spede,
I not what helpeth other dede.   (v, 4719 ff. [23])

The man who is not willing to be generous is scarcely likely to succeed:

Fulofte he faileth of his game
That wol with ydel hand reclame
His hauk, as many a nyce doth.   (v, 4723 ff.)

Parsimony and Love can never agree, but Mede and Love are close friends:

So was he wys that ferst yaf mede,
For mede kepeth love in house.   (v, 4798 f. [20])

Generous Croceus was able to win Viola from niggardly Balbio, and the story carries its moral:

Bot for men sein that mede is strong,
It was wel seene at thilke tyde.   (v, 4846 f. [18])

Ingratitude is another of Avarice's servants, and he has all too many devotees:

Thus hiere I many a man compleigne,
That nou on daies thou schalt finde
At nede fewe frendes kinde.   (v, 4912 f. [162a])

In the story of Adrian and Bardus, the latter received from a grateful serpent a precious stone, the nature of which was such that it came back to him after he had sold it. Naturally he did not spread this abroad, but the marvel soon became common property, for

so wel may nothing ben hidd,
That it nys ate laste kidd.   (v, 5123 f. [28b])

Rapine is exemplified by the story of Tereus, who fell in love with his sister-in-law Philomela. They were together on shipboard,

And fyr, whan it to tow aprocheth,
To him anon the strengthe acrocheth,
Til with his hete it be devoured,
The tow ne mai noght be socoured.   (v, 5623 ff. [67])

The Lover swears that nothing could be farther from his thoughts than rape. He loves his lady, and therefore he fears her, for

Men sein that every love hath drede.   (v, 6059 [177a])

Robbery, another subordinate of Avarice, is a tempting vice,

For other mennes good is swete.   (v, 6118)

Our Lover has never taken aught by stealth from his lady. He protests that even in private he never

laid hands on her to steal either this or that. His
heart is hers, and

as men sein, wher herte is failed,
Ther schal no castell ben assailed.   (v, 6573 f. [267])

Even if he had both ability and inclination, oppor-
tunity would be lacking. Danger is on guard, and

this proverbe is evere newe,
That stronge lokes maken trewe
Of hem that wolden stele and pyke.   (v, 6631 ff. [139])

The Lover confesses that he would have been
guilty of Sacrilege in trying to make love to his
lady in church, but that he hasn't been able to do
so. The Confessor blames his will, and reminds
him

That alle thing hath time and stede.   (v, 7187 [235a])

The punishment of Sacrilege appears in the story
of Paris and Helen. Priam, disturbed at the reports
which Antenor brought back from Greece, found
it difficult to sleep:

Bot for men sein that nyht hath reste,
The king bethoghte him al that nyht.   (v, 7296 f.)

He convoked a parliament on the following day,
and Hector spoke against war. The Trojans might
lose:

Wicke is to stryve and have the worse.   (v, 7353)

Gluttony is the theme of Book VI and it evokes
only four proverbs. With his customary skill in

introducing apparently extraneous matter the Confessor works in a few remarks on the efficacy of prayer. Supplication often helps:

He was no fol that ferst so radde,
For selden get a domb man lond:
Tak that proverbe, and understond
That wordes ben of vertu grete.   (vi, 446 ff. [45])

Delicacy may often be harmful. Men should eat things to which they are accustomed,

For in Phisique this I finde,
Usage is the seconde kinde.   (vi, 663 f. [136])

Lovers sometimes follow their lusts so far as to make use of Sorcery. This is very bad indeed, and also dangerous,

For often he that wol beguile
Is guiled with the same guile,
And thus the guilour is beguiled.   (vi, 1379 ff. [109a])

Zoroaster got into trouble on account of Sorcery and his reputation still suffers from it. Nothing can endure which is out of keeping with apodeictic faith:

An ende proveth every thing.   (vi, 2383 [4a])

Book VII is an educational handbook for kings. Perhaps Gower hoped that the first six books would so beguile Richard that he would absorb, unconsciously as it were, the lessons of the seventh. There are few proverbs in all this didacticism.

Kings ought to tell the truth, and so should be careful as to what they promise:

Avise him every man tofore,
And be wel war, er he be swore,
For afterward it is to late.   (vii, 1741 ff.)

The truthful man shall gain:

The proverbe is, who that is trewe,
Him schal his while nevere rewe.   (vii, 1961 f. [283])

The story of Rehoboam and his foolish young counsellors reminds the Priest that

Old age for the conseil serveth.   (vii, 4137 [71])

There is a time for everything, as we learn from a transitional phrase in the story of the Rape of Lucrece:

Bot every time hath his certein.   (vii, 4754)

Aruns, son of King Tarquin, urged himself on to the ravishing of Lucrece by reflecting that

Fortune unto the bolde
Is favorable forto helpe.   (vii, 4902 f. [204a])

In the end the new sin of Aruns was added to the old sins of his father,

So that the comun clamour tolde
The newe schame of Sennes olde.   (vii, 5115 f. [31b])

Book VIII opens with a few remarks on the laws of primitive marriage, thus gently leading up to the subject of incest. Incest was inevitable in Noah's family:

Men sein that nede hath no lawe,
And so it was be thilke dawe
And laste into the Secounde Age.   (viii, 75 ff. [131b])

Every man ought to take warning from the mistakes and woes of others, says the Confessor before opening the story of Apollonius:

And every man is othres lore.   (viii, 256)

When Apollonius was called back to Tyre the people of Pentapolis were greatly disturbed,

Bot nede he mot, that nede schal.   (viii, 1020 [132a])

After finishing this long story, which seems to have incited Chaucer's Man of Law to level a jibe at Gower's devoted head, the Confessor tells the Lover to renounce Love. The Lover, in reply, asserts that the Priest is hardly in a position to judge him:

The hert which fre goth on the launde
Not of an Oxe what him eileth.   (viii, 2160 f.)

In the first conclusion, dealing with Richard, Gower declares that his Muse has warned him to write no more of Love. He is glad to stop:

In his proverbe seith the wise,
Whan game is best, is best to leve.   (viii, 3086*f. [93])

Gower's use of proverbial material [4] is, as we can readily perceive, in sharp contrast to Chaucer's. There is no type of composition into which Chaucer did not introduce proverbs, and he made espe-

cially effective use of them in his narrative verse.
Gower, as we have seen, excludes them rigorously
from his stories. The overwhelming majority of
the proverbs are uttered by Genius, the priest of
Venus, and are intended to lead the Lover from sin
and to virtue. Sometimes the Lover uses a proverb or two, but this is relatively rare, and the Confessor occasionally pours out a whole stream, as
when, in reprehending Haste, he makes use of
five proverbs, four proverbial phrases, and six sententious remarks within a few lines.[5] We never
feel, however, that Genius is being characterized
in any way by this use of proverbs; he has no more
individuality than a didactic manual. Gower puts
proverbs in his mouth only to point a moral. Chaucer's use of proverbs, on the other hand, is seldom
merely didactic. We find cases, as at the end of
the *Manciple's Tale*,[6] where instruction or exhortation seems to be Chaucer's main object in introducing a mass of sayings, but such instances are rare.
Chaucer makes use of proverbs to advance a narrative, to prepare the reader for coming events, as
when Palamon and Arcite are to meet in the forest.[7]
Chaucer found in proverbs a ready means of characterization, and what a curiously assorted group
he distinguished by this means! Pandarus and
John the Clerk of the *Reeve's Tale*, and Cressida,
the Wife of Bath, and, strangest of all, the falcon

in the *Squire's Tale*! Gower was probably wise in
keeping proverbs out of his stories. His chief fame
to-day is that of a narrative poet, one who had an
appreciative eye for a good story and could tell
it without too much ado. If he had permitted
himself to indulge the fondness for sententiousness which won him the appellation "moral," the
chances are that he would have spoiled his tales.
An effective use of proverbs for purposes other
than instruction alone requires a sense of humor,
and that Gower lacked. Chaucer, however, was
well equipped with humor, and it does not often
appear to better advantage than when he plays
with proverbs, and brings forth a trite saying with
a lavish gesture and a quiet smile. Then, too,
Chaucer appreciated the salt and pithy wisdom of
proverbs, and understood that they were close to
life. Proverbs were a unit, and a not unimportant
unit, of Chaucer's literary make-up. Just as he
was fascinated by dreams and used them over and
over again in his poems, so from the time when
first he read and translated the *Roman de la Rose*
he made the use of proverbs an integral part of his
style.

CHAPTER VI

PROVERBIAL PHRASES

I HAVE divided Chaucer's proverbial phrases into comparisons and other proverbial phrases and have made an alphabetical arrangement under the most important word in the phrase. The French originals are given for such sayings in the *Romaunt* as were not introduced by the translator.

PROVERBIAL COMPARISONS

Right as an adamaunt, iwys,
Can drawen to hym sotylly —
The iren. (*Rom.* A 1182 ff.)
    Car trestot en autel maniere
    Con la pierre de l'aïmant
    Trait a soi le fer soutilment. (II, 60, ll. 1158 ff.)

As piled as an ape was his skulle. (I [A] 3935)

As round as appil was his face. (*Rom* A 819 [*H* p. 57])
    La face avoit, come une pome. (II, 42, l. 804)

Hir mouth was sweete as . . .
. . . hoord of apples leyd in hey or heeth. (I [A] 3261 f.)

Youre fader is in sleght as Argus eyed.
                (*T&C*, iv, 1459 [*H* 164])

And thow, Symois, that as an arwe clere
Thorugh Troie rennest. (*T&C*, iv, 1548 f.)

Thanne shal youre soule up to hevene skippe
Swifter than dooth an arwe out of a bowe. (IV [E] 1672 f.)

Ded wex hire hew, and lyk an ash to sene.   (*LGW* 2649)

Other colour then asshen hath she noon.   (*Anel* 173)

So woodly that he lyk was to biholde
. . . the asshen dede and colde.   (I [A] 1301 f.)

And with a face deed as asshen colde.   (VI [C] 209)

His hewe falow and pale as asshen colde.   (I [A] 1364)

And as an aungel hevenysshly she soong.   (I [A] 1055)

For trewely, ye have as myrie a stevene
As any aungel hath that is in hevene.
                                    (VII, 3291 f. [B 4481 f.])

He rolleth under foot as dooth a bal.   (I [A] 2614)

In trust of hir that turneth as a bal.   (*Truth* 9)

Hir heer was as yelowe of hewe
As ony basyn scoured newe.   (*Rom* A 539 f.)
     Cheveus ot blonz come uns bacins.   (II, 28, l. 527)

Ye been as boold as is Bayard the blynde,
That blondreth forth, and peril casteth noon.
He is as boold to renne agayn a stoon
As for to goon bisides in the weye.
                                    (VIII [G] 1413 ff. [S 288])

          for ay as bisy as bees
Been they, us sely men for to deceyve.   (IV [E] 2422 f.)

Lo, lyk a bisy bee, withouten gile.   (VIII [G] 195)

They murmureden as dooth a swarm of been.   (V [F] 204)

Right so as bees out swarmen from an hyve.   (III [D] 1693)

Alday as thikke as been fleen from an hyve.
                                    (*T&C*, iv, 1356)

For nevere yet so thikke a swarm of been
Ne fleigh, as Grekes fro hym gonne fleen.   (*T&C*, ii, 193 f.)

He rong hem out a proces lik a belle.   (*T&C*, ii, 1615)

And rynge it out as round as gooth a belle.   (VI [C] 331)

That they gonne as beres rore.   (*HF* 1589)

And blak as bery.   (*Rom* A 928 [*H* p. 58])
    E si estoit plus noirs que meure.   (II, 47, l. 914)

His palfrey was as broun as is a berye.   (I [A] 207 [*H* p. 58])

Broun as a berye.   (I [A] 4368)

They lyve but as a . . . beest,
In libertee.   (IV [E] 1281 f.)

This knyght ne stood nat stille as doth a best.   (III [D] 1034)

Wery and weet, as beest is in the reyn.   (I [A] 4107)

And for to drynken strong wyn, reed as blood.   (I [A] 635)

And therupon he hadde a gay surplys
As whit as is the blosme upon the rys.   (I [A] 3323 f.)

Ywympled wel, and on hir heed an hat
As brood as is a bokeler.   (I [A] 470 f.)

As doon thise loveres in hir queynte geres,
Now in the crope, now doun in the breres,
Now up, now doun, as boket in a welle.
                                   (I [A] 1531 ff. [*S* 218])

         upright as a bolt.   (I [A] 3264)

      the milleres doghter bolt upright.   (I [A] 4266)

Have hire in his armes bolt upright.   (VII, 316 [B 1506])

No lasse flaterynge in hir word,
That purely hir symple record
Was founde as trewe as any bond.   (*BD* 933 ff. [*H* p. 57])

How that an egle, fethered whit as bon.   (*T&C*, ii, 926)

He groneth lyk oure boor, lith in oure sty.   (III [D] 1829)

He looked as it were a wilde boor.   (III [D] 2160)

As wilde bores gonne they to smyte.   (I [A] 1658)

Al vinolent as botel in the spence.   (III [D] 1931)

So woodly that he lyk was to biholde
The boxtree.   (I [A] 1301 f. [*H* p. 55])

And pale as box she was.   (*LGW* 866 [*H* p. 55])

Hir mouth was sweete as bragot.   (I [A] 3261)

This Diomede, as fressh as braunche in May.
                        (*T&C*, v, 844 [*H* p. 57])

She rist hire up, and dredfully she quaketh,
As doth the braunche that Zepherus shaketh.   (*LGW* 2680 f.)

And sweete as is the brembul flour
That bereth the rede hepe.   (VII, 746 f. [B 1936 f.])

Lyk to the skyn of houndfyssh, sharp as brere.
                                   (IV [E] 1825)
Hir chere was symple as byrde in bour.
                        (*Rom* A 1014 [*H* p. 59])
      Simple fu come une esposee.   (II, 51, l. 1000)

They lyve but as a bryd . . .
In libertee.   (IV [E] 1281 f.)

Therto she koude skippe and make game,
As any . . . calf folwynge his dame.   (I [A] 3259 f.)

Syn ye be strong as is a greet camaille.   (IV [E] 1196)

Hir eyen twoo were cleer and light
As ony candell that brenneth bright.   (*Rom* B 3199 f.)

> Li ueil qui en son chief estoient
> Con deus estoiles reluisoient.   (II, 150, ll. 2981 f.)

And he hymself as sweete as is . . .
. . . any cetewale.   (I [A] 3206 f.)

Amydde a tree, for drye as whit as chalk.   (V [F] 409)

Hir flesh [as] tendre as is a chike.   (*Rom* A 541)
> La char plus tendre qu'uns poucins.   (II, 28, l. 528)

From every wight as fer as is the cloude
He was.   (*T &C*, iii, 433 f.)

As blak he lay as any cole.   (I [A] 2692 [*H* p. 58])

He hadde a beres skyn, col-blak for old.   (I [A] 2142)

Of col-blak silk.   (I [A] 3240)

Derk was the nyght . . . as the cole.   (I [A] 3731)

And she sproong as a colt dooth in the trave.   (I [A] 3282)

Wynsynge she was, as is a joly colt.   (I [A] 3263)

And quok for fere, pale and pitously . . .
. . . as the culver, that of the egle is smiten.
                              (*LGW* 2317-2319)

His coomb was redder than the fyn coral.
                              (VII, 2859 [B 4049])

And eke of loves moo eschaunges
Then ever cornes were in graunges.   (*HF* 697 f.)

For as the cristal glorious ye shyne.   (*To Rosemounde* 3)

As blak he lay as any . . . crowe.   (I [A] 2692 [*H* p. 58])

His steede was al dappull gray.   (VII, 884 [B 2074])

Hir forheed shoon as bright as any day.   (I [A] 3310)

Whit was his berd as is the dayesye.   (I [A] 332 [*H* p. 59])

But this as sooth as deth, certeyn.   (*HF* 502 [*H* p. 60])

Tok out hys blake trumpe of bras,
That fouler than the devel was.   (*HF* 1637 f.)

Hir flesh was tendre as dew of flour.   (*Rom* A 1013 [*H* p. 59])
    Tendre ot la char come rosee.   (II, 51, l. 999)

Thanne shaltou swymme as myrie, I undertake,
As dooth the whyte doke after hire drake.   (I [A] 3575)

And est and west upon the peple I bekke,
As dooth a dowve sittynge on a berne.   (VI [C] 396 f.)

And she was symple as dowve on tree.   (*Rom* A 1219)
    E fu simple come uns colons.   (II, 62, l. 1198)

And I lye as a draf-sak in my bed.   (I [A] 4206)

Have herte as hard as dyamaunt.   (*Rom* B 4385 [*H* p. 56])
    Aiez dedenz cuer d'aïmant.   (II, 200, l. 4011)

Ech (*leaf*) in his kynde, of colour fresh and greene
As emeraude.   (*PF* 174 f.)

And trowe hem as the Evangile.   (*Rom* B 5453)

    S'en glorefient e les croient
    Ausinc con ce fust evangile.   (II, 236, ll. 4878 f.)

Crul was his heer . . .
And strouted as a fanne large and brode.   (I [A] 3314 f.)

Ful ofte his lady from hire wyndow down,
As fressh as faukoun comen out of muwe.
                              (*T&C*, iii, 1783 f. [*H* p. 57])

Hir yen grey as is a faucoun.   (*Rom* A 546 [*H* p. 58])
    E les iauz vairs come uns faucons.   (II, 28, l. 533)

For shaft and ende, soth for to telle,
Were also blak as fend in helle.   (*Rom* A 973 f. [*H* p. 58])

Li fust estoient e li fer
Plus noir que deables d'enfer.   (II, 49, ll. 959 f.)

For as feele eyen hadde she
As fetheres upon foules be.   (*HF* 1381 f.)

Ne that a monk, whan he is recchelees,
Is likned til a fissh that is waterlees.

(I [A] 179 f. [*S* 211])

and ful eke of wyndowes,
As flakes falle in grete snowes.   (*HF* 1191 f.)

Ligurges doughter, fayrer on to sene
Than is the flour ageyn the bryghte sonne.   (*LGW* 2425 f.)

Her heed, for hor, was whyt as flour.   (*Rom* A 356)

Toute sa teste estoit chenue
E blanche con s'el fust florie.   (II, 19, ll. 346 f.)

His nekke whit was as the flour-de-lys.   (I [A] 238)

That frothen whit as foom for ire wood.

(I [A] 1659 [*H* p. 59])

His mouth as greet was as a greet forneys.   (I [A] 559)

As fayn as fowel is of the brighte sonne.

(I [A] 2437 [*H* 178; *S* 223])

As fowel is fayn whan that the sonne up riseth.

(VII, 51 [*B* 1241] [*S* 223])

But was as glad therof as fowel of day.   (VII, 38 [*B* 1228])

Was nevere brid gladder agayn the day.

(VIII [G] 1342 [*H* p. 71; *S* 223])

Gladeth, ye foules, of the morowe gray!

(*Com Mars* 1 [*H* p. 71])

For was ther nevere fowel so fayn of May.   (*T&C*, v, 425)

Grehoundes he hadde as swift as fowel in flight.   (I [A] 190)

His berd as any . . . fox was reed.   (I [A] 552)

But also cold in love towardes the
Thi lady is, as frost in wynter moone.   (*T&C*, i, 523 f.)

As cold as any frost now waxeth she.   (*LGW* 2683 [*H* p. 55])

As frost, hym thoughte, his herte gan to colde.
(*T&C*, v, 535)

For thou shalt brenne as ony fir.   (*Rom* B 2548)

But Troilus, though as the fir he brende.   (*T&C*, iii, 425)

desyr
That in his herte brende as any fyr.   (*LGW* 1750 f.)

sykes hoote as fyr.   (*PF* 246)

His eyes reed sparclyng as the fyr glowe.   (*Rom* B 3136)

S'ot les iauz roges come feus.   (II, 148, l. 2923)

For also seur as reed is every fir.   (*T&C*, iii, 1633)

That hadde a fyr-reed cherubynnes face.   (I [A] 624)

rubyes rede as fyr sparklynge.   (I [A] 2164)

Upon a courser stertlynge as the fyr.   (*LGW* 1204)

He on a courser, startlynge as the fir.   (I [A] 1502)

The woful teeris . . .
As bittre weren . . .
For peyne, as is . . . galle,   (*T&C*, iv, 1135 ff.)

So that ye men shul been as lewed as gees.   (IV [E] 2275)

With wawes grene, and brighte as any glas.
(I [A] 1958 [*H* p. 58])

For in the sterres, clerer than is glas,
Is writen.   (II [B] 194 f.)

Hir nose tretys, hir eyen greye as glas.   (I [A] 152 [*H* p. 58])

With kamus nose, and eyen greye as glas.   (I [A] 3974)

His heed was balled, that shoon as any glas.   (I [A] 198)

That shoone ful lyghter than a glas.   (*HF* 1289)

Caught with the lymrod coloured as the gleede.
(VII, 2384 [B 3574])

A thousand sikes, hotter than the gleede.   (*T&C*, iv, 337)

Twoo firy dartes, as the gledes rede.   (*LGW*, F 235, G 167)

The crueel Ire, reed as any gleede.   (I [A] 1997 [*H* p. 58])

Than sterve here as a gnat, withouten wounde.
(*T&C*, iv, 595)

Me thoghte most lyk gold hyt (*hair*) was.   (*BD* 858)

Hir heer, that oundy was and crips,
As burned gold hyt shoon to see.   (*HF* 1386 f.)

And lyk the burned gold was his colour.   (VII, 2864 [B 4054])

Crul was his heer, and as the gold it shoon.   (I [A] 3314)

For his crispe heer, shynynge as gold so fyn.   (III [D] 304)

Shoon (*Phoebus*) as the burned gold with stremes brighte.
(V [F] 1247)

With nayles yelewe and brighte as any gold.
(I [A] 2141 [*H* p. 59])

Gaillard he was as goldfynch in the shawe.   (I [A] 4367)

He was nat pale as a forpyned goost.   (I [A] 205)

His rode was reed, his eyen greye as goos.   (I [A] 3317)

A voys he hadde as smal as hath a goot.   (I [A] 688)

For al the world they stynken as a goot.   (VIII [G] 886)

That every word was gospel that ye seyde!   (*T&C*, v, 1265)

And therwithal he knew of mo proverbes
Than in this world ther growen gras or herbes.

(III [D] 773 f. [*H* 183])

And they were set as thik of nouchis . . .
As grasses growen in a mede.   (*HF* 1350–1353)

And lik a grifphon looked he aboute.   (I [A] 2133)

For strokes, whiche that wente as thikke as hayl.

(*LGW* 655 [*H* p. 57])

Swiche glarynge eyen hadde he as an hare.   (I [A] 684)

For thogh this Somonour wood were as an hare.

(III [D] 1327 [*S* 272])

  thise wedded men, that lye and dare
As in a fourme sit a wery hare.   (VII, 103 f. [B 1293 f.])

This false theef, this somonour, quod the Frere,
Hadde alwey bawdes redy to his hond,
As any hauk to lure in Engelond.   (III [D] 1338 ff.)

This cave was also as derk
As helle-pit overal aboute.   (*BD* 170 f. [*H* p. 58]

And hyt stank as the pit of helle.   (*HF* 1654)

   she
Had also fele upstondyng eres
And tonges, as on bestes heres.   (*HF* 1388 ff.)

He was as ful of love and paramour
As is the hyve ful of hony sweete.   (I [A] 4372 f.)

That is in mariage hony-sweete.   (IV [E] 1396)

That as an hors he snorteth in his sleep.   (I [A] 4163)

With thikke brustles of his berd unsofte,
Lyk to the skyn of houndfyssh, sharp as brere.

(IV [E] 1824 f.)

  thou janglest as a jay.   (II [B] 774)

As any jay she light was and jolyf.　(I [A] 4154)

His byle was blak, and as the jeet it shoon.

(VII, 2861 [B　4051])

Therto she koude skippe and make game,
As any kyde.　(I [A] 3259 f.)

He gan to speke as lordly as a kyng.　(I [A] 3900)

Right soo thi Sone list, as a lamb, to deye.

(*ABC* 172 [*H* p. 60])

For as the lomb toward his deeth is broght,
So stant this innocent.　(II [B] 617 f.)

As meke as evere was any lomb, to yow!　(VIII [G] 199)

And as a lamb she sitteth meke and stille.　(IV [E] 538)

I moorne as dooth a lambe after the tete.　(I [A] 3704)

And quok for fere, pale and pitously,
Ryght as the lamb that of the wolf is biten.　(*LGW* 2317 f.)

As lyghtly as I were a larke.　(*HF* 546)

Phebus wax old, and hewed lyk laton.　(V [F] 1245)

I feele me nowhere hoor but on myn heed;
Myn herte and alle my lymes been as grene
As laurer thurgh the yeer is for to sene.　(IV [E] 1464 ff.)

Now is it wan and of a leden hewe.　(VIII [G] 728)

And also grene as ony leek.　(*Rom* A 212)

E ausi vert come une cive.　(II, 11, l. 200)

And eke this hous hath of entrees
As fele as of leves ben in trees
In somer, whan they grene been.　(*HF* 1945 ff.)

Be ay of chiere as light as leef on lynde.

(IV [E] 1211 [*S* 276])

Right as an aspes leef she gan to quake.
>   (*T&C*, iii, 1200 [*H* 107a])

And quok as doth the lef of aspe grene. (*LGW* 2648 [*H* 107b])

That lyk an aspen leef he quook for ire. (III [D] 1667)

Fy

Upon a lord that wol have no mercy,
But been a leon, bothe in word and dede. (I [A] 1773 ff.)

Ne in Belmarye ther nys so fel leon,
That hunted is, or for his hunger wood,
Ne of his praye desireth so the blood,
As Palamon to sleen his foo Arcite. (I [A] 2630 ff.)

>   but if that I
Be lik a wilde leoun, fool-hardy. (VII, 1915 f. [B 3105 f.])

Withinne thyn hous ne be thou no leon. (III [D] 1989)

Ful lyk a fiers leoun, she sendeth heere. (VIII [G] 198)

With stoute Romeyns, crewel as lyoun. (*LGW* 627 [*H* p. 60])

As fiers as leon. (*I* [*A*] 1598)

In his fightyng were a wood leon. (I [A] 1656)

Yong, fressh, strong, and hardy as lyoun. (*T&C*, v, 830)

And as a leon he his lookyng caste. (I [A] 2171)

He looketh as it were a grym leoun. (VII, 3179 [B 4369])

For thogh he looked as a wood leon. (III [D] 429)

And in the feld he pleyde the leoun. (*T&C*, i, 1074)

Stibourn I was as is a leonesse. (III [D] 637)

And he up stirte as dooth a wood leoun. (III [D] 794)

The frere up stirte as dooth a wood leoun. (III [D] 2152)

And he hymself as sweete as is the roote
Of lycorys. (I [A] 3206 f.)

Tho woful teeris that they leten falle
As bittre weren, out of teris kynde,
For peyne, as is ligne aloes.   (*T &C*, iv, 1135 ff.)

That Emelye, that fairer was to sene
Than is the lylie upon his stalke grene.   (I [A] 1035 f.)

An egle tame, as any lilye whyt.   (I [A] 2178 [*H* p. 59])

As whyt as lylye . . .
Hir face.   (*Rom* A 1015 f.)

E blanche come flor de lis.   (II, 51, l. 1001)

As whit as is a lilye flour.   (VII, 867 [B 2057])

His nayles whitter than the lylye flour.   (VII, 2863 [B 4053])

And the almycanteras in her Astrelabyes ben streight as a
lyne.   (*Astr*, ii, 26, ll. 23 ff.)

But to his neces hous, as streyght as lyne,
He com.   (*T &C*, ii, 1461 f. [*H* p. 57])

Long as a mast.   (I [A] 3264)

And Jason is as coy as is a mayde.   (*LGW* 1548 [*H* p. 60])

Ye ryde as coy and stille as dooth a mayde
Were newe spoused.   (IV [E] 2 f.)

                    he sayde,
As curteisly as it had been a mayde.   (VII, 445 f. [B 1635 f.])

And of his port as meeke as is a mayde.   (I [A] 69)

That she was lyk the brighte morwe of May.   (IV [E] 1748)

Have hat of floures as fresh as May.   (*Rom* B 2277)

He was as fressh as is the month of May.   (I [A] 92)

And fressher than the May with floures newe.
                    (I [A] 1037 [*H* p. 57])

That highte Dianira, fressh as May.   (VII, 2120 [B 3310])

And been a feestlych man as fressh as May.   (V [F] 281)

That fressher was and jolyer of array,
As to my doom, than is the month of May.   (V [F] 927 f.)

Embrouded was he, as it were a meede
Al ful of fresshe floures, whyte and reede.   (I [A] 89 f.)

Hir mouth was sweete as . . . the meeth.   (I [A] 3261)

For thogh so be that lovers be as trewe
As any metal that is forged newe.
                          (*Com Mars* 200 f. [*H* p. 56])

An anlaas and a gipser al of silk
Heeng at his girdel, whit as morne milk.
                          (I [A] 357 f. [*H* p. 59])

A barmclooth eek as whit as morne milk.   (I [A] 3236)

The flesh was seen as whit as mylk.   (*Rom* A 1196 [*H* p. 59])

Janglynge is whan men speken to muche biforn folk, and
clappen as a mille, and taken no keep what they seye.
                          (X [I] 405)

        and chaunge as the moone.   (*Rom* B 3778)

And clere as the mone lyght.   (*Rom* A 1010 [*H* p. 59])

        Ainsi fu clere come la lune.   (II, 51, l. 996)

His brydel . . . shoon
. . . as the moone light.   (VII, 879 f. [B 2069 f.])

Somme to wexe and wane sone,
As doth the faire white mone.   (*HF* 2115 f.)

And she as fair as is the bryghte morwe.
                          (*LGW* 1202 [*H* p. 57])

As thikke as motes in the sonne-beem.   (III [D] 868)

I dar wel seyn, if she hadde been a mous,
And he a cat, he wolde hire hente anon.   (I [A] 3346 f.)

We faren as he that dronke is as a mous.
> (I [A] 1261 [H p. 60; S 214])

Thou comest hoom as dronken as a mous.
> (III [D] 246 [H p. 60; S 214])

This soun was so ful of japes,
As ever mowes were in apes. (*HF* 1805 f.)

Lyk to the naddre in bosom sly untrewe. (IV [E] 1786)

He syngeth, brokkynge as a nyghtyngale. (I [A] 3377)

And synge, ywis, as any nyghtyngale. (III [D] 458)

Thurgh out his armure it wole kerve and byte,
Were it as thikke as is a branched ook. (V [F] 158 f.)

And al day after hidde hym as an owle. (III [D] 1081)

For with a boor as gret as ox in stalle.
> (*T&C*, v, 1469 [H p. 57])

Though she were wis as Pallas. (VI [C] 49)

Whit was his face as payndemayn. (VII, 725 [B 1915])

And hoom he gooth, murie as a papejay.
> (VII, 369 [B 1559] [H p. 60])

Syngeth ful murier than the papejay. (IV [E] 2322)

Upon a thikke palfrey, paper-whit. (*LGW* 1198)

As any pecok he was proud and gay. (I [A] 3926)

As swifte as pelet out of gonne,
Whan fyr is in the poudre ronne. (*HF* 1643 f.)

Derk was the nyght as pich. (I [A] 3731)

They walwe as doon two pigges in a poke.
> (I [A] 4278 [S 301])

He is as angry as a pissemyre. (III [D] 1825)

That was al pomely grey and highte Scot. (I [A] 616)

His hakeney, that was al pomely grys.   (VIII [G] 559)

He was of foom al flekked as a pye.   (VIII [G] 565)

And ful of jargon as a flekked pye.   (IV [E] 1848)

Stibourn and strong, and joly as a pye.   (III [D] 456)

And forth she gooth as jolif as a pye.   (VII, 209 [B 1399])

And she was proud, and peert as is a pye.   (I [A] 3950)

        the janglynge pye.   (*PF* 345)

And thou shalt make hym couche as doth a quaille.
                                   (IV [E] 1206)

I is ful wight, God waat, as is a raa.   (I [A] 4086)

As leene was his hors as is a rake.   (I [A] 287 [*H* p. 57])

But though this arwe was kene grounde
As ony rasour that is founde.   (*Rom* B 1885 f.)

        Ele est agüe por percier,
        E trenchant con rasoirs d'acier.   (II, 95, ll. 1845 f.)

And out he caught a knyf, as rasour kene.
                        (*LGW* 2654 [*H* p. 57])

As any ravenes fethere it shoon for blak.
                        (I [A] 2144 [*H* p. 58])

His crispe heer lyk rynges was yronne.   (I [A] 2165)

The stalke was as rishe right.   (*Rom* A 1701)

        La queue est droite come jons.   (II, 87, l. 1665)

She semede lyk a rose newe
Of colour.   (*Rom* A 856 f.)

        El resembloit rose novele
        De la color sor la char tendre.   (II, 43, ll. 840 f.)

And she was fayr as is the rose in May.   (*LGW* 613 [*H* p. 57])

I koude walke as fressh as is a rose.   (III [D] 448)

Now reed as rose.   (*Rom* B 2399)

   and wex as red as rose.   (*T&C*, ii, 1256)

Agayn the sonne, that roos as red as rose.
      (*LGW* F 112 [*H* p. 57])

His lippes rede as rose.   (VII, 726 [B 1916])

   rose reed (*crown*).   (VIII [G] 254)

As whyt as . . . rose in rys,
Hir face.   (*Rom* A 1015 f.)

  E blanche come flor de lis.   (II, 51, l. 1001)

And lyke ruby ben your chekes rounde.   (*To Rosemounde* 4)

His heer, his berd was lyk saffroun.   (VII, 730 [B 1920])

O sodeyn hap! o thou Fortune unstable!
Lyk to the scorpion so deceyvable,
That flaterest with thyn heed whan thou wolt stynge.
      (IV [E] 2057 ff.)

Swiche salutaciouns and contenaunces
Passen as dooth a shadwe upon the wal.
    (VII , 8 f. [B 1198 f.] [*H* p. 60])

That passen as a shadwe upon a wal.
    (IV [E] 1315 [*H* p. 60])

and passen as a shadwe on the wal.   (X [I] 1067 [*H* p. 60])

That lene he wex and drye as is a shaft.
    (I [A] 1362 [*H* p. 57])

And with a soun as softe as any shryfte.   (*LGW* 745 [*H* p. 60])

And strawe hir cage faire and softe as silk.   (V [F] 613)

And eke the gravell, which that shoon
Down in the botme as silver fyn.   (*Rom* A 1556 f.)

E la gravele qui paroit
Au fonz, plus clere qu'argenz fins.   (II, 79, ll. 1526 f.)

Out goon the swerdes as the silver brighte.
                              (I [A] 2608 [*H* p. 59])

And blak as . . . ony slo.   (*Rom* A 928)

E si estoit plus noirs que meure.   (II, 47, l. 914)

And tho were bent and blake as any sloo.   (I [A] 3246)

And thow fordon, as snow in fire is soone.   (*T&C*, i, 525)

Hir throte, also whit of hewe
As snowe on braunche snowed newe.   (*Rom* A 557 f. [*H* p. 59])

La gorge avoit autresi blanche
Come est la nois desus la branche,
Quant il a freschement negié.   (II, 29, ll. 545 ff.)

But whit as snow yfallen newe.   (*Rom* A 1214 [*H* p. 59])

Ainz estoit blanche come nois.   (II, 62, l. 1193)

Upon an hors, snow-whit.   (IV [E] 388)

Snow white (*crown*)   (VIII [G] 254)

Whit was this crowe as is a snow-whit swan.   (IX [H] 133)

May,
As fressh as is the brighte someres day.   (IV [E] 1895 f.)

Or see your colour lyk the sonne bryght,
That of yelownesse hadde never pere.   (*Purse* 10 f.)

Among al these Anelida, the quene
Of Ermony, was in that toun dwellynge,
That fairer was then is the sonne shene.   (*Anel* 71 ff.)

Dido,
That whilom was the wif of Sytheo,
That fayrer was than is the bryghte sonne.   (*LGW* 1004 ff.)

His crispe heer lyk rynges was yronne,
And that was yelow, and glytered as the sonne.
(I [A] 2165 f.)

His brydel as the sonne shoon.   (VII, 879 [B 2069])

Up riseth fresshe Canacee hirselve,
As rody and bright as dooth the yonge sonne.   (V [F] 384 f.)

His steede, which that shoon as sonne brighte.   (V [F] 170)

His berd as any sowe . . . was reed.   (I [A] 552)

a toft of herys,
Reed as the brustles of a sowes erys.   (I [A] 555 f.)

And therto brood, as though it were a spade.   (I [A] 553)

And forth upon his wey he glood
As sparcle out of the bronde.   (VII, 904 f. [B 2094 f.])

and chirketh as a sparwe
With his lyppes.   (III [D] 1804 f.)

As hoot he was and lecherous as a sparwe.   (I [A] 626)

The sparwe, Venus sone.   (*PF* 351)

For as a spaynel she wol on hym lepe.   (III [D] 267)

a gay daggere
Harneised wel and sharp as point of spere.
(I [A] 113 f. [*H* p. 57])

He loketh as a sperhauk with his yen.   (VII, 3457 [B 4647])

Thou shalt me fynde as just as is a squyre.
(III [D] 2090 [*S* 274])

Ful longe were his legges and ful lene,
Ylyk a staf, ther was no calf ysene.   (I [A] 591 f.)

But, right as they were bounden to a stake,
They wol nat of that firste purpos slake.   (IV [E] 704 f.)

white alauntz,
Twenty and mo, as grete as any steer.   (I [A] 2148 [H p. 57])

As trust and trew as ony stel.   (Rom B 5146)

The wyse and worthi, secre, trewe as stel.   (PF 395 [H p. 56])

Trewe as stiel in ech condicioun.   (T &C, v, 831 [H p. 56])

trewe as stel.   (LGW 2582 [H p. 56])

That ben as trewe as ever was any steel.
                              (LGW F 334 [H p. 56])

as trewe as any steel
I have a wyf.   (IV [E] 2426 f. [H p. 56])

Moo than sterres ben in hevene.   (HF 1254)

His eyen twynkled in his heed aryght,
As doon the sterres in the frosty nyght.   (I [A] 267 f.)

The God of Love, blynde as stoon.   (Rom B 3703)

This Januarie, as blynd as is a stoon.   (IV [E] 2156 [H p. 55])

And fel a-swowne as cold as ston.   (BD 123 [H p. 55])

Ded as a ston.   (Com Pite 16 [H p. 55])

Therwith he wax as ded as stoon,
And seyde.   (BD 1300 f. [H p. 55])

And lith aswowne, deed and lyk a stoon.   (V [F] 474)

Domm as a ston.   (Rom B 2409)

And, also domb as any stoon.   (HF 656 [H p. 56])

To ride by the weye doumb as a stoon.   (I [A] 774)

To grounde ded she falleth as a ston.   (Anel 170 [H p. 55])

That doun he fil atones as a stoon.   (II [B] 670)

Thogh ye ben harder than is any ston.
                              (LGW 2554 [H p. 56])

That hath an herte as hard as any stoon.   (IV [E] 1990)

And set hire doun as stylle as any ston.
(T&C, ii, 600 [H p. 55])

To Troilus, as stille as any ston.   (<i>T&C</i>, ii, 1494 [<i>H</i> p. 55])

And stille as stoon.   (<i>T&C</i>, iii, 699 [<i>H</i>. p. 56])

Into the derke chambre, as stille as ston.
(T&C, iv, 354 [H p. 56])

And stant, astoned of thise causes tweye,
As stille as ston.   (<i>T&C</i>, v, 1728 f. [<i>H</i> p. 56])

And there he stod, as stille as stoon.   (<i>HF</i> 1605 [<i>H</i> p. 56])

As stille as any ston.   (<i>LGW</i> F 310, G 236 [<i>H</i> p. 56])

This Nicholas sat ay as stille as stoon.   (I [A] 3472)

In crepeth age alwey, as stille as stoon.   (IV [E] 121)

The bryde was broght abedde as stille as stoon.   (IV [E] 1818)

Stant in the court as stille as any stoon.   (V [F] 171)

That trusty is and trewe as ston.   (<i>Rom</i> B 5248)

As breme as blase of straw iset on-fire.
(T&C, iv, 184 [H p. 60])

But smothe it heeng as dooth a strike of flek.   (I [A] 676)

But of hir song, it was as loude and yerne
As any swalwe sittynge on a berne.   (I [A] 3257 f.)

walkynge as a swan.   (III [D] 1930)

That (<i>Skeat reads</i> Right as) with a swerd it stingeth to myn
herte.   (<i>LGW</i> 1729)

Thou fallest as it were a styked swyn.   (VI [C] 556 [<i>H</i> p. 60])

he sleep as a swyn.   (II [B] 745)

Thanne shal this cherl, with bely stif and toght
As any tabour.   (III [D] 2267 f.)

> an hat
As brood as is . . . a targe.   (I [A] 470 f.)

It is more swift than any thought.   (*Rom* B 5024)

And ever mo, as swyft as thought.   (*HF* 1924 [*H* p. 60])

And upon coursers, swift as any thought.
                    (*LGW* 1195 [*H* p. 60])

And north, as lowde as any thunder.   (*HF* 1681)

The se, by nyghte, as any torche it brende.   (*LGW* 2419)

Though I be hoor, I fare as dooth a tree
That blosmeth er that fruyt ywoxen bee.   (IV [E] 1461 f.)

And she, for sorwe, as doumb stant as a tree.   (II [B] 1055)

Styl as an ymage of tree.   (*Rom* B 2408 [*H* p. 56])

> Ausi come une image mue,
> Qui ne se crole ne remue.   (II, 117, ll. 2287 f.)

His voys was as a trompe thonderynge.   (I [A] 2174)

The wedded turtil, with hire herte trewe.   (*PF* 355)

The turtle trewe.   (*PF* 577)

That lik a turtel trewe is my moornynge.   (I [A] 3706)

Soul as the turtle that lost hath hire make.   (IV [E] 2080)

Joye of this world, for tyme wol nat abyde;
Fro day to nyght it changeth as the tyde.   (II [B] 1133 f.)

And as a crueel tigre was Arcite.   (I [A] 1657)

Ther nas no tygre in the vale of Galgopheye,
Whan that hir whelp is stole whan it is lite,
So crueel on the hunte as is Arcite.   (I [A] 2626 ff.)

And sklendre wyves, fieble as in bataille,
Beth egre as is a tygre yond in Ynde.   (IV [E] 1198 f.)

Sprang up the grass, as thicke yset
And softe as any veluët.   (*Rom* A 1419 f.)

And she ay sad and constant as a wal.   (IV [E] 1047 [*H* p. 57])

And founde hym stedefast as a wall.   (*Rom* B 5250)

This somonour, which that was as ful of jangles,
As ful of venym been thise waryangles.   (III [D] 1407 f.)

She was as digne as water in a dich.   (I [A] 3964)

The blod out of the wounde as brode sterte
As water, whan the condit broken is.   (*LGW* 851 f.)

But, as a wedercok, that turneth his face
With every wind, ye fare.
                    (*Against Women Unconstant* 12 f. [*S* 147])

As any wezele hir body gent and smal.   (I [A] 3234)

But certeynly, a yong thyng may men gye,
Right as men may warm wex with handes plye.
                                        (IV [E] 1429 f.)

This Pardoner hadde heer as yelow as wex.
                                        (I [A] 675 [*H* p. 58])

Fat as a whale.   (III [D] 1930)

And rage he koude, as it were right a whelp.   (I [A] 257)

As lowde as beloweth wynd in helle.   (*HF* 1803)

Ryght as a wolf that fynt a lomb alone.   (*LGW* 1798)

And softer than the wolle is of a wether.   (I [A] 3249)

For nakid as a worm was she.   (*Rom* A 454 [*H* p. 60])

      Qu'ele estoit nue come vers.   (II, 24, l. 445)

Lat me nat lyk a worm go by the weye.   (IV [E] 880)

How fairer been thy brestes than is wyn!   (IV [E] 2142)

OTHER PROVERBIAL PHRASES

Youre bagges been nat fild with ambes as,
But with sys cynk, that renneth for youre chaunce.
(II [B] 124 f.)

Now may I seyn that I is but an ape.   (I [A] 4202)

And seyd, that Loves servantz everichone
Of nycete ben verray Goddes apes.   (*T&C*, i, 912 f.)

He made the person and the peple his apes.
(I [A] 706 [*H* 136d])

And thus she maketh Absolon hire ape.
(I [A] 3389 [*H* 136b])

Right as hym liste, the preest he made his ape!
(VIII [G] 1313 [*H* 136c])

Lo, Argus, which that hadde an hondred yen.
(IV [E] 2111 [*H* p. 71])

Artow like an asse to the harpe?   (*Boece* I, pr. 4, 3)

Or artow lik an asse to the harpe.   (*T&C*, i, 731 [*H* 108])

Sin I am free, I counte him not a bene.
(*Merciles Beaute* 29, 39)

God helpe me so, I counte hem nought a bene!
(*T&C*, v, 363 [*H* p. 62])

This Absolon ne roghte nat a bene.   (I [A] 3772)

But nathelees, I recche noght a bene.   (II [B] 94)

If he wol serve thee, rekke nat a bene.   (VII, 2814 [B 4004])

Swiche argumentes ne ben naught worth a beene.
(*T&C*, iii, 1167 [*H* p. 62])

"Noon oother lyf," seyde he "is worth a bene."
(IV [E] 1263 [*H* p. 62])

She preyseth nat his pleyyng worth a bene.

> (IV [E] 1854 [*H* p. 62])

I yeve not of her harm a bene!   (*Rom* C 6464)

And lat se which of yow shal bere the belle,
To speke of love aright!   (*T&C*, iii, 198 f. [*H* 167; *S* 173])

Quod Pandarus, "Thow wrecched mouses herte,
Artow agast so that she wol the bite?"   (*T&C*, iii, 736 f.)

"Nay, dred the not therof," quod he;
"Hyt is nothing will byten the."   (*HF* 1043 f.)

With bleryng of a proud milleres ye.   (I [A] 3865)

For al thy waityng, blered is thyn ye.   (IX [H] 252)

For blood bitokeneth gold, as me was taught.   (III [D] 581)

She loveth so this hende Nicholas
That Absolon may blowe the bukkes horn.

> (I [A] 3386 f. [*H* p. 52; *S* 204])

In stede of blew, thus may ye were al grene.

> (*Against Women Unconstant* 7, 14, 21)

Before me stont, clad in asure,
To profren eft a newe asure
For to be trewe.   (*Anel* 330 ff.)

> this blewe ryng.   (*T&C*, iii, 885)

And covered it with veluettes blewe,
In signe of trouthe that is in wommen sene.   (V [F] 644 f.)

Ther nedeth me no care for to borwe.   (*Com Lady* 10)

I sette right noght, of al the vileynye,
That ye of wommen write, a boterflye!   (IV [E] 2303 f.)

Swich talkyng is nat worth a boterflye.

> (VII, 2790 [B 3980])

Although it be nat worth a botel hey.

(IX [H] 14 [*H* p. 62])

It is not worth a croked brere.   (*Rom* C 6191 [*H* p. 62])

Il ne vaut pas un coutel troine.   (III, 185, l. 11057)

Another day he wole, peraventure,
Reclayme thee and brynge thee to lure.

(IX [H] 71 f. [*H* p. 54])

But I ne kan nat bulte it to the bren.

(VII, 3240 [B 4430])

He yaf me al the bridel in myn hond.   (III [D] 813)

Tak with thy teeth the bridel faste,
To daunte thyn herte.   (*Rom* B 3299 f.)

Pren durement as denz le frein,
Si dente con cuer e refrain.   (II, 154, ll. 3067 f.)

Or casten al the gruwel in the fire.   (*T&C*, iii, 711 [*S* 177])

Thou shalt make castels thanne in Spayne,
And dreme of joye.   (*Rom* B 2573 f. [*H* 60])

Lors feras chastiaus en Espaigne.   (II, 124, l. 2442)

I fare as doth the song of *Chaunte-pleure*;
For now I pleyne, and now I pleye.   (*Anel* 320 f.)

Shal noon housbonde seyn to me "chek mat!"

(*T&C*, ii, 754)

Quod Pandarus, "Thow hast a ful gret care
Lest that the cherl may falle out of the moone!

(*T&C*, i, 1023 f.)

Lest Chichevache yow swelwe in hire entraille!

(IV [E] 1188)

I warne yow wel, it is no childes pley
To take a wyf.   (IV [E] 1530 f.)

And yet ik have alwey a coltes tooth.   (I [A] 3888 [S 229])

But yet I hadde alwey a coltes tooth.

(III) [D] 602 [S 229])

A wys wyf shal, if that she kan hir good,
Bere hym on honde that the cow is wood,
And take witnesse of hir owene mayde.   (III [D] 231 ff.)

I made hym of the same wode a croce.   (III [D] 484)

So longe mote ye lyve, and alle proude,
Til crowes feet be growen under youre yë.   (T &C, ii, 402 f.)

the cukkow ever unkynde.   (PF 358)

This crowe sang "Cokkow! cokkow! cokkow!"   (IX [H] 243)

Ther lakketh noght, oonly but day and place.   (IV [E] 1998)

God helpe me so, I was to hym as kynde
As any wyf from Denmark unto Ynde.   (III [D] 823 f.)

For thou shalt for this synne dwelle
Right in the devels ers of helle.   (Rom C 7575 f.)

Vous en ireiz ou cul d'enfer,
Se vous ne vous en repentez.   (III, 234, ll. 12248 f.) [1]

Murmure . . . whiche wordes men clepen the develes *Pater
noster*, though so be that the devel ne hadde nevere *Pater
noster*, but that lewed folk yeven it swich a name.

(X [I] 505 ff.)

A twenty devel-wey the wynd hym dryve!   (LGW 2177)

Oure Hoost answerde, "Tel on, a devel wey!"   (I [A] 3134)

And lat me slepe, a twenty devel wey!   (I [A] 3713)

And forth he goth, a twenty devel way.   (I [A] 4257)

Lat hym go honge hymself a devel weye!   (III [D] 2242)

And al the cost, a twenty devel waye.   (VIII [G] 782)

And we shal speek of the somwhat, I trowe,
Whan thow art gon, to don thyn eris glowe! (*T &C*, ii, 1021 f.)

Do wey youre barbe, and shewe your face bare.
(*T &C*, ii, 110)

For in this world nys dogge for the bowe
That kan an hurt deer from an hool yknowe
Bet than this somnour knew a sly lecchour. (III [D] 1369 ff.)

And eek to Januarie he gooth as lowe
As evere dide a dogge for the bowe. (IV [E] 2013 f.)

Such folk drinken gret mysese. (*Rom* C 6807)

Teus genz beivent trop de mesaise. (III, 205, l. 11535)

Oure wrecche is this, oure owen wo to drynke. (*T &C*, ii, 784)

But goodly drynketh up al his distresse. (*T &C*, iii, 1035)

For what I drye, or what I thynke,
I wil myselven al hyt drynke. (*HF* 1879 f. [*H* p. 69])

Withouten coppe he drank al his penaunce. (V [F] 942)

Nay, thou shalt drynken of another tonne,
Er that I go, shal savoure wors than ale. (III [D] 170 f.)

I am, til God me bettre mynde sende,
At dulcarnoun, right at my wittes ende.
(*T &C*, iii, 930 f. [*S* 181])

Dulcarnoun called is "flemyng of wrecches." (*T &C*, iii, 933)

And seyde, "Sires, what! Dun is in the myre!
(IX [H] 5 [*H* 180a; *S* 289])

The bacon was nat fet for hem, I trowe,
That som men han in Essex at Dunmowe.
(III [D] 217 f. [*H* p. 72])

And yet in bacon hadde I nevere delit. (III [D] 418 [*H* p. 72])

For all yede out at oon ere
That in that other she dide lere. (*Rom* B 5151 f. [*H* 41b])

Par l'une des oreilles giete
Quanque Raison en l'autre boute.   (II, 226, ll. 4640 f.)

Oon ere it herde, at tothir out it wente.
(T&C, iv, 434 [H 41a])

maugree hir eyen two.   (I [A] 1796)

God woot, they take it wisly, faire, and softe.
(T&C, v, 347)

But seyn in voice of flaterie,
That now apperith her folye,
Overall where so they fare,
And synge, "Go, farewel, feldefare."
(Rom B 5507 ff. [H 181; S 180])

the frosty feldefare.   (<i>PF</i> 364)

The harm is don, and fare-wel feldefare!
(T&C, iii, 861 [H 181; S 180])

Pandare answerde, "Be we comen hider
To fecchen fir, and rennen hom ayein?"
(T&C, v, 484 f. [S 202])

than have ye fisshed fayre!   (<i>T&C</i>, ii, 328)

This seyd by hem that ben nought worth two fecches.
(T&C, iii, 936 [H p. 61])

And for to lawghe as they were wod,
Such game fonde they in her hod.   (<i>HF</i> 1809 f.)

Thou lookest as thou woldest fynde an hare,
For evere upon the ground I se thee stare.
(VII, 696 f. [B 1886 f.])

Ye rekke not whether I flete or synke.   (<i>Com Pite</i> 110)

Him rekketh never wher she flete or synke.   (<i>Anel</i> 182)

The flour nyl seeden of my corn.   (<i>Rom</i> B 4344)

The goos seyde, "Al this nys not worth a flye!
(*PF* 501 [*H* p. 62])

Aleyn answerde, "I counte hym nat a flye,   (I [A] 4192)

As helpe me God, he is noght worth at al
In no degree the value of a flye.
(VII, 170 f. [B 1360 f.] [*H* p. 62])

      and swich folye
As in oure dayes is nat worth a flye. (V [F] 1131 f. [*H* p. 63])

Or somwhat elles, was nat worth a flye.
(VIII [G] 1150 [*H* p. 63])

For foot-hoot, in his felonye.   (*Rom* B 3827)

The mayster-hunte anoon, fot-hot,
With a gret horn blew thre mot.   (*BD* 375 f.)

That in his owene grece I made hym frye
For angre, and for verray jalousye.   (III [D] 487 f. [*S* 269])

And yf I slepe a furlong wey or tweye.   (*Anel* 328)

Or hyt a forlong way was old.   (*HF* 2064)

Ne nat a word was spoken in the place
The mountaunce of a furlong wey of space.
(*LGW* F 306 f., G 232 f.)

This John lith stille a furlong wey or two.   (I [A] 4199)

They seten stille wel a furlong way.   (I [A] 3637)

Fortune his howve entended bet to glaze!
(*T&C*, v, 469 [*S* 166, 201])

I wol nat wirche as muchel as a gnat.   (III [D] 347)

Noght worth to thee, as in comparisoun,
The montance of a gnat.   (IX [H] 254 f. [*H* p. 62])

Now artow hent, now gnaw thin owen cheyne!   (*T&C*, i, 509)

So he may fynde Goddes foyson there.   (I [A] 3165)

I rekke nevere, whan that they been beryed,
Though that hir soules goon a-blakeberyed!   (VI [C] 405 f.)

Thus goth the world.   (T&C, v, 1434)

Gras tyme is doon, my fodder is now forage.   (I [A] 3868)

Ne knewe hem more than myn olde hat!   (T&C, iii, 320)

And al withoute, the mewe is peynted grene,
In which were peynted alle thise false fowles.   (V [F] 646 f.)

Youre herte hangeth on a joly pyn!   (IV [E] 1516)

Al hadde folkes hertes ben of stones,
Hyt myght have maked hem upon hir rewe.
                    (LGW 1841 f. [H 163b])

It myghte han mad an herte of stoon to rewe.
                    (T&C, iii, 114 [H 163a])

"A ryng?" quod he, "ye, haselwodes shaken!"
                    (T&C, iii, 890)

"Ye, haselwode!" thoughte this Pandare.   (T&C, v, 505)

From haselwode, there joly Robyn pleyde,
Shal come al that that thow abidest heere.   (T&C, v, 1174 f.)

Nay, swiche abodes ben nought worth an hawe.
                    (T&C, iii, 854 [H p. 61])

Or calkulyng, avayleth nought thre hawes.
                    (T&C, iv, 1398 [H p. 61])

But al for noght, I sette noght an hawe
Of his proverbes n'of his olde sawe.   (III [D] 659 f.)

mawgree my hed.   (BD 1201)

malgre her hed.   (Com Mars 220)

Maugre hire hed.   (LGW 2326)

maugree his heed.   (I [A] 1169)

Maugree his heed.   (I [A] 2618)

Maugree thyn heed.   (II [B] 104)

Maugree youre heed.   (VII, 3412 [B 4602])

Her astat is not worth an hen.   (*Rom* C 6856)

Leur estaz n'est ne beaus ne genz.   (III, 206, l. 11576)

I counte nat a panyer ful of herbes
Of scole-termes.   (IV [E] 1568 f. [*H* p. 62])

If that he faught, and hadde the hyer hond.   (I [A] 399)

His newe lady holdeth him so narowe
Up by the bridil.   (*Anel* 183 f. [*H* p. 71])

For in oure wyl ther stiketh evere a nayl,
To have an hoor heed and a grene tayl,
As hath a leek.   (I [A] 3877 ff.)

We hoppen alwey whil the world wol pype.   (I [A] 3876)

Have at thee, Jason! now thyn horn is blowe!   (*LGW* 1383)

With hornepipes of Cornewaile.   (*Rom* B 4250)

As estives de Cornoaille.   (II, 195, l. 3900)

Although he sought oon in-tyl Ynde.   (*Rom* A 624)

Ne plus bel leu por soi joer
Ne porroit il mie troer.   (II, 32, ll. 613 f.)

To gete her love no ner nas he
That woned at hom, than he in Ynde.   (*BD* 888 f.)

For I ne kan nat fynde
A man, though that I walked into Ynde.   (VI [C] 721 f.)

Go fro the wyndow, Jakke fool.   (I [A] 3708)

Fro Jerusalem unto Burgoyne
Ther nys a fairer nekke, iwys.   (*Rom* A 554 f.)

Of paramours he sette nat a kers.   (I [A] 3756 [S 227])

And som men seyn he was of tonge large.
(T&C, v, 804 [H p. 68])

Sich love I preise not at a lek.   (Rom B 4830)

Que cete amour n'ont mie chiere.   (II, 216, l. 4390)

Men wole not sette by hym a lek.   (Rom B 5374)

And though they die, they set not a lek.   (Rom B 5730)

And seyden they yeven noght a lek
For fame.   (HF 1708 f. [H p. 62])

That every man that halt hym worth a leek.
(IV [E] 1350 [H p. 62])

And othere swiche, deere ynough a leek.
(VIII [G] 795 [H p. 62])

What sleighte is it, thogh it be long and hoot,
That Love nyl fynde it out in som manere?   (IV [E] 2126 f.)

God woot, no lussheburghes payen ye!
(VII, 1962 [B 3152] [H p. 54])

For love bigan his fetheres so to lyme.   (T&C, i, 353)

And moo berdys in two houres
Withoute rasour or sisoures
Ymad, then greynes be of sondes.   (HF 689 ff. [H 135c])

Yet kan a millere make a clerkes berd,
For al his art.   (I [A] 4096 f. [H 135a])

Yet koude I make his berd, so moot I thee!
(III [D] 361 [H 135b])

And maken hym a howve above a calle,
I meene, as love another in this while.   (T&C, iii, 775 f.)

And up he gooth and maketh it ful tough.
(VII, 379 [B 1569])

A theef he (*a miller*) was for sothe of corn and mele.
                                        (I [A] 3939)

My mouth hath icched al this longe day;
That is a signe of kissyng atte leeste.   (I [A] 3682 f.)

I shal nat faille surely of my day,
Nat for a thousand frankes, a mile way.
                                   (VII, 275 f. [B 1465 f.])

Ye, sterve he shal, and that in lasse while
Than thou wolt goon a paas nat but a mile.   (VI [C] 865 f.)

Hymsilf it availeth not a myte.   (*Rom* B 5762 [*H* p. 61])

He yeveth nat now therof a myte.   (*Rom* C 7550 [*H* p. 61])

    Il n'i donrait pas une escorce
    De chesne.   (III, 233, ll. 12224 f.)

He ne roghte not a myte for to dye. (*Com Mars* 126 [*H* p. 61])

Alas! ye rekke not a myte.   (*Anel* 269 [*H* p. 61])

And if to lese his joie he sette a myte,
Than semeth it that joie is worth ful lite.   (*T&C*, iii, 832 f.)

And with hire tales, deere ynough a myte.
                                   (*T&C*, iv, 684 [*H* p. 61])

It nas nat sene, deere ynogh a myte.   (*LGW* 741 [*H* p. 61])

Now highte I Philostrate, noght worth a myte.
                                   (I [A] 1558 [*H* p. 60])

Thomas, that jape nys nat worth a myte.
                                   (III [D] 1961 [*H* p. 60])

For in effect they been nat worth a myte.
                                   (VIII [G] 511 [*H* p. 60])

His overslope nys nat worth a myte.
                                   (VIII [G] 633 [*H* p. 61])

Of al his thretyng rekke nat a myte!   (VIII [G] 698 [*H* p. 61])

And I right now have founden al the gise,
Withouten net, wherwith I shal hym hente.
                    (*T&C*, iv, 1370 f.)

Nettle in, dok out, now this, now that, Pandare.
                    (*T&C*, iv, 461 [*H* 179; *S* 187])

Ek wonder last but nyne nyght nevere in towne.
                    (*T&C*, iv, 588 [*S* 188])

But thilke text heeld he nat worth an oystre.
                    (I [A] 182 [*H* p. 63])

For she knew all the olde daunce. (*Rom* B 4300)

  Qu'el set toute la vieille dance. (II, 197, l. 3936)

But Pandarus, that wel koude ech a deel
The olde daunce. (*T&C*, iii, 694 f.)

For she koude of that art the olde daunce. (I [A] 476)

And knowen wel ynough the olde daunce. (VI [C] 79)

But wel I wot, thow wolt answere and saye:
"Lo! olde Grisel lyst to ryme and playe!" (*Scogan* 34 f.)

Who peyntede the leon, tel me who? (III [D] 692)

But in Pilates voys he gan to crie. (I [A] 3124)

Syngeth *Placebo*, and "I shal, if I kan." (III [D] 2075])

Flatereres been the develes chapelleyns, that syngen evere
Placebo. (X [I] 616)

Of whiche that oon was cleped Placebo. (IV [E] 1476)

But kanstow pleyen raket, to and fro. (*T&C*, iv, 460)

Ful prively a fynch eek koude he pulle. (I [A] 652)

And yet as proud a pekok kan he pulle.
                    (*T&C*, i, 210 [*H* p. 60])

Withoute scaldyng they hem pulle. (*Rom* C 6820)

Senz eschauder touz vis les plument.   (III, 205, l. 11548)

He yaf nat of that text a pulled hen.   (I [A] 177 [H p. 63])

As proude Bayard gynneth for to skippe
Out of the weye, so pryketh hym his corn.   (T &C, i, 218 f.)

The monk putte in the mannes hood an ape,
And in his wyves eek, by Seint Austyn!
                (VII, 440 f. [B 1630 f.] [H 136a])

By God! in erthe I was his purgatorie.   (III [D] 489)

Paraunter she may be youre purgatorie!   (IV [E] 1670)

But Troilus, thow maist now, est or west,
Pipe in an ivy lef, if that the lest!
                (T &C, v, 1432 f. [H 169b; S 204])

That oon of yow, al be hym looth or lief,
He moot go pipen in an yvy leef.
                (I [A] 1837 f. [H 169a; S 204])

But that tale is nat worth a rake-stele.
                (III [D] 949 [H p. 62])

His resons, as I may my rymes holde.   (T &C, iii, 90)

Noot I nought what, al deere ynough a rysshe,
As he that nedes most a cause fisshe.   (T &C, iii, 1161 f.)

Thorughout the world my belle shal be ronge!
                (T &C, v, 1062)

And doun gooth al; he foond neither to selle,
Ne breed ne ale, til he cam to the celle.   (I [A] 3821 f.)

And yet this Manciple sette hir aller cappe.
                (I [A] 586 [H p. 54])

How that a clerk hath set the wrightes cappe.
                (I [A] 3143 [H p. 54])

Thogh I answere, and somdeel sette his howve.
                (I [A] 3911)

But manly sette the world on six and sevene.
(T &C, iv, 622 [H 175; S 190])

This sevene yer.   (LGW 2120)

Thise seven yeer.   (I [A] 1452)

> seventhe yer.   (I [A] 1462)

Hir brother, which that seven yeer was of age.   (IV [E] 780)

> seven yeer,   (VIII [G] 720)

That he may shake hem be the biles.   (HF 868 [H p. 54])

The clerk, whan he is oold, and may noght do
Of Venus werkes worth his olde sho.   (III [D] 707 f.)

He was tho glad his hornes in to shrinke.   (T &C, i, 300)

Where as thise bacheleris synge "allas."   (IV [E] 1274)

For Absolon may waille and synge "allas."   (I [A] 3398)

For I may synge "allas and weylawey,
That I was born."   (VII, 118 f. [B 1308 f.])

For which his song ful ofte is "weylaway!"   (T &C, iv, 1166)

That many a nyght they songen "weilawey!"   (III [D] 216)

Or was to bold, to synge a fool a masse.   (T &C, iii, 88)

Ye, fare wel al the snow of ferne yere!
(T &C, v, 1176 [S 203])

Be war also to sporne ayeyns an al.   (Truth 11 [S 143])

He wolde sowen som difficulte,
Or springen cokkel in our clene corn.   (II [B] 1182)

For though that Absolon be wood or wrooth,
By cause that he fer was from hire sight,
This nye Nicholas stood in his light.   (I [A] 3394 ff.)

And plongeth hem in poverte,
As a stepmoder envyous.   (Rom B 5472 f. [cf. 5417 f.])

E leur assiet, come marrastre,
Au cueur un doulereus emplastre.   (II, 236, ll. 4897 f.)

"Straw!" quod the thridde, "ye been lewed and nyce."
                                    (VIII [G], 925)

A straw for alle swevenes signifiaunce!
                                    (T&C, v, 362 [H p. 70])

Straw for thy Senek, and for thy proverbes!   (IV [E] 1567)

"Straw for youre gentillesse!" quod oure Hoost.   (V [F] 695)

Al hir compleynt ne al hir moone,
Certeyn, avayleth hir not a stre.   (HF 362 f. [H p. 61])

God wot, she acounted nat a stree
Of al my tale.   (BD 1237 f. [H p. 61])

For he ne counted nat thre strees
Of noght that Fortune koude doo.   (BD 718 f. [H p. 61])

Algate she ne roughte of hem a stree!   (BD 887 [H p. 61)]

I sette nat a straw by thy dremynges.   (VII, 3090 [B 4280])

I holde that wyssh nat worth a stree!   (BD 671 [H p. 61])

yet be they nat worth a stree.   (VII, 1336 [B 2526] [H p. 61])

> elles ne vallent riens se elles ne sont deffendues. (*Mellibée*
> in *Le Méagier de Paris*, ed. J. Pichon, Paris, 1846, I,
> 209.)

al be the cause nat worth a straw.   (X [I] 600 [H p. 61])

But as the swan, I have herd seyd ful yore,
Ayeins his deth shal singen his penaunce.
                                    (*Anel* 346 f. [H 153b; S 137])

The jelous swan, ayens his deth that syngeth.
                                    (PF 342 [S 137])

"Ryght so," quod she, "as that the white swan
Ayens his deth begynnyth for to synge."
>   (*LGW* 1355 f. [*H* 153a; *S* 137, 210])

Take every man hys turn, as for his tyme.   (*Scogan* 42)

Ne sette I nat the montance of a tare.
>   (I [A] 1570 [*H* p. 62])

But therof sette the millere nat a tare.   (I [A] 4000)

Of al hir art I counte noght a tare.   (I [A] 4056 [*H* p. 62])

   thurgh thikke and thurgh thenne.   (I [A] 4066)

But I wol kepe it for youre owene tooth.   (III [D] 449)

Thy drasty rymyng is nat worth a toord!
>   (VII, 930 [B 2120] [*H* p. 61])

He hadde moore tow on his distaf
Than Gerveys knew.   (I [A] 3774 f. [*S* 228])

Ne lasteth not the twynkelyng of an ye.
>   (*Com Mars* 222 [*H* p. 63])

But as it were a twynklyng of an ye.   (IV [E] 37)

That they had ofte, for the nones,
Two heedes in oon hood at ones.   (*Rom* C 7385 f.)

   Que deus testes avait ensemble
   En un chaperon, ce me semble.   (III, 227, ll. 12063 f.)

Ne were worthy unbokelen his galoche.   (V [F] 555 [*H* 160])

I hadde the prente of seinte Venus seel.   (III [D] 604)

He song; she pleyde; he tolde tale of Wade.   (*T &C*, iii, 614)

And eek thise olde wydwes, God it woot,
They konne so muchel craft on Wades boot.
>   (IV [E] 1423 f.)

That oother weep as she to water wolde.   (V [F] 496)

So was hir joly whistle wel ywet.   (I [A] 4155)

What manere wyndes gydeth yow now here?
(*T&C*, ii, 1104)

I see wel that som thyng ther is amys;
Ye looken as the wode were ful of thevys.   (III [D] 2172 f.)

Swiche as men clepen a word with two visages.
(*T&C*, v, 899)

I trowe that ye dronken han wyn ape,
And that is whan men pleyen with a straw.
(IX [H] 44 f. [*H* p. 71])

NOTES

CHAPTER I

1. This belief, with an appropriate exception, is admirably stated in the latest and most valuable handbook on the proverb: "Proverbs are used freely in writings which make an appeal to the folk and in those in which the folk is characterized; in those classes of literature which are far removed from the folk, proverbs rarely occur. . . . Writings which make a conspicuous effort at literary style generally avoid them except as details characterizing the folk. . . . Yet we must not carry these distinctions too far: Chaucer's *Troilus*, a very sophisticated, anti-popular poem, bristles with proverbs." (A. Taylor, *The Proverb* [Cambridge, Massachusetts, 1931], p. 172.)

2. *Siege of Thebes*, ed. A. Erdmann and E. Ekwall, EETS., ES., CVIII, CXXV (London, 1911–1930), I, 3, ll. 51 f.

3. *Political, Religious and Love Poems*, ed. F. J. Furnivall, EETS., XV (London, 1903), 307.

4. Speght points out a proverb by means of a small hand in the margin; as an indication of what he considered proverbial I list the sayings so designated in the *Wife of Bath's Prologue* (III [D] ll. 1–886): Ll. 52, 67, 71 f., 89, 180 f., 209 f., 227 f., 231 f., 269 f., 278 ff., 326 f., 333 f., 349 ff., 361, 386, 389, 401 f., 414, 415, 441 f., 465 f., 467 f., 477 f., 484, 487, 517 ff., 522 ff., 572 ff., 602, 655 ff., 692, 707 ff., 775 ff., 778 ff., 782 ff., 835 f. It has been held probable that it was this edition of Speght which suggested to William Painter his *Chaucer new Painted* (c.1623). This volume, recently discovered in the Huntington Library and described by L. B. Wright ("William Painter and the Vogue of Chaucer as a Moral Teacher," *Modern Philology*, XXXI (1933), 165 ff.), is a collection of proverbs, few or none of which seem to come

from Chaucer, set in a frame. Mr. Wright's article gives a valuable account of Elizabethan appreciation of Chaucer's proverbial wisdom.

5. For examples, see C. F. E. Spurgeon, *Five Hundred Years of Chaucer Criticism and Allusion* (Cambridge, 1925), I, 117, 142, 220, 239, 316; *The Diary of John Manningham, 1602–03*, ed. J. Bruce, Camden Society, XCIX (London, 1868), 11.

6. Spurgeon, I, 228 f.

7. *A Comment Upon the Two Tales of . . . Chaucer*, ed. C. F. E. Spurgeon, Chaucer Society, 2d Series (London, 1901).

8. Notice of Chaucer's proverbs by critics and editors could probably be extended greatly, but it hardly merits more space.

9. *Sermons*, ed. G. E. Corrie, Parker Society (Cambridge, 1844), I, 106 f.

10. *Miscellaneous Writings and Letters*, ed. J. E. Cox, Parker Society (Cambridge, 1846), II, 198.

11. For other occurrences, see Spurgeon, *Five Hundred Years*, I, 111, 116(2), 119, 122, 175, 178, 203, 239, 311(2), 366, 383, 408, 424; III, 60; R. D[ixon], *Canidia, or the Witches* (London, 1683), iii, 171; *British Apollo*, I (1708), no. 103, sig. Lllll (v), II (1709), no. 56, sig. Kkk (v); *Diary of John Thomlinson* (1717), in *Six North Country Diaries*, ed. J. C. Hodgson (Surtees Soc. 118, Durham, 1910), I. 71; W. Byrd, *Histories of the Dividing Line*, ed. W. K. Boyd (Raleigh, N. C., 1929), p. 64.

12. F. Grose, ed. E. Partridge, *A Classical Dictionary of the Vulgar Tongue* (London, 1931), s.v. "Canterbury Story."

13. Spurgeon, I, 116, 144(2), 162, 179, 185(2), 219; III, 48, 61.

14. *Das Sprichwort bei Chaucer*, Erlanger Beiträge, VIII (Erlangen and Leipzig, 1890). This work is referred to hereafter as *H*. It was reviewed by E. Koeppel, *Anglia Beiblatt*, II (1891), 169–173, who made many additions. Other omissions were supplied by A. Andrae, *Anglia Beiblatt*, III (1892), 276–282; IV (1893), 330–341.

15. Berlin, 1893.

16. Oxford, 1910. This work is referred to hereafter as *S*.

17. See *infra*, pp. 199 ff., for proverbs in the *Filostrato*.

18. On proverbs from Deschamps illustrative of passages in Chaucer, see J. L. Lowes, *Romanic Review*, II (1911), 116 ff.

19. H. L. Cohen, *The Ballade* (New York, 1915), p. 94. Miss Cohen discusses Deschamps briefly on pp. 95 f.

20. The proverbs of Deschamps have been isolated by E. Fehse, *Sprichwort und Sentenz bei Eustache Deschamps und Dichtern seiner Zeit* (Erlangen, 1905). This work is by no means satisfactory; it is incomplete, proverbial phrases are scarcely considered, and we find listed as proverbs many things which appear to be sententious remarks. I have given his number after each saying which he included, for the sake of his parallels.

21. See Appendix A for proverbial material in Deschamps. All references are to the edition published by the Société des Anciens Textes Français, ed. Le Marquis de Queux de Saint-Hilaire and Gaston Raynaud, 11 vols. (Paris, 1878–1903).

22. V, 402 f., MXCIII.

23. VII, 133 f., MCCCL.

24. I, 205 f., XCVII.

25. I, 210 f., C.

26. I, 154 f., LX, ll. 8, 16, 24.

27. III, 109 f., CCCLXVI, ll. 8, 16, 24, 32, 40, 46.

28. V, 398, MXC, ll. 10, 20, 30.

29. VI, 40 ff., MCXXIV, ll. 12, 24, 36, 48, 60, 66.

30. I, 181 f., LXXIX, ll. 8, 16, 24, 28.

31. II, 134 f., CCLXXXII, ll. 10, 20, 30, 34.

32. III, 183 f., CCCXCIX, ll. 10, 20, 30, 40, 50, 56.

33. III, 232 f., CCCCXXVII, ll. 8, 16, 24, 28.

34. The *Boece* and the *Astrolabe*.

35. My remarks and quotations are based on A. de Montaiglon and G. Raynaud, *Recueil Général des Fabliaux* (Paris, 1872–1890), 6 vols. The proverbs in the *fabliaux* were collected after a fashion by Johannes Loth (*Die Sprichwörter und Sentenzen der altfranzösischen Fabliaux* [printed in two programs of the Königl. Friedrich-Wilhelms-gymnasium at Greifen-

berg in Pomerania, 137, 138, 1895, 1896]). This work does not include any proverbial phrases and does contain many quotations which no stretch of the imagination could call proverbial or sententious (cf., for example, pp. 7, 8, 11, 12). As Loth's illustrative material is of little or no value I do not give his numbers.

36. See Appendix B for quotations.

37. See E. Faral, *Les Arts Poétiques du XIIe et du XIIIe Siècle* ([Bibliothèque de l'École des Hautes Études. Sciences Historiques et Philologiques, 238] Paris, 1924); C. S. Baldwin, *Medieval Rhetoric and Poetic* (New York, 1928); and Whiting, "The Nature of the Proverb," *Harvard Studies and Notes in Philology and Literature*, XIV (1932), 284 ff.

38. Baldwin, pp. 185 ff.; Faral, p. 113.

39. Baldwin, pp. 187 ff., 221, n. 31; Faral, pp. 201 ff.

40. Arguments based on the *Canterbury Tales* all too often confuse the speakers. A good example of this is in J. M. Manly's Warton Lecture on English Poetry, "Chaucer and the Rhetoricians," *Proceedings of the British Academy* (London, 1926), XII, p. 97, "And certainly the humorous citation by Chauntecleer and Pertelote of 'Daun Catoun,' and 'the hooly doctour Augustyn, Or Boece, or the bishop Bradwardyn' does not imply any lack of respect for those eminent authorities." Manly follows this with a warning against confusing the remarks of the characters with those of Chaucer.

41. In addition to Manly's pioneer paper, see Traugott Naunin, *Der Einfluss der mittelalterlichen Rhetorik auf Chaucers Dichtung* (Bonn, 1929).

42. *PF*, l. 1; *Truth*, ll. 3 f.; *T & C*, Bk. ii, ll. 21, 28, 35 f., 42; *Legend of Phyllis, LGW*, ll. 2394 f. See Manly, p. 100.

43. *Bukton*, ll. 27 f.; *Reeve's Prologue*, I [A], 3919 f.; *Reeve's Tale*, I [A] 4319 ff.; *Shipman's Tale*, VII, 427 ff. [B 1617 ff.]; Balthasar in *MT*, VII, 2241 ff. [B 3431 ff.]; *Maunciple's Tale*, IX [H] 320 ff. See Manly, p. 101.

44. Pp. 32–34, 43.

45. G. L. Kittredge, *Chaucer and his Poetry* (Cambridge, Massachusetts, 1915), pp. 13 f.

46. "Til that the brighte sonne loste his hewe;
    For th'orisonte hath reft the sonne his lyght, —
    This is as muche to seye as it was nyght!"
                                            (V [F] 1016 ff.)
47. See Manly, pp. 107 ff.
48. See Naunin, pp. 53 f.

CHAPTER II

1. See D. S. Fansler, *Chaucer and the Roman de la Rose*
(New York, 1914), pp. 175–202. Fansler points out instances
where proverbs in the *Roman de la Rose* appear in Chaucer's
work outside the *Romaunt*. On the general matter of proverbs
in English translations from the French I may call attention
to my article "Proverbs in Certain Middle English Romances
in Relation to Their French Sources," *Harvard Studies and
Notes in Philology and Literature*, XV (1933), 75–126.
2. I give the original French from the edition of Ernest
Langlois, Société des Anciens Textes Français (Paris, 1914–
1924).
3. See pp. 89 f. above.
4. The authenticity of these quatrains is by no means established.
5. See p. 68.

CHAPTER III

1. *Opere Volgari di G. Boccaccio*, ed. I. Moutier (Florence,
1831), XIII.
2. E benchè l' uom non prenda buon consiglio, / Donar lo
puote nell' altrui periglio (ii, 10); E come io udii già sovente
dire, / Il nuovo amor sempre caccia l'antico (iv, 49); la fortuna aiuta / Chiunque è ardito, e' timidi rifiuta (iv, 73);
Amor promessa non cura nè fede (iv, 75).
3. Ma come noi, per continova usanza, / Per più legne
veggiam fuoco maggiore, / Così avvien crescendo la speranza
/ Assai sovente ancor cresce l'amore (ii, 85).

4. Che quei che sè non sa guardar dal tosco, / Altrui per buon consiglio salvo tiene: / E già veduto s'è andare il losco / Dove l'alluminato non va bene (ii, 10); Sol una volta ha nel mondo ventura / Qualunque vive, se la sa pigliare; / Che lei vegnente lascia, sua sciagura / Pianga da sè senz' altrui biasimare (ii, 44); (Pandaro) Disse: questo è a pensar nuova cosa, / Che quel che più dalle donne è bramato, / Di ciò ciascuna e ischifa e crucciosa / Si mostra innanzi altrui (ii, 112); I sogni e le paure caccia via, / In quel che son lasciali andar ne' venti (v, 32).

5. Anima mia, i' udii, ragionando / Già è assai, se mi ricordo bene, / Che amore è uno spirto avaro, e quando / Alcuna cosa prende, sì la tiene / Serrata forte e stretta con gli artigli, / Ch'a liberarla invan si dan consigli (iii, 48); Ed oltre a questo, vo' che tu riguardi / A ciò che quasi d'ogni cosa avviene; / Non è cosa sì vil, se ben si guardi, / Che non si faccia disiar con pene, / E quanto più di possederla ardi, / Più tosto abominìo nel cor ti viene, / Se larga potestade di vederla / Fatta ti fia, e ancor di ritenerla (iv, 152); L'aspettar tempo è utile talvolta / Per tempo guadagnare, anima mia (iv, 159); L'uom dee guardare / Tempo e stagion quand' altri vuol pigliare (vi, 31).

6. Oimè! chi molto perde piange assai (v, 36); Oimè che tu di' vero! Troilo disse, / Or così va, cotanto mi trasporta / Quel ch'io vorrei ch'al presente avvenisse (vii, 9); Perocchè fior caduto è tosto bruno (vii, 93).

7. Le cose andavan si come di guerra, / Tra li Troiani e' Greci assai sovente, *etc.* (i, 16); O cecità delle mondane menti, / Come ne seguon sovente gli effetti / Tutti contrarii a' nostri intendimenti! (i, 25); che amore a molti aperto / Noia acquistava, e non gioia per merto (i, 36); che tutt' eran fole / Che perdeansi ne' venti (i, 57); L'acqua furtiva, assai più dolce cosa / È che il vin con abbondanza avuto: / Così d'amor la gioia, che nascosa / Trapassa assai, del sempre mai tenuto / Marito in braccio (ii, 74); Guarda che fai; che il senno da sezzo / Nè fu, nè è, nè fia mai d'alcun prezzo (ii, 76); Gli disse: speglio mio, le nuove spose / Son la notte primiera vergognose (iii, 31); La fama velocissima, la quale / Il falso e'l

vero ugualmente rapporta, / Era volata con prestissim' ale / Per tutta Troia (iv, 78); Ma come noi veggiam che egli avvienne, / Che l'una donna all' altra a visitare / Ne' casi nuovi va se le vuol bene (iv, 80); e vada dove gire / Ne vuole il fumo, e ciò che può seguirmi / Di ciò ne segua (vi, 7).

8. i, 22, 53, 56; ii, 62, 108; iii, 91; iv, 27, 41, 138, 140; v, 37; vi, 23; vii, 30, 80.

9. ii, 50, 83; iv, 16, 85, 89; vii, 10.

10. E. Spenser, *The Shepherd's Calendar*, ed. W. L. Renwick (London, 1930), p. 3; see also, J. C. *Alcilia* (1595) in E. Arber, *Garner* (London, 1897), IV, 272.

11. The method here adopted of taking up the various groups involves some repetition of setting, but this seems preferable to mixing the proverbs and sententious remarks together.

12. I do not intend to discuss the proverbial phrases at length or to reproduce them here, but it is instructive to note that Pandarus uses two comparisons (ii, 193 f.; iv, 595) and twenty-two other proverbial phrases (i, 731, 912 f., 1023 f.; ii, 110, 328, 1021 f.; iii, 198 f., 711, 775 f., 854, 861, 890, 936; iv, 588, 622; v, 347, 362, 363, 484 f., 505, 1174 f., 1176).

13. iv, 1356, 1548 f.

14. ii, 754, 784, 1104; iii, 885, 931, 1035, 1167; iv, 1370 f., 1398; v, 1062.

15. i, 524 f.; iv, 1459; v, 425, 1265.

16. i, 509; iv, 460 f.

17. See R. K. Root, *Troilus and Criseyde* (Princeton, 1926), p. 449.

18. v, 899.

19. v, 1469.

20. See pp. 11 ff. above.

21. i, 1074; ii, 600 (also ii, 1494; iii, 699, iv, 354; v, 1728 f.), 926, 1256, 1461 f., 1615; iii, 425, 1200, 1784; iv, 184, 337, 1135 ff.; v, 535, 830, 831, 844.

22. i, 210, 218 f., 300, 353; iii, 88, 90, 114, 614, 694 f., 1161 f.; iv, 434, 1166; v, 469, 804, 1432 f., 1434.

CHAPTER IV

1. See p. 66 above.

2. I have often wondered why no one has commented upon the trueness to life and type of this ribald scholar. Abuse he could bear, and repay, but violence to a book, especially "right as he radde," demanded and received condign punishment.

3. The only printed text of this tract, probably by neither Jean de Meun or Renaud de Louens, to both of whom it has been ascribed, is in [J. Pichon], *Le Ménagier de Paris* (Paris, 1846), I, 186 ff. For the relation of the French original to Chaucer's translation see J. S. P. Tatlock, *Development and Chronology of Chaucer's Works* (Chaucer Society, 2d Series, 37 [London, 1907]), pp. 188 ff.

4. See Tatlock, p. 191, n. 2.

5. Cf. *T & C.*, i, 956. See Tatlock, p. 193 f.

6. Pp. 192 f.

7. See p. 88 above.

8. See p. 113 above.

CHAPTER V

1. *The Complete Works of John Gower*, ed. G. C. Macaulay, 4 vols. Oxford, 1899–1902.

2. The proverbial phrases and sententious remarks are given in Appendix C (I). The proverbial material in Gower was isolated by Gotthart Walz, *Das Sprichwort bei Gower* (Nördlingen, 1907). Walz's collection is not complete, and omits the proverbial phrases almost completely, but his parallels are valuable and I give his numbering in brackets in all cases.

3. Gower's French works are of less interest in relation to Chaucer, but I give in Appendix C (II) line references to the various items.

4. There are seven sententious remarks in the 385 lines of *In Praise of Peace:*

And more than god may no man justefie.   (l. 11)

The werre hath set his cart on thilke whieles
Wher that fortune mai noght be believed.   (ll. 115 f.)

For everemor the werste is forto doute.   (l. 138 [140])

Of that the heved is siek, the limes aken.   (l. 260 [241a])

That now is up, to morwe is under grave.   (l. 292 [215])

Men sein the wolle, whanne it is wel sponne,
Doth that the cloth is strong and profitable,
And elles it mai nevere be durable.   (ll. 299 ff. [276])

   the trouthe can noght feine.   (l. 312)

   5. See p. 142 above.
   6. See pp. 130 f. above.
   7. See p. 79 above.

CHAPTER VI

   1. Cf. III [D] 1674 ff., and G. L. Kittredge in *Harvard Studies and Notes in Philology and Literature*, I (1892), 21.

APPENDICES

APPENDIX A

PROVERBS IN DESCHAMPS

THE following quotations are taken from *Oeuvres Complètes de Eustache Deschamps*, edited by the Marquis de Queux de Saint-Hilaire and Gaston Raynaud (Société des anciens textes français), 11 vols. (Paris, 1878–1903). The numbers in brackets refer to Erich Fehse's *Sprichwort und Sentenz bei Eustache Deschamps und Dichtern seiner Zeit* (Erlangen, 1905).

PROVERBS

Ceuls s'accusent qui dicnt mal d'autrui.   (I, 98, ll. 8, 16, 24)

Grant chose est d'acoustumance.   (II, 203, l. 1 [92])

Car qui a pechier s'accoustume
Une foiz, legierement tume
La seconde, la tierce et quarte,
Ce nous dit la divine quarte.   (VIII, 323, ll. 2481 ff. [92])

Car qui une fois s'acoustume
A pechier, legierement tume
Les autres foiz ou grief pechié.   (IX, 57, ll. 1671 ff. [92])

Qui a delit acoustumé,
Tantost est en autre tumé
Et usaige fait la coustume
Que d'un pechié en autre tume
Souventefoiz l'acoustumant.   (IX, 351, ll. 10925 ff. [92])

Car puis qu'elle change une foys,
Son lit certes ne deux ne trois
A homme ne refusera,
Et ainsis honnie sera.   (IX, 57, ll. 1667 ff.)

Car qui tant l'aime, tant l'achete.   (VIII, 48, l. 134 [68])

Car je voy bien: Qui aime, a tart oublie.
                        (VII, 124 f., ll. 10, 20, 30, 34 [67])

On est amé tant c'om fait fruit.
                        (I, 168 f., ll. 8, 16, 24, 28 [7])

On ne peut estre amé de tous.
                        (V, 173 f., ll. 10, 20, 30, 36 [66])

Bonne est la chose qui amende.   (VIII, 53, l. 32 [100])

Et la clarté d'Amour perdre et perir
Qui onques jour n'ama bien seignourie,
Que les frans cuers souloient conjouir.   (I, 225, ll. 15 ff.)

Mal fait mangier a l'appetit d'autruy.
                        (VII, 81 f., ll. 10, 20, 30, 36 [57])

Chascun est hardi en son art.   (VII, 71 f., ll. 10, 20, 30, 36)

Et lors vint a moy un bossus
Qui me dit: 'Dieu gart le varlet
Qui prant les asnes a la glus!'   (I, 205 f., ll. 5 ff.)

Celle qui veult son aumosne donner
Ne le doit pas faire deux foys attendre.
                        (IV, 93, ll. 1 f., 7 f. [103])

Barat toudis les barateurs conchie.   (II, 88, l. 15 [134])

Car tel prant qui puis est prins.   (II, 340, l. 144 [134])

Car au derrain est prins qui autre prent.
                        (IV, 296, l. 12 [134])

Ou tu t'es mis, dont le proverbe est voir:
Deceveurs sont deceus communement.
                        (IV, 353 f., ll. 7 f., 16, 24 [134])

Toudis se craint tricheur qui a trichié. (VIII, 155, l. 7 [134])

A grant moqueur fault grande moqueresse.

(V, 50 f., ll. 9, 18, 27)

Que qui de glaive fiert autrui,
A glaive yra le corps de lui.   (IX, 372, ll. 11575 f. [140])

Telz a pou blef qui a assez pain cuit.

(I, 293 f., ll. 8, 16, 24 [9])

Trop me merveil comme uns homs contrefais
Ose boiteux un autre homme appeller.   (I, 98, ll. 1 f. [43])

Et neantmoins un proverbe si dist
Que bon compains a trop sur lui a dire.

(VI, 114 f., ll. 7 f., 16, 24, 28 [131])

On dit qu'om doit les bons suir:
Pour ce prouverbe poursuir.   (VII, 253, ll. 1 f. [99])

Foulz est li homs qui bon conseil ne croit.

(I, 118 f., ll. 8, 16, 24, 30 [227])

Foulz suy, foulz est qui se conseille
Et ne veult bon conseil tenir.   (IX, 187, ll. 5690 f. [227])

Qu'om ne doit nulle chose faire
Sanz conseil, car qui de lui euvre,
A bonne fin vient de son euvre.   (IX, 19, ll. 502 ff. [228])

Bonne vie fait a bonne fin tendre.

(II, 8 f., ll. 8, 16, 24 [95])

La male vie a male fin se tent.   (IV, 296, l. 13 [95])

Et moult long temps a que je lui
Que beaus chastois est par autrui.

(IX, 221, ll. 6781 f. [229])

Qui son chien het, on li met sus la raige.

(V, 402 f., ll. 10, 20, 30, 36 [18])

Prince, qui sert sanz querir avantage,
Quant il est vieulx, on lui met sus la rage.

(III, 341, ll. 25 f. [18])

Qui povres est, l'en ly met sus la rage. (X, xxxiii, l. 21 [18])

Par faire mal n'aprivois'on pas chien!

(V, 281 f., ll. 8, 16, 24, 28 [17])

Deux chiens sont mauvais a un os.

(VII, 133 f., ll. 8, 16, 24 [16])

Le croire legierement
Fait decepvoir et perdre mainte gent.   (II, 25, ll. 21 f.)

On se deçoit par legierement croire.   (II, 61 f., ll. 8, 16, 24)

Qui legier croit, certes c'est grant folie,

(II, 88, ll. 9, 17, 26, 32 [122])

C'est grant peril de legierement croire.

(VI, 48 f., ll. 10, 20, 30, 36)

On ne doit pas croire a tout homme.

(VII, 85 f., ll. 8, 16, 24, 30)

On ne doit pas croire chascun.

(VIII, 147 f., ll. 8, 16, 24, 30 [122])

Toute parole n'est pas voire.   (IX, 105, l. 3138)

Pour ce est trop foulz qui en cuidier se fonde.

(II, 156 f., ll. 10, 20, 30, 36 [123])

De deux celles le cul a terre.

(V, 383 f., ll. 10, 20, 30, 36 [38])

Que homs a deux seigneurs servir
Ne puet pas bien et le plesir
De tous deux faire absolument.   (IX, 353, ll. 10981 ff. [167])

Ainsi dit on, mais on ne le fait mie.

(II, 62 f., ll. 8, 16, 24 [124])

Amis sanz don pour autre dort.

(II, 45 f., ll. 8, 16, 24, 30 [195])

Car amours par dons vit et dure.   (VIII, 236, l. 784 [195])

Car eschaudés craint eaue jour et nuit.   (II, 155, l. 33 [29])

Chaude yaue craint cilz qui a esté ars.   (III, 140, l. 21 [29])

On dit qu'eschaudez yaue craint,
Poissons batu fuit le fillé,
Et cerf que a esté empaint,
Et chaz qui a le cul brulé.   (V, 30, ll. 1 ff. [29])

Caz eschaudez craint eaue jour et nuit.   (V, 264, l. 33 [29])

Espoir le fait endurer.   (IV, 162, l. 27)

A l'omme expert creez, ce dit le saige.
   (III, 107 f., ll. 8, 16, 24, 32, 40, 46 [230])

Mais au faire gist toute la maniere.
   (II, 92 f., ll. 9, 18, 27 [124])

Trop grant familiarité
Nourrist et engendre contemps.   (VI, 245, ll. 1 f. [127])

Car familiarité gendre
En ce cas a humble contant.   (IX, 297, ll. 9198 f. [127])

Car priveté sy engendre contens.
   (X, xxiv, ll. 8, 16, 24, 29 [127])

Nulz ne puet avoir povre office,
Qui sert femmes a leur talent.   (IX, 301, ll. 9330 f. [157])

Saiges est, qui a la fin pense.   (I, 182, l. 27 [221])

Des oeuvres doit homs la fin regarder.   (I, 214, l. 17 [221])

Il fault penser et regarder la fin.   (II, 22, l. 9 [221])

Car sages homme la fin voit et regarde.
   (II, 66 f., ll. 8, 16, 24 [221])

Et pour ce un ver dit le saige en latin
Qui se conclud en disant par telz mos:
Fay saigement et regarde la fin.
   (III, 163 ff., ll. 8 ff., 20, 30, 39, 49, 55 [221])

Qui regardast les diz de Salemon
Au commencier de quelconque besongne,
Feist saigement, que son propos fust bon
Et que la fin ne lui donnast vergongne.

(VI, 198, ll. 1 ff. [221])

Salemon . . .
Qui disoit assez plainement:
'Se tu faiz rien, fay saigement,
Et resgarde en tous temps la fin.'   (IX, 19, ll. 496 ff. [221])

Il n'est chose qui ne viengne a sa fin.

(V, 378 f., ll. 10, 20, 30, 40, 50, 56 [208])

On dit que fol ne doubte jusqu'il prent.

(III, 145 ff., ll. 8, 16, 24, 32, 40, 46 [115])

Foulz ne doubte jusqu'il se voit ferir.   (V, 375, l. 24 [115])

De ce que fol pense souvent remaint.   (X, lxiii, l. 1 [117])

Quant fruit fault, desserte s'en va.

(VI, 270 f., ll. 10, 20, 30, 36 [7])

Goute d'yaue fait la pierre caver.   (V, 152, l. 7 [2])

On dit partout que les honneurs,
Quant on y puet estre monté,
Font a aucuns muer les meurs.   (X, ix, ll. 1 ff. [198])

Qui jeusne sainctist, viez enrrage.

(VII, 47, ll. 10, 20, 30, 36 [42])

Et si dit on communement
Que, s'un homme a une jument,
Que quelque estalon qui l'assaille,
Que droit li est acquis sanz faille,
Si tost qu'elle a le ventre plain,
Que sien en sera le poulain.   (IX, 349, ll. 10861 ff. [20])

A main lever ne gist pas li esplois.

(III, 281 f., ll. 8, 16, 24 [197])

Princes, foulz est qui a noble maison,
Et par non sens la change a une grange.   (I, 86, ll. 25 f.)

Cilz qui a chois de prandre et departir
N'est pas saiges, s'il ne prant le meilleur.

(I, 72, ll. 1 f. [224])

Qui est a choiz de deux choses avoir,
Eslire doit et choisir la meillour.   (IV, 257, ll. 1 f.)

Et l'en doit de deux maulx le mendre
Ensuir, j'ay oy reprandre.   (IX, 313, ll. 9725 f. [224])

Je prandray le milleur des deux.   (IX, 340, l. 10573)

Tele la mere com la fille.   (IX, 107, l. 3201)

Car voulentiers tient, par saint Pere
Le chemin fille de sa mere.   (IX, 107, ll. 3203 f. [87])

Qui monte haut il puet cheoir a val.   (V, 312, l. 17 [207])

Et monter hault pour descendre trop bas.   (V, 385, l. 8)

Car qui s'abaisse Dieux l'acrout,
Et qui se hauce plus qu'a point,
Cheoir le fault en petit point.   (IX, 300, ll. 9280 f. [207])

De necessitez font vertuz.   (II, 96, l. 9 [114])

Et si ay veu ailleurs escript
Un proverbe, qui sur ce dit
Que les grans noces font li sot
Et li saige homme sanz escot
Les nopces de ces foulz manguent.   (IX, 50, ll. 1457 ff.)

Maint ont grans oeulx et si ne voient goute!

(V, 389 f., ll. 10, 20, 30, 36 [55])

Tout n'est pas or ce qui reluit.

(II, 96 f., ll. 8, 16, 24, 30 [4])

D'un pain mangé vous savés qu'on s'ennuye!

(X, lxxv, l. 9 [176])

N'aiez paour, il n'est nul qui la praingne,
Dist le villain, elle vault hault logier.   (III, 86, ll. 27 f.)

Beau parler fait ire appaisier.   (VIII, 244, l. 1053 [84])

Au mol pasteur va li loups brebis prendre.

(III, 158, l. 24 [21])

Qui le sien pert, en lui tourne l'oye.   (I, 289, l. 7 [195])

Et plus proufite les poissons
Aux mangeurs en toutes saisons
Qui est grans, vieulx, parcreuz, gros,
Que li jeunes au maigre dos;
Mieulx nourrit et est moins visqueux
Que li petit, ce scevent queux,
Et quant plus vit, et tant mieulx vault;
Et la vielle beste deffault,
Qui est dure et qui ne vault rien.

(VIII, 311, ll. 2087 ff. [58])

C'est bien dit, on n'en veult riens faire:
L'en ne fait pas tout ce qu'on presche.

(VI, 173 f., ll. 9, 20, 30, 36)

Grant honte avoir doit le docteur qui presche
Faire vertus, quant il fait le contraire.   (VII, 125, ll. 1 f.)

Car si saiges n'est pas, j'en doubt,
Qui aucune fois n'ait folie.   (IX, 319, ll. 9910 f. [118])

    on dit que tout a sa saison.   (X, xxix, l. 4 [208])

Il ne scet rien qui ne va hors.   (VII, 69 f., ll. 10, 20, 30, 36)

Une jument n'aroit d'un toreaux cure,
Ne la chievre n'a cure du sangler.
Chascun se doit a son per assembler,
Pour bien vivre non dissemblablement.

(I, 117, ll. 3 ff. [91])

Gay contre gay doivent estre en usaige.   (II, 62, l. 21 [91])

Chose semblant l'une a l'autre se lie.   (II, 110, l. 14 [91])

Toute chose het son contraire
Et a son semblable se trait.   (II, 166, ll. 11 f. [91])

Deux contraires ne se puellent amer.   (V, 248, l. 18 [91])

Serf eslever est chose perilleuse.
> (III, 135 f., ll. 8, 16, 24, 32, 40, 46)

En ce monde n'a nul plus grand peril
Que d'eslever un povre homme en estat,
Ne qui par tout puist tant faire debat.
> (IV, 122, ll. 1 ff., 6 f., 11 ff.)

Servir a Dieu est regner, si c'om dit.
> (I, 176, ll. 8, 16, 24, 28 [139])

Souffisance est un tresriches tresors.
> (III, 10 ff., ll. 10, 20, 30, 40, 50, 56 [101])

Car qui sueffre en la fin vaincra. (IV, 253, l. 16 [106])

Mais l'en dit, qui trop veult souffrir
Quant on se repute trop mendre. (IX, 297, ll. 9196 f. [106])

On parle a eulx hault, qu'ilz sont sourt. (V, 159, l. 14)

Puis c'uns homs de court partira,
De lui ne souvendra jamais. (I, 111, ll. 7 f.)

Ne m'oubliez, pour ce se je suis hors. (IV, 126, l. 2)

Ne m'oubliez se de vous sui lointains. (IV, 131, l. 2)

Le temps passé ne mettez en oubli
Pour autrui biens, souveingne vous de my.
> (IV, 146, ll. 1 f., 6 f., 11 f.)

Ne m'oubliez pour ce se ne vous voy. (IV, 146, ll. 3, 13)

Li Souverains regne sur toutes loys.
> (III, 12 f., ll. 8, 16, 24, 32, 40, 46 [160])

Princes, mieulx vault encor tart que jamais. (I, 208, l. 31)

Face ent le mary pourveance,
Car j'en ay veu plusieurs de ciaulx
A tart venir a repentence. (VI, 239 f., ll. 8 ff., 20, 30, 36)

  la gloire souveraine
Fust a m'ame. Tart est que me repente. (VII, 63, ll. 25 f.)

Vous vault il mieulx tart que jamais.   (VIII, 38, l. 41 [225])

Soy departir vault mieulx tart que jamais.
                    (VIII, 152 f., ll. 10, 20, 30, 36 [225])

Ancor vault mieux tart que jamais
Sou marier pour avoir hoirs.   (IX, 16, ll. 396 f.)

Qu'encor vault mieulx tart que jamais
Soy repentir de ses meffais.   (IX, 232, ll. 7133 f. [225])

Mais c'est trop tart pour repentir.   (IX, 358, l. 11119)

Il fault prandre le temps si comme il est.
                    (I, 145 f., ll. 8, 16, 24 [110])

Prangne chascun le temps tel qu'il vendra.
                    (VI, 220, l. 11 [110])

Pren le temps come il peut venir.   (X, xx, l. 4 [110])

Tiers hoir ne jouist de chose mal acquise.
                    (II, 129 f., ll. 9, 18, 27, 30 [191])

Qui fuit toudis treuve bien qui le chace.
                    (V, 105 ff., ll. 10, 20, 30, 40, 50, 54 [54])

Et ne voit nul ce qui lui pent a l'ueil.
                    (III, 153 f., ll. 8, 16, 24, 32, 40, 46 [212])

Pour ce dit on communement:
Tant vault ly hons, tant vault sa terre.
                    (X, xviii, ll. 7 f., 15 f., 23 f. [186])

Nulz n'est villains se du cuer ne lui muet.
                    (VI, 67 f., ll. 8, 16, 24, 28 [89])

Nul n'est chetis s'il ne le cuide estre.
                    (II, 123 f., ll. 10, 20, 30 [89])

Tuit voir ne sont pas bel a dire.
                    (III, 105 f., ll. 10, 20, 30, 40, 50, 56 [108])
De vuide main la sourde oreille.   (II, 46, l. 19 [56])

PROVERBIAL COMPARISONS

De mon buisson sailli comme une beste.   (II, 212, l. 261)

Et se consent comme une beste
A l'ort pechié, vil, deshonneste.   (IX, 57, ll. 1659 f.)

Ta femme seroit comme beste.   (IX, 108, l. 3225)

Domptez fut com beuf a charrue.   (IX, 32, l. 905)

Prins et lié comme le beuf.   (IX, 189, l. 5780)

Autant sui seur qu'a la bouche d'un four,
J'ay tout perdu, ma fournée est bruie.   (II, 82, ll. 22 f.)

Quant li temps est frès comme burre.   (IX, 44, l. 1269)

Plus aspre qu'aguillons de fer.   (IX, 190, l. 5804)

Mais plus doulz devint c'uns aigniaux.   (IX, 32, l. 902)

Royne y aura parée comme un ange.   (III, 89, l. 12)

Brodez de bran et noirs comme arremens.   (IV, 327, l. 2)

Ou je mourray com canne a bourbeter.   (V, 59, l. 30)

Qui n'a en lui de moisteur ne que cendre.   (V, 133, l. 18)

N'estaindre comme la chandelle
Son renom et vie charnelle.   (IX, 337, ll. 10475 f.)

Elle est plus glote que la chate.   (IX, 119, l. 3580)

Il het les bons, il est gloux comme un chat.   (IV, 122, l. 9)

Ainçois mangiez comme un cheval.   (VIII, 25, l. 22)

Legiers estes comme uns chevreaulx.   (VI, 118, l. 17)

Il souloit saillir com chevriaux.   (IX, 32, l. 901)

Mourir le fist enrragié comme un chien.   (I, 126, l. 20)

Dont je suis huez comme uns chiens.   (VI, 11, l. 28)

Ils sont huez au monde comme chien.   (VII, 74, l. 18)

Pour estre mort et tiré comme un chien!   (V, 194, l. 6)

Alez vous ent, vous puez comme un chien.   (VI, 234, l. 9)

  cilz runge comme chiens
Le bien commun.   (VI, 286, ll. 22 f.)

Je ne me puis trop merveillier
De ce qu'om dit communement
Quant on veult aucun desprisier:
Ne qu'un chien n'a d'entendement,
Il ne scet riens; mais vraiement
Chiens par droit doit bien estre saige.   (VIII, 94, ll. 1 ff.)

S'iert comme une chievre vacant.   (IX, 107, l. 3212)

Yeux de corbaut, noire comme une choe.   (IV, 318, l. 2)

Je fonderay comme cire.   (IV, 171, l. 20)

Elle sonne comme une cloche.   (V, 111, l. 4)

Crasse et orde, noire com cornillat.   (VII, 81, l. 12)

Et doulce comme columbelle.   (IX, 27, l. 730)

Tresdoulce flour, humble com coulombelle.   (III, 214, l. 25)

Les yeulx avoit plus rouges que corail.   (X, xlii, l. 9)

Les crins avez plus noirs que cramillie.   (VI, 210, l. 11)

Tu chantes comme li cucus
Qui s'estonne et gaste son plet.   (I, 206, ll. 13 f.)

Par le viez tronc cuer plus dur d'aymant.   (III, 6, l. 34)

Et plus ferme (*fleur*) que n'est le dyament.   (III, 214, l. 26)

Mais se tu dis aussi voir qu'euvangille.   (I, 173, l. 32)

Seigneur des choses incredibles
Pronuncées comme Euvangiles.   (VII, 347, ll. 3 f.)

En clarté comme estincelles.   (II, 300, l. 608)

Et reluist comme une estincelle.   (IX, 249, l. 7680)

De beauté la souveraine,
Comme estoille trasmontaine
De toutes pars regardée.   (II, 183, ll. 16 ff.)

Qui leur fera droit comme une faucille.
                              (I, 172 f., ll. 10, 20, 30, 34)

Plus dure que fers ne fus.   (IV, 189 f., ll. 1, 28)

Et le bon nom demourra comme fleur.   (II, 114, l. 28)

Mannette blanche comme fleur de lis.   (V, 187, l. 12)

Plus doubteus que n'est flos de mer.   (I, 115, l. 4)

  mais comme uns gluis
Se ploie.   (V, 87, ll. 20 f.)

Groing de pourcel, long coul comme une grue. (V, 32, l. 3)

Sa proye prins comme un hobé.   (IX, 67, l. 1968)

Mais crasse et noire que housiaux.   (VII, 89, l. 36)

Doulz comme let ou comme craime.   (I, 117, l. 33)

Tousjours aguette comme uns leux.   (IX, 199, l. 6072)

Braie brairoit comment uns leux.   (VIII, 72, l. 31)

Et es desers demourray comme uns leux.   (III, 224, l. 21)

Quant je suis par envieux
Comme un leux.   (IV, 28, ll. 10 f.)

Villains en fais et goufres comme uns leus.   (II, 53, l. 6)

Il faut hurler avec les leux.   (IX, 342, l. 10614)

Plain de pité comme est uns leux.   (V, 170, l. 3)

Plus despent loups que brebiz ne oustarde.   (II, 64, l. 14)

Et par la bouche comme uns loux.   (IV, 278, l. 7)

Qui haioient comme brebis loux
Les femmes par merancolie.   (IX, 338, ll. 10502 f.)

Et m'en fouy comme lievre couars.   (III, 139, l. 12)

Couardement et trop acouardis
Est mon las cuer, comme lievres couars.
                                    (IV, 151, ll. 1 f., 6 f., 11 f.)

Et si suy couart comme un lievre.   (VIII, 233, l. 702)

Par tout couroit comme uns lins
Du monde li pelerins.   (II, 334, ll. 285 f.)

Jeunes homs a com lins la veue ague.   (VII, 234, l. 1)

Telz fu gouteux qui sault comme lipars.   (III, 140, l. 20)

Ainçoiz feussion hardis com liepart.   (III, 274, l. 5)

Qui plus froide est que le ray de la lune.   (I, 290, l. 14)

Mais, tout ainsi comme la lune
Resplendist plus que les estoilles.   (IX, 319, ll. 9902 f.)

Et plus crueulx que gueule de lyon.   (III, 316, l. 7)

Mais neantmoins fu dur come uns lyons.   (III, 145, l. 7)

Oultrecuidez et plus fier que lyon.   (III, 133, l. 13)

Et plus fors que n'est uns lions.   (VI, 118, l. 6)

Hardis estoit et fiers comme lyons.   (X, lxxix, l. 10)

A cuer plus noir que meure.   (V, 123, l. 29)

Doulce (dame) com miel, blanche com fleur de lis.
                                    (III, 244, l. 1)

Et plus doulz que miel en rée.   (IV, 227, l. 23)

Et plus doulz que n'est miel en rée.   (V, 81, l. 2)

Qui semble doulz com miel ou lait.   (VII, 86, l. 18)

"Encor," dit-il, "regarde et pense
Que leurs bouches samblent le miel
En douçour, mais c'est piz que fiel."   (IX, 185, ll. 5656 ff.)

Et buvez com fait un Normant. (VIII, 25, l. 23)

Qu'elle le rouille comme un œuf. (IX, 189, l. 5779)

Tendres et molz comme un petit oison! (IV, 288, l. 14)

Suis plus frans que l'oisel du raim. (IX, 20, l. 528)

Et se boute la hart ou coul
Plus que l'oisel qu'om prant au voul. (IX, 189, ll. 5787 f.)

Pure comme li fins ors. (IV, 226, l. 9)

Car vostre chief a toute gent agrée,
Blont com fin or. (V, 186, ll. 9 f.)

Garder et amer com fin or. (IX, 5, l. 74)

Tu seras plus hideux c'uns ours. (II, 282, l. 399)

Nous rechignons l'un l'autre, comme un ours.
(III, 275, l. 17)

Car chascun d'eulx veult mangier comme uns ours.
(VIII, 107, l. 9)

Comme paille s'est tost esvannouy. (V, 337, l. 21)

Comme paille mis au neant. (VIII, 40, l. 107)

Il est vray com le Patenostre. (VIII, 57, l. 89)

Comme pie, qu'il se soit maintenu
A bien jangler. (I, 174 f., ll. 13 f.)

Leur cuers, qui fut durs com pierre. (II, 173, l. 65)

Qui m'a navré plus que pierre de fonde. (III, 285, l. 14)

Certes, c'est moy, qui fu froit comme pierre. (III, 355, l. 8)

Qui sont plus souefs que pimens. (IX, 234, l. 7188)

Et, en a fin, com le poisson a l'ain,
Le lasse et prant a dolente pasture. (I, 70, ll. 28 f.)

Et va saillant comme uns poissons. (V, 81, l. 6)

Grosse de corps, ronde comme une pomme.	(IV, 318, l. 1)
Et, se ferme est comme un pommier.	(IX, 68, l. 1994)
Pitié, amour n'avons ne que pourceaulx.	(III, 32, l. 39)
Et en alant comme uns pourceaulx rouffler.	(IV, 144, l. 10)
Et assommez comme uns pourceaulx.	(VII, 36, l. 35)
Couchier, mangier, comme pourceaulx.	(VII, 88, l. 6)
Le ventre en ay emflé comme uns pourceaux.	(VII, 219, l. 13)
Et se melle comme uns pourceaux.	(IX, 57, l. 1661)
Honteux comme uns pors aux abays.	(I, 112, l. 22)
Et ainsi vivez comme pors.	(II, 149, l. 9)
Les chaça comme on fait pors.	(II, 330, l. 167)
Qui dort et romfle comme uns pors!	(VII, 260, l. 223)
Leur vie est a ung pot de terre Comparée.	(IX, 70, ll. 2072 f.)
Aussi tendre comme un poucin.	(V, 81, l. 1)
Langue trenchant, com rasoir afilée.	(VII, 5, l. 10)
Laissent Paris, fuient comme renars.	(III, 139, l. 18)
Plus tost muevent que roe de moulin.	(V, 21, l. 10)
Coulourée comme rose vermeille.	(III, 244, l. 2)
Et plus blanche que rose de rosier.	(III, 346, l. 11)
Plus fresche que rose en may.	(IV, 184, l. 11)
Charongne a vers, povre fragilité, Qui puez estre comparée a la rose.	(V, 204, ll. 1 f.)
Bien dançans, parez comme un roys.	(IV, 276, l. 12)
Car vous m'avez fait plus riche d'un roy.	(IV, 207, l. 3)

L'autre s'en vest vermeil com sanc.   (IX, 57, l. 1652)

Jaunes, flairans comme santine.   (VII, 4, l. 22)

Aux gens font pis que Sarrazins.   (VII, 68, l. 17)

Dont l'en vous sieut au flair comme un sengler.
                                             (IV, 318, l. 6)

Venymeux sont plus qu'ydre le serpent.   (III, 316, l. 5)

Qui venimeux sont plus que nul serpent.   (III, 364, l. 2)

Contre ma mort feray un chant de plour
Com le signe.   (III, 218, ll. 22 f.)

Fronciez est comme singesse.   (II, 266, l. 259)

Ou je mourrai transiz comme une souche.   (III, 290, l. 20)

L'un machoit gros, l'autre comme souriz.   (V, 16, l. 20)

Il te fault le vin avaler
Chascun jour comme en une tonne!   (VII, 185, ll. 320 f.)

Fort et hardys, courageux come ung tor.   (X, xxxvi, l. 6)

Comme un torel avez chascune joe.   (IV, 318, l. 18)

Par tout courir comme uns toriaux.   (VI, 229, l. 7)

Recevez moy, loial com turterelle.   (III, 214, l. 27)

Grans queues portent comme veaulx.   (III, 196, l. 39)

Plus tost change que le vert
Ou que temps n'a efflouré.   (II, 347, ll. 83 f.)

Separez sont comme blanc est du noir,
Et comme vin de l'eaue, a droit comprandre.
                                             (III, 39, ll. 10 f.)

Ce sont deux ymages de terre,
Luisans aussi cler comme voirre.   (X, lxxxviii, ll. 16 f.)

Emflez soit comme est une yraigne!   (VII, 33, l. 10)

Ne faictes mie com l'yraingne.   (IX, 150, l. 4535)

Other Proverbial Phrases

Lors la prant li homs prins a l'ain.	(IX, 124, l. 3738)
Veulz tu doy arer les champs?	(I, 206, l. 9)
Et qui n'acomptent deux baloces.	(IX, 245, l. 7540)
Tu bas bien l'eaue d'un pilet.	(I, 206, ll. 8, 16, 24, 28)
Tu bas froit fer, tu es deçus.	(I, 206, l. 12)
Ou il fault batre le cabas.	(VIII, 12, l. 18)
Ainsi comme on bat le cabas.	(IX, 115, l. 3450)
Ainsis seult on le cabas batre.	(IX, 115, l. 3458)
Qui promet blanc et baille noir.	(I, 116, l. 9)
Car ilz veulent faire acroire Que blanche brebiz est noire.	(II, 219, ll. 173 f.)
D'autre part frans a femme franche Ne puet batre blef sur sa granche, A gloser honnourablement.	(VIII, 38, ll. 19 f.)
Ne bate blef en aultrui grange.	(IX, 38, l. 1072)
Mais parti d'autre coulour, En honnour, De loyauté fine et pure: C'est de bleu.	(IV, 200, ll. 6 ff.)
En lieu de bleu, qui porte la figure De loyauté.	(X, lix, ll. 1 f.)
Lors ne la prise un bouton.	(II, 320, l. 164)
Ne dorroie un bouton.	(IV, 347, l. 14)
Qui au jour d'ui lui vaille .ii. boutons.	(V, 222, l. 35)
Mais pour toy ne fait un bouton.	(V, 399, l. 9)

Encor n'ont pas brebiz souppé.
> (III, 47 ff., ll. 8, 16, 24, 32, 40, 46)

Nulz ne m'y sçaroit que respondre
Par raison; voist les brebis tondre
Ton Repertoire de Science.   (IX, 318, ll. 9863 ff.)

cilz est bien sur brese.   (IX, 74, l. 2194)

Met donc ceste bride a tes dens.   (VIII, 183, l. 28)

Il me convient prendre la bride au dens.
> (IV, 53, ll. 2, 7, 12)

Faictes bien la cate catie.   (IX, 123, l. 3693)

Au cul de l'asne fais tes chans.   (I, 206, l. 11)

Autant vaudroit batre son cul au chaut.   (I, 210, l. 7)

Chantez a l'asne, il vous fera des pès.
> (I, 210 f., ll. 10, 20, 30, 34 [25])

Aroit il pas chapeau de vert?   (VIII, 114, l. 48)

Qui pendra la sonnette au chat?
> (I, 151 f., ll. 8, 16, 24, 28 [124])

Mais il convient, comme dist la souris,
Vir qui pandra la cloquette au mynon.   (V, 389, ll. 13 f.)

Veulz tu espouser chat en sac.   (IX, 284, l. 8758)

Pluseurs sanz cause on mal en leurs cheveulx.
> (VIII, 155 f., ll. 8, 16, 24, 30)

Mais chien n'a ne roix pour tempter
Ce tro.   (VIII, 224, ll. 412 f.)

Vous et autres le sçavez bien,
Et pour ce en sont batu li chien.   (VIII, 39, ll. 53 f.)

Chievre gratant (les Anglais).   (I, 315, l. 4 [28])

Non fait, car tout ne vault un chol.   (III, 22, l. 9)

Les clochettes de Gallien.   (VIII, 124, l. 328)

Soubz bel armé qui ne vault par un cor.   (VI, 97, l. 26)

Qu'elle le trait a sa cordelle.   (IX, 32, l. 900)

Donnez leur l'ordre du cordier.
                        (V, 103 ff., ll. 10, 20, 30, 40, 50, 54)

Li cornuz empeliçonnez
Dont li deduis ne plaist c'un po.   (IX, 124, ll. 3744 f.)

Un coup vendra qui paiera tout.   (II, 68 f., ll. 7, 14, 21)

N'as tu leu que c'est d'estre coux.   (VIII, 12, l. 32)

Fors seulement que le chant du cucu.
                               (III, 296 f., ll. 8, 16, 24)

Car li cucus pourra pour moy chanter.   (V, 91, l. 26)

Je lui feray, sanz jardiner,
Avoir cucu en son mesnaige.   (VI, 236, ll. 8 f.)

Sur lui chantera li cucus.   (VII, 265, l. 374)

      et comprandre
Le chant de l'oisel qui parole
Aux mariez ou temps qu'il vole
Es moys d'avril, juing et juillet.   (VIII, 191, ll. 15 ff.)

Bon dos, bon cul de Paris.   (IV, 8, l. 15)

Parler a vous atout les dens.   (IX, 123, l. 3711)

Tu faiz voler par mi les dens.   (IX, 358, l. 11124)

Tais toy; les dens devant sont bons.
                             (V, 159 f., ll. 10, 20, 30, 36)

En jouant vous changoit les dez.   (VIII, 114, l. 47)

Certes, tout ce ne vault une escaloingne.   (III, 63, l. 27)

Eschac et mat a ce jour lui dirons.   (III, 77, l. 49)

Et que les eufs soient velus.   (I, 206, l. 18)

Saiges, preudoms, ne vaillans un festu
N'y conquerront avoir, jour de leur vie.   (I, 175, ll. 21 f.)

Tout ce ne vault pas deux festus.   (IX, 284, l. 8784)

Veulz tu planter bois de festus?   (I, 206, l. 10)

Pourrez vous bien le cours du firmament
Faire muer? eaue devenir cendre,
Et d'un pourcel creer une jument,
Et faire Dieu en la terre descendre?   (I, 211, ll. 21 ff.)

Pour ce ne valent un flajol
Povres saiges.   (III, 23, ll. 32 f.)

Las! je fus né a la foire aux quetis.   (V, 69, l. 20)

L'en treuve hostel de Froitvaulx.   (IX, 287, l. 8865)

Mais je ne voy ne Gautier, ne Colin.   (I, 178, l. 5)

Te fault hanter le bas couvent.   (VIII, 15, l. 118)

Et fusse la, vaillant un harenc sor
N'en venrroit pas vers moy vif un frelin.   (V, 137, ll. 13 f.)

Ne n'aquerra vaillant .II. harens sors.   (V, 203, l. 25)

Grant robe avoir n'y vault un harenc sor.   (VI, 97, l. 17)

Belle chose est de contenter son hoste.
                         (VI, 256 f., ll. 10, 20, 30, 36)

Hurter ne veult plus a mon huis derriere.
                         (V, 79, ll. 8, 16, 24)

C'est droitement Jhesus sur une pele.   (V, 10, ll. 7, 14, 21)

Et font jouer aux esbahis
Pluseurs moines, prieurs et clers.   (IX, 164, ll. 4990 f.)

Vous avez langue dorée.   (II, 180, l. 297)

Et tout chascun crie sur lui au lart.   (IV, 37, l. 9)

Cilz ci n'a pas mangié le lart.   (V, 110, l. 29)

Vous me direz qui a mangié le lart.   (VII, 29, l. 5)

Bruneval, par force de vin
Crioit sur tous comme enrragié,
Sine dubio, c'est latin.
                    (VII, 120 f., ll. 8 ff., 18 ff., 28 ff., 36 ff.)

Et vo harnois ne vault une lentille.   (V, 63, l. 19)

Il vauldroit mieulx garder trois leux
Que prandre rumoreux n'yvrongne.   (V, 199, ll. 19 f.)

Ba! si ferez; il ne met a lever
En trestous temps plus de lieue et demie.   (V, 26, ll. 10 f.)

Car damps Lopins chascun jour y a court.   (II, 109, l. 11)

Je le regni, ne le prise une mite.   (I, 133, l. 26)

Leur souverain n'ont prisié une mite.   (III, 41, l. 12)

Ainsi va des choses du monde.   (V, 310 f., ll. 12, 24, 36, 42)

Si, comme on dit, chascuns sert .iiii. moys
Des serviteux qui sont en ordonnance.   (IV, 301, ll. 1 f.)

Qui maintefoiz n'a vaillent une moufle.   (V, 37, l. 6)

L'en congnoist mal le mouton a la layne.   (V, 10, l. 11)

Et pour ce vueil porter la mule
Si qu'om ne me tiengne pour chievre.   (V, 38, ll. 5 f.)

Et qui n'a vaillant un navet.   (IV, 212, l. 20)

Et les amer, ou il ne vault une oistre.   II, 42, l. 14)

Et son pere doiz tu a l'ongle
Honourer, amer, conjouir.   (IX, 61, ll. 1774 f.)

Par l'une entre, par l'autre oreille sault
Ce qu'on lui dit, n'est que riote et plès.   (I, 211, ll. 27 f.)

Qui estoit assez sur le lart
Pour faire sonner l'oreloge.   (VIII, 46, ll. 70 f.)

Mon aage est finé
De jeunesce; ay cuit mon pain;
Viellesce d'ui a demain.   (II, 187, ll. 167 ff.)

Je lui feray d'autel pain souppe.
                              (VIII, 176, ll. 8, 16, 24, 30)

Ne leur laira la vaillance d'un pal
Pour leurs pechiez et leur mauvese erreur.   (V, 406, ll. 28 f.)

C'est droictement la pie qui parole.
                              (II, 103 f., ll. 10, 20, 30)

Que j'ay un pié deschaux, l'autre chaucié.
                              (III, 314 f., ll. 8, 16, 24)

D'avoir a court un pié hors et l'autre ens.
                              (II, 30 f., ll. 7, 14, 21)

D'avoir deux piez de tous poins hors de court.
                              (VI, 9, ll. 10, 20, 30)

S'il veult des pois on lui donra du chol.   (V, 64, l. 24)

Qu'es biens mondains n'a vaillant une pomme.
                                          (I, 242, l. 22)

Et qui ne vault une pomme pourrie.   (III, 142, l. 34)

.xiiii. fois lui bati sa pouppée.   (V, 361, l. 7)

Il ne lui vault prune.   (II, 270, l. 296)

Qui a une puce en l'oreille.   (IX, 280, l. 8634)

Certes la queue d'un goupil,
Afin que dedens son corps n'entre
Chose qui mal lui face ou ventre.   (IX, 119, ll. 3574 ff.)

Car deux tonneaux portent (les Anglais) adès
Et une queue proprement.   (IV, 130, ll. 5 f.)

Mais leur queue mettent comme un mastin
Soubz leur jambes.
                                          (V, 20, ll. 13 f.)

Levez vostre queue, levez!　　　　　(V, 48 f., ll. 8, 16, 24)

Lors dis: 'Oil, je voy vo queue.'　　　(V, 80, ll. 10, 20, 30)

Plus laide n'a de vous de cy a Rome.　　(IV, 318, l. 17)

Rouges sont dessoubz l'ele.　　　　(V, 10, l. 13)

Ou il n'a ryme ne raison.　　　　(VII, 351, l. 113)

Mais Saint Pierre s'i est fait apporter,
Sur les creniaulx veult son pouoir estendre.　(I, 215, ll. 19 f.)

C'est que: il se sauve qui puet!　　(I, 122 f., ll. 8, 16, 24)

VII. ANS.　　　　　(I, 248, l. 20; VI, 12, l. 17; VI, 42, l. 57
　　　　　　　　IX, 82, l. 2419; IX, 103, l. 3076)

Jus la gettay, j'entray en sa rouyere
Et commençay forment a tabourer.　　(V, 132, ll. 5 f.)

Et se tourne avecques le vent.　　　(IX, 5, l. 44)

Autant vault le vent d'un souflet.　　(I, 206, l. 22)

SENTENTIOUS REMARKS

Toudis advient ce qui doit advenir. (VI, 89, ll. 10, 20, 30, 34)

Et que mieulx vault amis qu'argent.　　(II, 45, 1. 2)

Amor vincit omnia.　　　(X, xlv, ll. 7, 14, 21 [60])

Adès fine il qui a argent.
　　　　　(III, 22 f., ll. 8, 16, 24, 32, 40, 44 [192])

Il n'est amis au jour d'uy que l'argent.
　　　　　(X, xxx f., ll. 8, 16, 24, 28)

En armes vault plus advis et prudence
Que foul hardi qui veult estre chaulz homs.
　　　　　(II, 117 f., ll. 17 f.)

Pour ce dit on: quant avoir vient, corps fault.
　　　　　(II, 15 f., ll. 8, 16, 24, 28)

Si riche n'est qui ait que sa ventrée!   (V, 293, l. 12)

Qui aises sist sur basse selle.   (V, 383, l. 6)

Petiz bas lieux sont trop moins a doubter.   (VI, 9, l. 21)

Bon fait toudis penser a sa besongne.
                        (III, 26 ff., ll. 10, 20, 30, 40, 50, 56)

Dont bons ne puet au monde bien avoir.
                        (I, 212 f., ll. 8, 16, 24, 28 [98])

Car ja prodoms n'ara bien en ce monde.
                        (II, 110 f., ll. 10, 20, 30, 34 [98])

Char a espée ne vault rien.   (V, 161, ll. 8, 16, 24, 28)

Ne prenez pas char a espée,
Trop chiere est et si ne vault rien.   (V, 162, ll. 1 f.)

Char a espée au jour d'uy ne vault rien.
                        (V, 194, ll. 8, 16, 24, 30)

Homme ne voy chevauchier c'un cheval.
                        (II, 20 f., ll. 8, 16, 24)

Mal chief fait les membres doloir.
                        (V, 276 ff., ll. 10, 20, 30, 40, 50, 56 [35])

Et desliez, car leur recours
Y ont clers qui n'ont que tonsure.   (VII, 161, ll. 188 f.)

On dit qu'il fait bon avoir compaignie.   (V, 300, l. 1)

Avec bonne compaingnie
Fait il bon joye mener.   (VII, 192, ll. 487 f.)

Noble chose est que de constance avoir.
                        (III, 299, ll. 8, 16, 24)

Par Convoitier mainte terre est perie.
                        (I, 83 f., ll. 10, 20, 30, 34 [132])

Qui trop convoite, il vit dolentement.   (II, 16, l. 27 [132])

Ne soiez pas si convoitous.   (II, 149, ll. 10, 20, 30, 36 [132])

Marchans, bourgois, ne facent comme chiens
Qui tout mangue et ne veult donner riens.   (V, 117, ll. 16 f.)

Pour les convoiteux, qui au chien
Sont comparez, d'orgueil prochien.   (V, 155, ll. 36 f.)

Cil qui plus a de richesce en baillie,
Tant plus couvoite.   (X, xxxiv, l. 11 [196])

Li couraiges croist par meffais
D'aulcuns.   (VIII, 219, ll. 243 f.)

Toudis font gens de court l'estrange.
(II, 163 f., ll. 10, 20, 30, 36)

Es grans cours n'a siege qui soit certains.
(V, 242 f., ll. 10, 20, 30, 34)

Le cuer noble croit toudiz bon conseil.   (III, 133, l. 19 [227])

Dieux n'a pas fait chascun d'une jointure.   (I, 180, l. 21)

Car ilz usent en trestoutes saisons
D'un droit pour eulx et d'un pour leurs voisins.
(VII, 127 f., ll. 9 f., 19 f., 29 f.)

Car a chascun doit rendre sa droiture.
(III, 98 f., ll. 8, 16, 24, 32, 39, 43 [141])

Eaue desrivant s'est tantost enrrivée.   (II, 51, l. 23)

N'eaue si grant ne se puist espuisier.
(VI, 6 ff., ll. 10, 20, 30, 40, 50, 60)

D'yvre varlet et d'enrragié qui tue,
Et d'ennemi privé et domestique.   (VI, 131, ll. 3 f.)

Petit conseil puent donner enfans.   (II, 68, l. 10)

Mais pour tes maulx enfant roy te donrray.   (I, 316, l. 17)

Las! toy, terre gouvernée d'enfans!   (II, 34, l. 11)

Et l'en voit ja que chascune lignie
A enfant roy pour terre estre envahie.   (III, 30, ll. 37 f.)

Et roys enfans es regnes principaulx.   (III, 31, l. 29)

Et si leur donrrons enfant roy,
Juesne lyon, pour leur desroy.   (VIII, 271, ll. 789 f.)

Car comme uns asnes couronnez
Est uns rois terriens sanz lettre.   (IX, 269, ll. 8314 f.)

Un chien, un chat, un lievre et un conin,
Un esprevier, un oisel de riviere,
Et les poissons refusent a l'engin;
Quant prins y sont en aucune maniere,
S'ilz eschapent, ilz se traient arriere,
D'y rembatre n'ont nulle fois envie.   (III, 54, ll. 1 ff.)

Envie . . . ne dort.   (IV, 14, l. 12)

Envie est en cloistre et en court.
                    (V, 175 f., ll. 10, 20, 30, 36 [136])

Envie ne mourra jamais.   (VI, 275 f., ll. 8, 16, 24, 30 [136])

Envie court comme entre chien et chienne
En mains pays, en mainte region.   (VII, 115, ll. 21 f.)

Princes, queue d'escorpion
Ou li venins gist, ce dit on,
Eschuez, que ne vous traisse.   (VI, 47, ll. 31 ff. [34])

Avise au venimeux serpent
Qui en la douce herbe se trait.   (VII, 85, ll. 9 f.)

Ne je ne sçay rien en ce monde estable.   (III, 12, l. 2 [232])

C'est tout noient en la conclusion.
                    (I, 154 f., ll. 8, 16, 24 [232])

Riens estable ne say dessoubz la nue.
                    (III, 109 f., ll. 8, 16, 24, 32, 40, 46 [232])

Ainsis va chascuns a sa fin.   (V, 398, ll. 10, 20, 30)

C'est tout neant des choses de ce monde.
                    (VI, 40 ff., ll. 12, 24, 36, 48, 60, 66 [232])

L'exploit n'est pas a grant quantité estre.

(III, 35 ff., ll. 8, 16, 24, 32, 40, 46)

Bien faire est souvent despité. (VIII, 131, l. 27)

Toudis qui fait bien, le treuve il. (IX, 107, l. 3197)

Fay ce que doiz, et aviengne que puet.

(I, 152 f., ll. 8, 16, 24, 28 [104])

Fay tousjours ce que tu doys. (IV, 23, l. 1 [104])

Tel meschief (*que le mal des dens*) n'a femme pour travailler.

(V, 4, l. 8 [44])

Servir a femme et a enfans
Et a peuple est moult grant peril
A tout homme, tant soit soutil,
Car en ces trois a pou de sens.

(VII, 10 f., ll. 1 ff., 6 f., 11 ff.)

Femme est plus fort lien qui soit.

(VIII, 197 f., ll. 10, 20, 30, 36 [150])

Eureux, se Salemon ne ment,
Est cilz qui treuve bonne fame! (IX, 11, ll. 248 f. [156])

Et par Dieu si sera li leux,
S'il a femme, doulz et piteux,
Et le verrez encor hermite. (IX, 36, ll. 1009 ff. [42])

A paine pourroit belle fame
Sanz grant bonté eschuer blame. (IX, 56, ll. 1635 f.)

Se tu prans femme qui soit riche,
C'est le denier Dieu et la briche
D'avoir des reprouches souvent. (IX, 60, ll. 1755 ff.)

Belle femme est trop perilleuse. (IX, 91, l. 2718)

Beau tresdoulz fils, bonne chançon
Ne fut onques ne n'yert chantée
De femme qui soit enfermée. (IX, 106 f., ll. 3186 ff.)

Que vuides chambres les (*femmes*) font sotes.

(IX, 291, l. 8989 [155])

Et n'est il escript es proverbes:
Femme fole est fosse parfonde? (IX, 198, ll. 6068 f.)

Bien doit estre villains tenuz
Qui escript ne dit de sa bouche
Laidure de femme ou reprouche. (IX, 294, ll. 9084 ff.)

En tous temps est Fortune decepvable.
(I, 316 f., ll. 8, 16, 24 [211])

Et ce proverbe fonde m'entencion
Que par raison nul ne doit esperer
Que grant fortune puist longuement durer.
(X, xxix f., ll. 5 ff., 14, 21)

Pour ce que foul ne doubte jusqu'il prant.
(V, 289 f., ll. 10, 20, 30, 36 [115])

Fouls est congnus a tele ensaingne:
Jusqu'il prant ne craint l'ennemi,
Pour ce ne treuve nul ami
En sa dolour, ne qui le plaingne. (V, 368 f., ll. 45 ff. [115])

Noble chose est que de franchise avoir.
(II, 100 f., ll. 10, 20, 30 [202])

Pour trestout l'or qui est et qui sera
Ne porroit pas Franchise estre vendue.
(IV, 135, ll. 1 f., 7 f. [202])

Franchise amer, car qui fait villenie,
Par faire mal n'aprivois'on pas chien. (V, 282, ll. 23 f.)

Car il n'est riens qui vaille franche vie.
(VI, 278 f., ll. 10, 20, 30, 36)

Habis fourrés, grant pencion d'argent,
Maistre de non ne font pas l'omme saige.
(X, xxxii, ll. 1 f. [184])

On ne congnoist aux robes la pensée.
(I, 233 f., ll. 10, 20, 30, 34)

Ou hault sommet de la haulte montaigne
Ne fait pas bon maison edifier,

Que li grant vens ne la gaste et souspraingne.

(I, 185, ll. 1 ff.)

Car en hault lieu ventent li vent a plain.   (V, 206, l. 11)

Car es hauls lieux sont les vens trop mauvès.   (V, 385, l. 9)

Car les hauls lieux sont perilleux.   (V, 387, l. 7)

Deux fois huchier ne se font pas, mais cent.   (VII, 19, l. 15)

Mais par l'imparfaicte est veue
Vraie, parfaite et congneue,
Et si est cler et general
Qu'om congnoist le bien par le mal.   (IX, 320, ll. 9931 ff.)

Il fault ploier contre force le jonc.   (III, 140, l. 22)

Joue qui veult, qui veult labeure.   (VIII, 215, l. 119)

L'en ne doit pas par tout jugier de l'oeil.

(VI, 72 f., ll. 8, 16, 24, 28)

Chascun juge selon son sentement.

(III, 58 f., ll. 8, 16, 24, 32, 40, 44)

Car un chascun fait du sien a sa guise.

(V, 326 f., ll. 8, 16, 24, 28)

Laissent le mal, facent le bien.

(VIII, 166 f., ll. 10, 20, 30, 36)

Fay le mieulx, laisse le piour.   (IX, 338, l. 10494)

De la langue chascun s'i playe.   (V, 407, l. 17)

Toute la premiere vertu
Est de sa langue refrener,
Car taire en temps a plus valu
A pluseurs que le trop parler,
Qui nuist souvent.   (VIII, 165 f., ll. 1 ff. [121])

Trop parler nuyt.   (X, xx, l. 15 [119])

Mais .xv. loups puellent mangier
Une brebis, quant prinse l'ont,

Legierement, et ainsis font
Pluseurs vices un homme prandre.   (IX, 344, ll. 10686 ff.)

Mais on rent mal en lieu de bien souvent.
                                        (I, 120 f., ll. 8, 16, 24)

Qui se marie, il a mal en sa teste.   (VII, 108, ll. 7, 14, 21)

Car quant maulx vient tous biens cesse.   (IV, 13, l. 40)

Car un mauvais un mauvais gendre.   (VIII, 321, l. 2403)

Bon fait fuir qui a mauvaise grace.   (V, 106, l. 48)

Car menteur a cuer villain.   (II, 317, l. 91 [133])

Maint mentent qui jurent.   (VII, 262, l. 273)

Car mieulx vault que li homs se taise
Que se qu'il mente par faveur.   (IX, 145, ll. 4382 f.)

Baillis, prevos, sergens, merencolie
N'aiez des clers; la bourse est leur amie
Qui les purge de mourdre et traison.   (VII, 31, ll. 51 ff.)

Cui il meschiet, tous jours on lui mesofre.
                                        (I, 291, ll. 8, 16, 24)

Car, chascun jour, meschiet il qui que soit.
                                        (V, 311 f., ll. 9, 18, 27, 31)

Compaignons en leur grant misere.   (VIII, 40, l. 89)

Benoist de Dieu est qui tient le moien.
                                        (I, 185 f., ll. 8, 16, 24 [159])

Le moien doit vouloir et desirer.   (II, 72, l. 29)

Tiengne en tous estas le moien.   (V, 240, l. 6 [159])

Bon fait faire par atrempance
Ne trop ne po.   (VII, 47, ll. 34 f. [107])

Tousjours sent le mortier les aulx.
                                        (II, 77 f., ll. 8, 16, 24, 30)

Advise qu'il te fault mourir.   (I, 181 f., ll. 8, 16, 24, 28 [49])

Que chascun muert et ne puet sçavoir quant.
                                (II, 134 f., ll. 10, 20, 30, 34 [48])

Tuit y mourront, et li fol et li saige.
                            (III, 183 f., ll. 10, 20, 30, 40, 50, 56 [48])

Car homme n'est qui ait point de demain.
                                (III, 232 f., ll. 8, 16, 24, 28 [47])

Que vous servez de la nappe ploye
A ces amens qui font sy le joly.   (V, 11, ll. 19 f.)

Oiseuse . . .
Que nulz homs ne doit pourchacier
Comme chose fausse et amere
Qui de tous maulx est droicte mere.
                            (IX, 299 f., ll. 9273 ff. [120])

Et certes qui n'oste la paille,
Qui l'embrasement du feu baille
Et l'esteule, ne cessera
Ce feu, ançois alumera
Tant comme les deliz charnelz
Seront en la char encharnez.   (IX, 199, ll. 6097 ff.)

Par pitié, qui ne s'acorde
Que nobles cuers soit crueux.   (II, 184, ll. 51 f.)

Le plain chemin vault mieulx que la bruiere.
                                        (III, 366, l. 21)

Qui povres est, on le rigole.   (V, 369, l. 68)

Povre robe a mauvais pourpoint.   (VIII, 131, l. 28)

Que vault preschier au sourt qui goute n'oit?
Que vault semer sur pierre le froument?
Que vault monstrer a cellui qui ne voit?
Que vault le lire a cellui qui n'apprant?
Que vault enter sur tron qui ne reprant?   (III, 5, ll. 1 ff.)

Chasun est moqué qui recule.   (V, 38, l. 7)

En po de temps gens reformez.   (V, 110, l. 28)

Ne jamès jour la regle ne faurra.   (II, 6 f., ll. 8, 16, 24)

Rien n'ay acquis, et ne puis durer longues,
Fors que renom, c'est le vent de soulerre.   (II, 65, ll. 22 f.)

Plus que fin or vault bonne renommée.
                     (VII, 139 f., ll. 8, 16, 24)
Et certes nulz n'emportera
De ce monde, quant il mourra,
Que .ii. choses, si com moy semble:
C'est bien fait, bon renom ensemble.
Le bien fait pour l'ame sera;
Bon renom aux hoirs demourra
Exemple, afin d'eulx exempler
De leur bon pere ressembler.   (IX, 80, ll. 2381 ff. [113])

Et disoit on communement
Que beste estoit tresbien rentée
Qui fust sur tresor assignée
Mieulx que de prandre par sa main.   (VIII, 258, ll. 370 ff.)

Ne fay passer despens ta revenue.
            (I, 141 f., ll. 8, 16, 24 [102])
Ta despense ne soit tenue
Si grande com ta revenue.   (IX, 115, ll. 3469 f. [102])

Mieulx vault restraindre son estat
Un petit que cheoir tout plat
En povreté.   (IX, 116, ll. 3491 ff.)

Ja riches homs n'yra en paradis.   (I, 73 f., ll. 10, 20, 30, 34)

Que ce seroit aussi fort chose
Passer par le tro d'une aguille
Un chamel, texte est d'euvangille,
Com d'un riche mondain seroit
Qui en paradis entreroit.   (IX, 353, ll. 10962 ff. [197])

Que vault richesse mondayne
Mal acquise? n'est pas sayne.   (IV, 23, ll. 18 f.)

La male acquise n'est pas tele,
Qui petit ou neant profite.   (VIII, 255, ll. 262 f.)

Saiges n'est pas qui trop s'i fie.   (IX, 334, l. 10368)

Pour ce est saiges qui a ces poins regarde,
Car d'un festu mis a part, quoy qu'il tarde,
Puet un chascun ains l'an avoir mestier.   (V, 118, ll. 4 ff.)

Saiges sont donc ceuls qui se tiennent
Arrier de ce qui les puet nuire
Et du feu qui ne les puet cuire.   (IX, 342, ll. 10624 ff.)

Plus saiges est que Salemon
Et plus riches que ne fut Crise.   (II, 164, ll. 1 f.)

Qu'est devenu David et Salemon,
Mathussalé, Josué, Machabée, *etc.*   (III, 113 f., ll. 1 ff.)

Se je savoie autant com Salemon.   (III, 166, l. 1)

Force de corps, qu'est devenu Sanson?
Ou est Auglas, le bon practicien? *etc.*   (III, 182, ll. 1 ff.)

Crisès est mort . . . *etc.*
(Salomon, Sanson Fortin, Absalon, Alixandre)
                                               (III, 233, ll. 17 ff.)

A Salomon puet estre comparez, *etc.*
(Absalon, Hector, Sanson, Seneques, Paris)   (III, 239, ll. 9 ff.)

Large est con fu Charlemaine.   (IV, 164, l. 22)

Ne d'estre preux ou Julius Cesars
Ou comme furent Alixandre et Daviz,
  Ne du sans de Salomon,
Ne que j'aye la beauté d'Absalon.   (IV, 347, ll. 3 ff.)

Ou est Nembroth le grant jayant, *etc.*
                                               (VIII, 149 f., ll. 1 ff.)

Caton plain de phillosophie.   (VIII, 149, l. 22)

Tu n'es pas plus fort de Sanson
Ne plus saiges de Salemon, *etc.*   (IX, 181, ll. 5529 ff.)

Se d'Absalon la grant beauté humaine,
De Salomon tout le senz sanz demy,
D'Alixandre l'avoir et le demaine
Des .ix. preux eusse et leur prouesce aussy.

(X, xlix, ll. 9 ff.)

Ne quier veoir la beauté d'Absalon, *etc.*   (X, liv, ll. 1 ff.)

Puis dist Robins: 'Marion, deshonneste
Sont grans mangiers et cilz qui les apreste
En peril est qu'il n'en muire en la fin;
Plus eureux vif que ne font, par ma teste,
Ces grans seigneurs qui ont tant de moleste
Et qui doubtent la poison d'un coquin
Et en aguet vivent soir et matin.
Mon pain est bon; ne faut que nulz me veste;
L'eaue est saine qu'a boire sui enclin;
Je ne doubte ne tirant ne venin;
Le boys me craint dont je couppe la creste:
J'ay franc vouloir sanz os et sanz arreste,
Plus riche sui que Roy ne palazin.   (II, 212 f., ll. 274 ff.)

Princes, mieulx vault, se Salemon ne ment,
Un mors de pain qui est pris liement
Qu'une grant court de viande planiere
Ou tristesce est et envie souvent.   (III, 120, ll. 41 ff. [101])

Beau filz, mieulz vault faire silence
Que promettre.   (I, 127, ll. 25 f.)

La souris qui est en son tro
Scet petit fors l'estrain rungier.   (IX, 301, ll. 9316 f.)

Cilz pert son temps qui tele euvre pourchace,
Combien qu'aucuns dient communement.   (III, 6, ll. 6 f.)

Au petit ru boit teurterelle
Plus aise qu'en riviere isnelle,
Son nif en lieu moien enserre.   (V, 384, ll. 26 ff.)

On ne tient pas toudis ce qu'en convente.

(II, 24 f., ll. 8, 16, 24 [125])

C'est trop bien dit, mais querez qui le face.
                    (III, 6 f., ll. 8, 16, 24, 32, 40, 46)

Mais telz dit un qui autre chose a faicte.
                    (IV, 141, ll. 3, 13 [124])

Pou vault promesse qui ne l'acomplira.
                    (IV, 335 f., ll. 8, 16, 24 [125])

C'est trop bien dit, pour quoy ne le fait on?   (V, 389, l. 15)

Tout ne vault rien puis qu'executez n'est.   (V, 389, l. 19)

Pleges vault mieulx, qui y puet advenir.
                    (VII, 21 f., ll. 10, 20, 30)

C'est bien dit, mais on n'en fait rien.
                    (VII, 242 f., ll. 10, 20, 30, 36 [124])

De paroles et non de fait
Est maint ami qui ainsi fait.   (IX, 5, ll. 65 f.)

Qu'en ce monde n'a fors que Vanité.
                    (I, 239, ll. 7, 14, 21 [232])

Rien violent ne puet durer au fort.   (I, 109, l. 26 [205])

Chose qui vient par accident soudain
Et violant, n'a pas longue durée.   (II, 50, ll. 1 f. [205])

Rien violent ne puet estre durable.   (III, 12, l. 7 [232])

Pou dure chose violent.   (V, 185 f., ll. 10, 20, 30, 34)

Chose n'ara longue durée
Qui violemment est menée.   (VIII, 254, l. 221 [205])

APPENDIX B

PROVERBS IN THE FABLIAUX

THE following quotations are taken from A. de Montaiglon & G. Raynaud, *Recueil Général . . . des Fabliaux*, 6 vols. (Paris, 1872–1890). An * before a saying indicates that it occurs at or near the end of a poem, and ** indicates its position at or near the beginning. In giving line references I follow the count indicated at the top of a given page, despite the fact that the figures are often wrong from page to page.

PROVERBS

***Li abis ne fait pas l'ermite.* (III, 263, l. 1)

Car fort chose est d'acoustumance. (I, 325, l. 217)

Amors demande hardement. (II, 100, l. 271)

*Par la raison de cest flabel
Monstré ai essanple novel
As vallez et as damoiseax,
Qui d'Amors mainent lor cenbeax,
Que, qant auront lor cuer doné
As dames de très grant beauté,
Que il la doit tot arroment
Requerre molt hardiement. (II, 112 f., ll. 644 ff.)

Amur est celi qui tut veint. (II, 221, l. 225)

*Quar qui por amor sueffre maus
Bien li set merir ses travaus

Que loiaumant sueffre por li.
Veritez est, et je le di,
Qu'amors vaint tout et tout vaincra
Tant com cis siecles durera. (V, 262, ll. 592 ff.)

Qu'il n'est si fort ne si siens
Qui contre amour se puist deffendre. (VI, 267, ll. 18 f.)

Li asniers une chose pensse,
Et li asnes pensse tout el. (I, 120, ll. 104 f.)

Assez est bone, lessez ester. (II, 251, l. 306)

**Car on dist, et c'est chose vraie,
Que bonne atent qui bonne paie. (III, 247, ll. 7 f.)

*Rutebuez dit, bien m'en souvient:
Qui barat quiert, baraz li vient. (III, 226, ll. 154 f.)

"Bien vous en croy, quar *en sentier*
Qui est batus ne croist point d'erbe."
Cilz qui oïrent cest proverbe,
Commencierent si grant risée. (III, 249 f., ll. 107 ff.)

Qar qui biau dit, biau veut oïr,
Et qui mal dit et qui mal fait,
Il ne puet estre qu'il ne l'ait. (I, 84, ll. 50 ff.)

Que Salemon dist en son tens
Qu'entre la bouche et la cuillier
Avient sovent grant encombrier. (VI, 47, ll. 61 ff.)

—"Comment?" — fait-elle. "Ne doit boire
Le vin malveis qui tel le brasse?" (II, 87, ll. 1257 f.)

Que il est bien droiz et reson
Que *qui le brasce si le boive.* (VI, 129, ll. 381 f.)

*L'en dit: *Qui bien chace, bien trueve.* (III, 208, l. 267)

**Et cil ne fet mie folie
Qui d'autrui mesfet se chastie. (III, 199, ll. 5 f.)

Car grant sens gist en cortoisie:
Preuz est qui d'autri se chastie. (VI, 31, ll. 256 f.)

Li vilains reproche du chat
Qu'il set bien qui barbes il lèche. (I, 174, ll. 196 f.)

Miex velt estre sanz compaignie
Qu'avoir compaignon à amie. (V, 407, *variant*)

Mès miex vaut compaignon que nient. (I, 205, l. 229)

*Mès en la fin fin di en apert:
Cil qui tot covoite, tout pert. (V, 36, ll. 144 f.)

*Richart Bonier dit en apert,
Qui tot coveite trestot pert. (VI, 41, ll. 234 ff.)

Mal est couvert cui le cul pert. (III, 23, l. 679)

*Segnors, ce dist Colins Malès:
Teus cuide cunchier autrui,
Qui tout avant cunchie lui. (IV, 127, ll. 451 ff.)

Car *qui trop despent, il s'endete.* (III, 217, l. 85)

Pur ce dit um molt sovent
Qe petit ad e petit prent
Et velt despendre largement,
Ne purra durer longement,
Et pur ce il fet qe sage
Qe se prent à le avauntage. (VI, 198, ll. 25 ff.)

Entre .ii. boires .i. soupir
I doit on faire seulement. (III, 149, ll. 163 f.)

Car de .ii. maus prent-on le mieux. (II, 50, l. 144)

Le maindre mal deit hom eslire
Pur eschure cel ke est pire. (II, 226, ll. 348 f.)

Sovent ai oï amentoivre
Et dire et conter en main leu:
Li domages qui bout au feu
Vaut miaus que cil qui ne fet aise. (V, 155, ll. 147 ff.)

Droit à droit revient. (IV, 105, l. 393)

*Li vileins dit en son proverbe
Que mains hom a le tort requis
Qui par plaidier aura conquis;
Engiens a fauxée droiture,
Fauxers a veincue nature;
Torz vait avant et droiz aorce:
Mielz valt engiens que ne fait force.   (III, 214, ll. 173 ff.)

Et on dit bien en reprovier
Que *Trop estraindre fait chier.*   (III, 104, ll. 78 f.)

*Rutebues dist en cest fablel:
Quant fame a fol, s'a son avel.   (III, 198, ll. 174 f.)

*Por ce vos di, tot en apert,
Que son tens pert qui felon sert.
Raembez de forches larron,
Quant il a fait sa mesprison,
Jamès jor ne vous amera,
Ains à tousjours vous haïra.   (I, 303, ll. 67 ff.)

Moult est ore fols qui demande
Chose que l'en ne puet avoir.   (I, 99, ll. 62 f.)

Fols est qui chace la folie.   (II, 104, l. 393)

Fols est qui fol conseil demande.   (I, 284, l. 882)

*Car um puet oyr sovent
Un fol parler sagement.
Sage est qe parle sagement,
Fols come parle folement.   (II, 256, ll. 440 ff.)

Molt remaint de ce que fous pense.   (V, 227, l. 399)

Bien se porra tenir por fol
Qui sentira combien il poise.   (I, 274, ll. 578 f.)

Qui fait folie sel conpert.   (V, 141, l. 299)

Fous est qui de ce me mescroit.   (V, 82, l. 77)

*Je meïsmes li ai fet leu:
La male garde pest lo leu.   (V, 156, ll. 178 f.)

*Par ce nos veut Haiseaus moutrer
Qu'il se fet bon de tot garder.   (VI, 50, ll. 17 f.)

*Por ce vous di, seignor baron:
Male est compaignie à larron.   (IV, 111, ll. 536 f.)

Bien est lerres qui larron emble.   (IV, 96, l. 125)

*Bon larron est qui autre[s] emble.
          (V, 316, *variants after* l. 287)

*Dist on encor: *Maint fol paist duis.*   (III, 57, l. 87)

De ma mance m'a ters mon nés.   (III, 245, l. 570)

Nus ne se marie qui ne s'en repente.   (I, 137, l. 53)

S'il n'est bien droit c'on le deçoive:
Qui merde brasse, merde boive.   (IV, 119, ll. 246 f.)

De ceste chose me sovient
Que li mesaiges trop tost vient
Qui la male novele aporte.   (II, 102, ll. 340 ff.)

*Qui plus met en aus, plus i pert.   (I, 244, l. 189)

Murtres ne puet estre celé.   (VI, 125, l. 285)

*Par cest conte savoir poez,
Que nus murtres n'iert ja celez.   (VI, 253, ll. 30 f.)

Plus muet on le fiens, plus il pust.   (VI, 132, l. 485)

**.1. proverbes dit et raconte
Que *tout n'est pas ors c'on voit luire.*   (III, 263, ll. 14 f.)

Qui outrage quiert, il li vient.   (IV, 211, l. 128)

Cest fabliaus nos dit et raconte
Q'an son respit, dit li vilains,
*Que à celui doit l'an del pain
Q'on ne cuide jamais veoir.*   (V, 200, ll. 265 ff.)

De ma paste m'a fet tortel.   (III, 245, l. 574)

A mol pastor chie lous laine.   (III, 262, l. 305)

*Or puet hon le proverbe ci
Metre à point que jadis oï:
Soventes foiz avient à court
Que tieus ne peche qui encourt.　　　(VI, 45, ll. 80 ff.)

*Et li rois si a respondu:
'*Qui a perdu, si ait perdu.*'　　　(III, 174, ll. 156 f.)

Sachiez que li enfes qui fet
Contre le voloir de son père,
Sovient avient qu'il le compère.　　　(I, 137, ll. 47 ff.)

Car *il pert assez à l'esteule*
Que bons n'est mie li espis.　　　(III, 248 f., ll. 79 f.)

*Que *L'en pert bien par trop atendre.*　　　(V, 36, l. 143)

Or oiez .i. proverbe estable
Qui en mainz leus, ce m'est vis, cort,
Que tel ne pesche qui encort.　　　(IV, 76, ll. 295 ff.)

*L'avanture de cest proverbe
Retrai por riches homes hautz
Qui plus sont desloiaus et faus;
Lor san et lor parole vandent,
A nule droiture n'entandent,
Chacuns à prandre s'abandone:
Povres n'a droit, se il ne done.　　　(V, 158 f., ll. 77 ff.)

*Ja povres hons qui n'a avoir
N'avra par eus droit en sa vie.　　　(V, 36, ll. 129 f.)

Car qui trop prent et trop acroit
Ains qu'il ne veut caitis se voit.　　　(II, 61, l. 496)

Car ki se taist, il se repose.　　　(IV, 10, l. 302)

*Je di: *Cil se repent trop tart,*
Qui se repent quant a perdu.　　　(V, 36, ll. 139 f.)

Tu vendras tart au repentir.　　　(I, 20, l. 222)

Si m'en repent, mais ch'est à tart.　　　(II, 71, l. 783)

*L'en dit pieça: Qui va, il lesche,
Et qui toz jors se siet, il sèche.   (I, 317, ll. 381 f.)

*Si dist à soi: "*Qui siet, il seche,*"
Et puis si dist: "*Qui va, il leche,*"   (III, 207, l. 288 f.)

Qui toz jorz se tait rien ne valt.   (V, 92, l. 302)

**Pour çou dist on en un reclaim:
Tant as, tant vaus, et je tant t' aim.   (VI, 53, ll. 19 f.)

Par foi, tierce foie droiz est.   (I, 213, l. 452)

Tierce foiée, quar c'est droiz.   (IV, 44, l. 126)

La tierce fie, c'est le drois.   (V, 328, l. 19)

On dit sovent; l'uevre se prueve.   (I, 84, l. 54)

*C'est de tel vente tel marchié.   (II, 240, l. 197)

PROVERBIAL COMPARISONS

Et plus grosse qu'une baschoe.   (I, 252, l. 204)

Et il remest plus chaut que brese.   (IV, 170, l. 162)

Ains est plus dolce que canelle.   (II, 202, l. 172)

Tu me harroies plus c'un chien.   (III, 69, l. 75)

Si a la teste plus mellée
Assez que ne soit chiens de Flandres.   (IV, 155, ll. 55 f.)

Or seroit il pire que chiens.   (V, 88, l. 180)

Hors le traient com .i. mort chien.   (I, 123, l. 198)

Ele est plus noire c'une choe.   (I, 252, l. 203)

Lor cuer samblent cochet au vent.   (I, 24, l. 17)

Tant que tu fusses ausi mox
Com une coille de mouton.   (I, 6, ll. 154 f.)

Les iex ot vairs come cristal.   (I, 238, l. 11)

Front poli plus cler de cristal.   (V, 249, l. 227)

Que il estoit nuz com .i. dains.   (II, 22, l. 429)

Car pire est, ce dient les genz,
I tel maus que n'est mal des denz.   (V, 47, ll. 154 f.)

Cil qui estoit plus fel qu'Erodes.   (III, 266, l. 111)

Con faucons vairs ieus et rians.   (VI, 180, l. 20)

Mes barons a le vit plus noir
De fer, et la coille plus noire
Que chape à moinne n'à provoire.   (VI, 92, ll. 89 ff.)

Autre eure plus rouge que feus.   (I, 234, l. 99)

Venuz c'en est plus droit que flesche.   (VI, 125, l. 261)

S'est plus blanche que flor d'espine
La pucele.   (II, 19, ll. 342 f.)

Blanche ot la char con flor d'espine.   (V, 28, l. 154)

Blanche fu comme flors de lis.   (VI, 180, l. 16)

Quar il ot une longue jambe
Plus noire que forniaus de chambe.   (III, 65, ll. 236 f.)

Tremblant com une fueille d'arbre.   (II, 22, l. 437)

Tremblaunt come fueille menue.   (II, 191, l. 271)

Entra en trenblant comme fueille.   (VI, 81, l. 428)

Et fust chevaliers de sa main
Meillor c'onques ne fu Gavain.   (III, 75, ll. 222 f.)

Plus blanche estoit que n'est gelée.   (II, 48, l. 94)

Lor cul erent plus noir que fros
Qui mout estoient près à près.   (IV, 193, ll. 841 f.)

Cler (vin) comme larme.   (II, 57, l. 365)

Par cest example voil moustrer
C'on doit ainçois le leu huer
Des bestes qu'il y soit venuz.   (I, 237, ll. 173 ff.)

Hideus comme leu ou lupart.   (II, 50, l. 141)

Iex de liepart, cuer de lyon.   (II, 130, l. 8)

Tout aussi tremble comme lièvres.   (II, 65, l. 593)

A la dame va environ
Comme levriers qui lievre cache.   (V, 119, ll. 141 f.)

A dames est plus dous que miel.   (II, 174, l. 102)

Une eure est plus blanche que nape.   (I, 234, l. 98)

Rouges come oingnon de Corbueil.   (I, 232, p. 33)

Or vous ai je dit du Vallet
Qui d'aise à mallaise se met,
Que si faisoit le cretelet,
Et qui resamble l'oiselet
Qui, ains qu'ait elles, veut voler,
Et puis si demeure afolés.   (II, 169 f., ll. 404 ff.)

Si cheveil resambloient d'or,
Tant estoient luisant et sor.   (II, 48, ll. 96 f.)

Les cheveus tex qui les veïst,
Qu'avis li fust, s'estre poïst,
Que il fussent tuit de fin or.   (II, 95, ll. 114 ff.)

Qui se cuidoient hui matin
Plus esmerées que or fin.   (III, 28, ll. 834 f.)

Ensi luisanz comme fins ors
Lo chief sa fame resenbloit.   (V, 137, ll. 197 f.)

Blondès cheveus et bien soians,
Luisans con or.   (VI, 180, ll. 40 f.)

Ausi con uns ostoirs muiers
Ki se va par l'air enbatant,
Se va la dame deportant.   (II, 201, ll. 163 ff.)

Avoir vient et va comme paille.   (V, 87, l. 163)

Largece amoit plus ke Paris
N'amaist onkes nul jor Helaine.   (III, 134, ll. 351 f.)

Que ele sanbloit passerose.   (II, 95, l. 130)

Le vit fut roides com pel.   (I, 236, l. 143)

Il est plus roides que .i. pel.   (IV, 205, l. 214)

Sempres ert mol comme pelice.   (V, 205, l. 158)

Il n'est ne pie ne calandre
Qui me séust pas gosillier
Ce qui me fet si merveillier.   (I, 148, ll. 24 ff.)

Toz jorz fustes plus durs que pierre.   (III, 210, l. 61)

Le Prestre prenra à la nasse
Ausin com l'en prent le poisson.   (II, 12, ll. 138 f.)

Cui primes point la mamelete
Enmi le piz com une pomme.   (II, 11, ll. 84 f.)

Li poignoient .ii. mameletes
Auteles comme .ii. pommetes.   (II, 95, ll. 138 f.)

Je sui plus sain que une pomme.   (III, 168, l. 382)

Et li vilains, comme porciaus,
S'encressoit.   (III, 200, ll. 78 f.)

D'ame furent com rat en moie.   (I, 295, l. 32)

Qu'il i laissa les .ii. coillons
Autresi granz con .ii. roignons.   (V, 169, ll. 302 f.)

Qu'il est plus aspres c'une ronsce.   (IV, 168, l. 80)

Rose qui est encolorée
Ne se prent pas à sa color.   (I, 138, ll. 90 f.)

Et plus tornans et plus isnele
Ke ne soit rute ne venvole.   (II, 202, ll. 173 f.)

Sa bouche resanloit fin sanc.	(II, 48, l. 103)
Et chante cler comme seraine.	(II, 84, l. 1186)
Il est si pris en la teinture Qu'il est plus teint et plus vermeil Qu'au matinet n'est le soleil Au jor quant il doit plus roier.	(VI, 21, ll. 431 ff.)
Lor cul erent plus noir que torbes.	(IV, 194, l. 873)
Et frit con tourtiaus em paiele.	(VI, 262, l. 2)
Tristans, tant com fu en cest monde, N'anma autant Ysoue la blonde Cum si .ii. amans s'entr'emmerent.	(I, 319, ll. 29 ff.)
Denz de sengler, isniaus com tygre.	(II, 130, l. 9)
Et, s'il vient à une bataille, Ainsi com li vens fet la paille, Les fet fuir par devant lui.	(II, 131, ll. 52 ff.)
Lors avoirs va aussi ke vens.	(II, 206, l. 315)
De dames iert legiers con vens.	(VI, 264, l. 3)
Et les dens drus, et bien assis, Blanc con yvoire.	(VI, 180, ll. 34 f.)

OTHER PROVERBIAL PHRASES

Ne vaus pas certes .ii. chiez d'aus.	(II, 259, l. 103)
Il ne prisoit ne pris ne los, Ne chevalerie .ii. auz.	(III, 253, ll. 73 f.)
**De la plus bele criature Que hom puisse troveir ne querre De Paris juqu'en Aingleterre.	(III, 263, ll. 18 ff.)
Ne de ci jusqu'en Alemaingne.	(I, 35, l. 340)
Car ne prisoit pas une amande Tot l'autre jeu.	(IV, 137, ll. 153 f.)

Arrivés estes à boin port.   (II, 89, l. 1333)

Qu'ele ot tost la honte béue
Qu'ele avoit à premiers héue.   (I, 324, ll. 189 f.)

Après le conte doit on boire.   (II, 59, l. 415)

*Qui ceste rimme ont escoutée
Et celui qui l'a devissée.
Done-moi boire, si t'agrée.   (II, 122, ll. 285 ff.)

Seignor, ne vous vaut .I. bouton.   (I, 225, l. 162)

Ne el Realme de Castele,
Où les plus belles dames sont.   (II, 94, ll. 91 f.)

Le jor de demain au matin,
Chanteras-tu d'autre Martin,
Que je ne te pris deux mellenz.   (I, 104, ll. 227 ff.)

Cesti ne vaut plus que un chien.   (II, 254, l. 386)

Bien savez le coc chaponnez
Est as gelines mal venus.   (III, 250, ll. 133 f.)

Dont prent son cul parmi l'oreille.   (II, 72, l. 820)

Il n'a meillor de ci en Cypre.
                    (III, 94, l. 209 [cf. III, 100, l. 397])

Chi ne ferés vous vos besoigne
Vaillant le pris d'une escaillongne.   (II, 52, ll. 209 f.)

Qu'i donnast vaillant un espi.   (II, 175, l. 129)

Grant cose a en *Faire l'estuet*.   (VI, 61, l. 283)

Tu ne sez vaillant .II. festuz.   (I, 1, l. 7)

**Je ne pris mie .II. festus
Son habit.   (III, 263, ll. 4 f.)

Tot ce ne prise il .I. festu.   (VI, 10, l. 93)

Tu ne sez vaillant une figue.   (I, 5, l. 106)

Or est li Prestres fors de foire.   (II, 238, l. 110)

Lor commence à paller latin
Et postroillaz et alemant,
Et puis tyois et puis flemmanc, . . .
Li vins l'avoir fet roi de France.   (II, 238 f., ll. 135 ff.)

Mès il parla mout faus latin,
Et les servi mout bien de gangles.   (VI, 124, ll. 235 f.)

Que tu ne valz une letue.   (I, 3, l. 48)

Ne de ci jusqu'en Loheraine.   (I, 35, l. 326)

.ii. besanz valent .i. mangon.   (II, 112, l. 637)

Cesti ne vaut plus qe un mastyn.   (II, 254, l. 384)

Il n'a home jusqu'à Neele.   (I, 5, l. 116)

N'a tel larron jusqu'à Nevers.   (IV, 96, l. 123)

Ne li soit à vaillant .iii. noiz.   (V, 16, l. 474)

Que il n'a si bon chevalier
De moi de si en Normendie.   (IV, 60, ll. 133 f.)

.i. œf ne prise tout son mal.   (I, 124, l. 228)

Ne péust pas .i. oef d'aloe
Estre entre l'enclume et la cane.   (I, 149, ll. 70 f.)

N'en retint qui vausist .ii. oes.   (II, 2, l. 24)

Il n'a mie valhant douz œz.   (II, 202, l. 195)

Ja mar en serez en esmai,
Ne plus que por .i. oef de quaille.   (IV, 174, ll. 285 f.)

Biau parolt, si soit saje et cointe,
Se la paume li avoit ointe.   (V, 158, ll. 52 f.)

Nient plus ne vault que fet paille.   (V, 313 l. 12)

Qui li vendi paille por grain
Et changa por le forment l'orge.   (II, 18 f., ll. 320 f.)

Tu es el paradis Bertran;
Ou pués-tu chanter de Tristran,
Ou de plus longue, se tu sez.   (I, 108, ll. 321 f.)

Quar ele ne valt mie une piere.   (II, 249, l. 235)

Que ja n'i aura gaaingnié
A son oes vaillant une poire.   (III, 42, ll. 257 f.)

Tu ne sai pas vaillant un pois.   (I, 6, l. 137)

Ge ne pris pas .i. trox de pome.   (I, 2, l. 44)

De che n'en poise pas sa vie
Vaillant une pume pourrie.   (II, 77, ll. 960 f.)

Vus ne valez pas un purry poume.   (II, 249, l. 257)

De Monpellier dessi à Roie
Ne trouvissiés pas .ii. plus beles.   (II, 48, ll. 89 f.)

    qu'il ait homme
Qui sont mananz de si à Romme.   (I, 145, ll. 266 f.)

Entre si e Leons sur Rone
N'ad nulle meilour.   (II, 246, ll. 167 f.)

Pour jouer au *roy qui ne ment.*   (III, 248, l. 54)

Jà vous chantaisse putes Laudes,
Fet-il, foi que je doi saint Ladre.   (I, 190, ll. 66 f.)

Il n'a homme dusqu'à Samur.   (III, 164, l. 287)

Il n'a homme de si à Sens.   (III, 137, l. 1)

.vii. anz.   (I, 84, l. 56; II, 92, l. 12; II, 99, l. 246;
                        III, 245, l. 578; V, 60, l. 276)

Fet-il, tu ne vaus une tarte.   (I, 242, l. 141)

Quant il la vit, moult ot grant joie,
Com se il fust sire de Troie.   (I, 172, ll. 127 f.)

Je n'ai vaillant une vendoise.   (I, 91, l. 270)

Sententious Remarks

J'en ai cure
Que pour musart ja tenuz soie
D'acheter chose que ne voie.   (VI, 131, ll. 461 ff.)

**Or vous voel dire sans atente
Pourquoi cest provierbe commence,
Car il n'afiert mie c'on mence,
Ains doit on ensievir le voir.   (VI, 263, ll. 10 ff.)

Bien est amors et sire et mestre
Quant du monde le plus poissant
Fet si humble et obeissant
Qu'il ne prent nul conroi de lui,
Ainz s'oublie tot por autrui.
C'est droiz, qu'amors est de tel pris,
Que, puis qu'ele a .i. home pris,
N'i doit avoir nul desroi,
Qu'autant a amors sor un roi
De droit pooir, ce est la somme,
Comme sor tout le plus povre homme
Qui soit en Champaigne n'en France,
Tant est sa seignorie franche.   (V, 246 f., ll. 131 ff.)

*Tels cuide avancier qui recule.   (I, 134, l. 72)

Si li a dit: "A grant besoing
Doit l'en bien son ami aidier."   (VI, 12, ll. 153 f.)

J'ai oï dire en reprovier
Grant pieça que duel de noient
Seut acorer chetive gent.   (III, 24, ll. 729 ff.)

Nus ne set que bons avoirs vaut,
S'il ne set qui sont li assaut
Et li travail du pourcacier.   (VI, 54, ll. 66 ff.)

Lors avoirs va aussi ke vens.   (II, 206, l. 315)

*Cis fabliaus moustre en bon endroit,
Qui enseigne à chascun provoire

Que il se gardent bien de boire
A tel hanap comme cil burent,
Qui par lor fol sens ocis furent,
Et par lor grant maléurté.   (I, 218, ll. 606 ff.)

*Contre le con ne vaut engin.   (II, 139, l. 59)

Molt seroit malvais au civé
Li connins que li fuirons chace.
Molt est fox qui tel connin trace;
Mielz li venroit trover deus lievres,
Quar cil connins est si enrievres
Qu'il ne puet faire bele chiere
S'il n'a fuiron en sa tesniere.   (II, 239 f., ll. 165 ff.)

*Por çou vous di en la parfin:
Teus cuide avoir le cuer mout fin
Et mout repoint, n'est pas mençoigne,
Qui set mout peu à le besoigne.   (V, 178, ll. 252 ff.)

Nule riens à bele dame ne se prent.   (I, 138, l. 86)

Ne jà ostel n'ert à honor
Dont la dame se fet seignor.   (I, 185, ll. 201 f.)

"Hélas!" fait-il, "comme gaaingne
Fait chix qui autrui veut dechoivre;
Tex cuide sour autruï boire
Qui boit sour li, sour sa compaingne."   (II, 74, ll. 869 ff.)

*Durans, qui son conte define,
Dist c'onques Diex ne fist meschine
C'on ne puist por denier avoir.   (I, 22, ll. 285 ff.)

Ne se doit nus desnaturer.   (V, 42, l. 53)

Li doulousers seroit huiseuse,
Ne rien n'i puet on conquester.   (IV, 8, ll. 245 f.)

Quar en trop grant duel demener
Ne puet-il avoir nul conquest.   (I, 166, ll. 116 f.)

Mais esperance l'an deçoit.   (IV, 135, l. 103)

Molt a qui bone feme prent,
Qui male prent, ne prent nient.   (VI, 102, ll. 250 f.)

Quar qui sa bone amie pert
Molt a perdu, ce m'est avis; . . .
Et cil qui part sa desloiaus,
Dont ne doit il estre molt liez.   (III, 28, ll. 823–830 ff.)

Et si le dis tout as preudommes:
Pour chou si [nous le vous] dissommes
C'ains Dieus ne fist li mal avoir
Comme de male femme avoir,
Que femmes font et mal et bien:
On nes puet tenir en loiien.
Qui bone l'a, si le maingtienne
Et la mauvaisse son frain tiengne.   (V, 302, l. 13)

*Qui fame croit, si est desvés.   (III, 122, l. 130)

*Seignor, fols est qui fame croit
Fors tant comme il l'ot er la voit.   (III, 75, ll. 216 f.)

*Mès li fabliaus dist en la fin
C'on doit por fol tenir celui
Qui mieus croit sa fame que lui.   (IV, 216, ll. 121 ff.)

*Par cest fablel poez savoir
Que cil ne fet mie savoir
Qui mieus croit sa fame que lui:
Sovent l'en vient honte et anui.   (V, 207, ll. 208 ff.)

*Por ce tieng je celui à fol
Qui trop met en fame sa cure.   (III, 122, ll. 124 f.)

Cuidiez-vous por nule poverte
Que preude fame se descorge?
Nenil, ainz se leroit la gorge
Soier à un trenchant rasoir,
Qu'ele féist jà por avoir
Chose dont ses sire éust blasme.   (I, 218, ll. 596 ff.)

Meson ne clos ne ount durée
Vers femme, qar son engyn pase
Tot ce qe autre engyn compasse.   (II, 183, ll. 14 ff.)

**Par cest fablel prover vous vueil
Que cil fet folie et orgueil
Qui fame engingnier s'entremet;
Quar qui fet à fame .ɪ. mal tret,
Ele en fet .x. ou .xv. ou .xx.   (I, 254, ll. 283 ff.)

Quant li femme entre en le reddie,
U faice savoir u folie,
Anchois mangeroit fer ou boise
Qu'ele ne vainque ù qu'ele voisse.   (II, 161, ll. 140 ff.)

*Fame est de trop foible nature,
De noient rit, de noient pleure,
Fame aime et het en trop poi d'eure;
Tost est ses talenz remuez.   (III, 122, ll. 126 ff.)

**Hues Piaucele, qui trova
Cest fablel, par reson prova
Que cil qui a fame rubeste
Est garnis de mauvèse beste.   (I, 97, ll. 1 ff.)

Voir dit qui dist ne fu pas fous:
Fame soferoit plus de cous
Que une asnesse de .ɪɪ. anz
De mal et de poine .ɪɪ. tanz.   (V, 140, ll. 272 ff.)

Fame a trestout passé Argu;
Par lor engin sont decéu
Li sage dès le tens Abel.   (I, 120, ll. 85 ff.)

Fame est plaine de sanc agu;
Par lor engin ont deceü
Les sages dès lo tans Abel.   (IV, 136, ll. 116 ff.)

Fols est qui fame espie et guète.   (I, 259, l. 118)

*Quant li sage lor dient:
Homme qui fame prent,
S'il n'a estorement,
N'est ja tenuz por sage
A poissant ne à large.   (II, 156, ll. 273 ff.)

**Au biau faucon lanier mauvès
Resamble maint homme de fès.   (III, 86, ll. 1 f.)

*Tel gent ne doit on pas amer,
Ainz le doit on mout desprisier
Qu'il resamble de son mestier
Au faucon lanier, ce m'est vis,
Qui par sa perece est honis.   (III, 87, ll. 63 ff.)

Le feu qui tout adès alume
Ne peut estaindre, n'i vaut rien.   (I, 326, ll. 230 f.)

*Par cest fablel vueil enseignier
Que tels cuide bien chastier
Sa fille de dire folie,
Et quant plus onques le chastie,
Tant le met l'en plus en la voie
De mal fere, se Dieus me voie.   (V, 108, ll. 206 ff.)

Li fils doit resambler le pere.   (II, 260, l. 137)

Molt par est fols qui nule en croit,
Que chascune le sien deçoit.   (III, 18, ll. 534 f.)

Quar cil est fous, par saint Germain,
Que ce que il tient en sa main
Giete à ses piez en nonchaloir.   (VI, 76, ll. 276 ff.)

Fox est li hom qui croit musarde.   (III, 101, l. 435)

Fous est qui en vain se travaille.   (V, 87, l. 162)

*Je di des homes mariez,
Et c'est provée veritez,
Quant de lour fames sunt jalous,
Ce est de ceus qui plus sont cous,
Que cele qui pense folie,
C'est cele qui plus aplanie
Son baron, et oste la plume,
Et plus le deçoit par costume,
Et oste le poil du mantel.   (VI, 31 f., ll. 258 ff.)

*En petit d'eure Dieus labeure,
Tels rit au main qui au soir pleure,

Et *tels est au soir corouciez*
Qui au main est joianz et liez.   (IV, 92, ll. 142 ff.)

*Pur ce est droit qe mal purchace
Qe à la foiz mal à ly face.   (II, 192, ll. 264 f.)

Or voi ge bien que marcheant
Ne sont pas toz jors bien cheant.   (III, 225, ll. 130 f.)

*Car vos meymes savez bien
Qe nul trop valt rien:
Qy par mesure tote ryen fra
Ja prudhome ne l'y blamera,
Par mesure meenement
Come est escrit apertement,
E le latin est ensi:
Medium tenuere beati.   (II, 256, ll. 430 ff.)

Qui sueffre aucune fois mesaise,
Il est mius puis conjoïe l'aise.   (VI, 54, ll. 72 f.)

Gens sont coustumier de mesdire.   (III, 89, l. 62)

*Se cils ne ment qui fist che dit,
On se doit mout bien aviser
S'il a sour lui que deviser,
Ains que sour autrui on mesdie.
Or querrés qui plus vous en die.   (VI, 269, ll. 19 ff.)

Nous morrons tuit, ce sez-tu bien.   (I, 85, l. 80)

Mais li Mors, qui roi, duc ne conte
N'espargne.   (III, 106, l. 12)

Quar perte puet l'on recovrer,
Mais mort ne puet on restorer.   (V, 218, ll. 114 f.)

Boen gesir fait desor notre herbe;
Miauz valt char d'oe o de plovier
Que braon d'asne por mangier:
Nature passe norriture,
Fauseté a morte droiture.   (III, 401, *variant*)

Quar teus paiera nostre escot
Qui de tot ce ne sait or mot.   (VI, 79, ll. 352 f.)

*Par ceste chançon vous puis tesmoignier
Que du petit ueil se fait bon guetier:
Ex oculo pueri noli tua facta tueri.　　　　(II, 30, ll. 187 ff.)

*Par ceste fable moustrer voilg
Que l'en se gart dou petit eulg
Autresinc bien, comme del grant;
De fol et de petit effant
Se fait touz jors mout bon garder,
Car il ne sevent riens celer.　　　　(VI, 151, ll. 114 ff.)

*De cest exanple n'i a mès,
Ne mais itant dire vos voil
Que l'on se gart do petit oil
Et de larron qui est prové,
Car ainz avra assez emblé
Que l'en s'en soit aperceü.　　　　(IV, 149, ll. 63 ff.)

*Segnor, à çou vous en tenés:
Si est mais li siecles menés
Que li fius engigne le pere,
Si n'ert mais jors qui ce ne pere
Ci et aillors, si com je cuit,
Car plus sont li enfant recuit
Que ne sont li viellart barbu,
C'avint au vilain de Farbu.　　　　(IV, 86, ll. 154 ff.)

*Por le siecle fali et vuit,
Qui mal se preuve et est provés
Chaitis en cest siecle est trovés.　　　　(IV, 40, ll. 1175 ff.)

Por recouvrer le tens perdu.　　　　(I, 327, l. 260)

Car hom dit trop plus de la choze
Que on n'i trueve à la parcloze.　　　　(III, 217, ll. 98 f.)

*Dont je trai Chaton à garant
Qui fet l'auctorité parant,
Qui bon clers fu et sages hom:
Turpe est doctori, cum culpa redarguit ipsum.
Chatons dist en cest vers la glose

Que, quant on est repris de chose
C'on a blasmé à fere autrui,
Puis c'on en a blasme et anui,
C'est grant folie qui ce fet.   (V, 260, ll. 547 ff.)

*Por ce deffent à toute gent,
Qui se vantent de maint afere
Dont il ne sevent à chief trere,
Qu'il lessent ester lor vantance:
Et je vous di bien sanz faillance,
Quant il s'en vantent, c'est folie.   (IV, 66, ll. 291 ff.)

Mès cuers qui gist en la viellèce
Ne pensse pas à la jonèce
Ne au voloir de jone éage;
Grant difference a el corage
De viel au jone, ce m'est vis.   (I, 37, ll. 391 ff.)

Huet, cil ne gaaingne mie
Qui fait conquest par vilonnie.   (VI, 177, ll. 17 f.)

Quar vilain vient de vilonie.   (I, 268, l. 407)

Moult dit bien voir qui ce retret:
Qui vilain fet honor ne bien,
Celui het-il sor toute rien;
Tel loier a qui ce encharge.   (I, 268, ll. 392 ff.)

Communement dient entre els:
"Marchéandise a devorée
Li vin, qui lor art la corée."   (II, 141, ll. 51 ff.)

Doit bien vivre qui si bien emble.   (IV, 95, l. 103)

*Vous qui oez
Cestui conte, entendre poez
Que li voir gas ne valent rien.   (III, 251, ll. 146 ff.)

*Qui moult savoit de la chevance,
Quar apris l'avoit de s'enfance;
S'ele n'éust besoing éu,
Ele n'éust jamès séu
Le grant besoin de sa voisine.   (I, 131, ll. 145 ff.)

APPENDIX C

PROVERBIAL MATERIAL IN GOWER'S ENGLISH AND FRENCH WORKS

THE following quotations are from G. C. Macaulay's edition of Gower's works. Numbers in brackets refer to G. Walz, *Das Sprichwort bei Gower*, Nördlingen, 1907.

I

PROVERBIAL PHRASES AND SENTENTIOUS REMARKS FROM THE *CONFESSIO AMANTIS*

PROVERBIAL COMPARISONS

Al specheles and on the gras Sche glod forth as an Addre doth.	(v, 3966 f.)
And lich an Angel sang withal.	(viii, 1671)
Singende he harpeth forth withal, That as a vois celestial Hem thoghte it souneth in here Ere, As thogh that he an Angel were.	(viii, 779 ff.)
Bot as Baiard the blinde stede, Til he falle in the dich amidde, He goth ther noman wole him bidde; He stant so ferforth out of reule, Ther is no wit that mai him reule.	(vi, 1280 ff.)
For as it semeth that a belle Lik to the wordes that men telle Answerth.	(i, 1949 [40a])

Ther mai nothing his tunge daunte,
That he ne clappeth as a Belle.   (i, 2390 f. [40b])

And clappe it out as doth a belle.   (v, 4640 [40c])

Withoute soun as doth the belle,
Which hath no claper forto chyme.   (iv, 346 f.)

That he ne roreth lich a Bere.   (ii, 160)

Noght as a man bot as a beste,
Which goth upon his lustes wilde.   (i, 1240 f.)

And as it were a wilde beste,
The whom no reson mihte areste,
He ran Ethna the hell aboute.   (ii, 161 ff.)

And thus lich to a beste wod
Thei knowe noght the god of lif.   (iii, 1106 f.)

Lich to these othre bestes die.   (iii, 2476)

And take lust as doth a beste.   (viii, 2025)

And thanne he scheweth his tempeste
Mor sodein than the wilde beste.   (iii, 861 f.)

Whan he is worse than a beste.   (iii, 2598)

And lived worse than a beste,
Whom Pite myhte noght areste.   (vii, 3491 f.)

Ther was no beste which goth oute
More wylde than sche semeth ther.   (v, 4080 f.)

Into his bath he wente anon
And wyssh him clene as eny bon.   (v, 3805 f.)

Lich to the chaced wylde bor,
The houndes whan he fieleth sor,
Tothroweth and goth forth his weie,
In such a wise forto seie
This worthi kniht with swerd on honde
His weie made.   (vii, 5255 ff.)

Bot as a bridd which were in Mue
Withinne a buissh sche kepte hire clos.   (iii, 1412 f.)

Mor jolif than the brid in Maii
He makth him evere freissh and gay.   (i, 2703 f.)

Bot as a cock among the Hennes,
Or as a Stalon in the Fennes,
Which goth amonges al the Stod,
Riht so can he nomore good,
Bot takth what thing comth next to honde.   (viii, 159 ff.)

With fetheres blake as eny cole.   (v, 6204)

Evere afterward colblak therfore.   (iii, 808)

And also siker as the crede.   (v, 2912)

The beaute of hire face schon
Wel bryhtere þan þe Cristall ston.   (iv, 1321 f. [*MS* A])

With that the water in hire yhe
Aros, that sche ne myhte it stoppe,
And as men sen the dew bedroppe
The leves and the floures eke,
Riht so upon hire whyte cheke
The wofull salte teres felle.   (vii, 4830 ff.)

For as an Egle with his winges
Fleth above alle that men finde,
So doth this science in his kinde.   (vii, 630 ff.)

And wax so ferforth womannyssh,
That ayein kinde, as if a fissh
Abide wolde upon the lond.   (vii, 4321 ff.)

He seth hire face of such colour,
That freisshere is than eny flour.   (vi, 767 f.)

As he which is the worldes ẙe,
Thurgh whom the lusti compaignie
Of foules be the morwe singe.   (vii, 805 ff.)

Thin entre lich the fox was slyh.   (ii, 3033)

He routeth with a slepi noise,
And brustleth as a monkes froise,
Whanne it is throwe into the Panne.   (iv, 2731 ff.)

And lich the fyr which tunder hente,
In such a rage, as seith the bok,
His Moder sodeinliche he tok.   (ii, 1274 ff.)

            thi desir,
Thogh it brenne evere as doth the fyr.   (v, 5211 f.)

          a gret desir,
The which is hotere than the fyr.   (vi, 209 f.)

Hire herte is hot as eny fyr.   (viii, 846)

And as a man the blase of fyr
With water quencheth, so ferd I.   (viii, 2444 f.)

          and as a fyre
Which fleth out of a myhti bowe,
Aweie he fledde.   (ii, 150 ff.)

That other biter as the galle.   (vi, 341)

So that I brenne as doth a glede
For Wrathe.   (iii, 39 f.)

Bot lay oppressed and desesed,
As if a goshauk hadde sesed
A brid, which dorste noght for fere
Remue.   (v, 5643 ff.)

Thei fledde, as doth the wylde Hare.   (vii, 3776)

Awey he skulketh as an hare.   (iv, 2720)

That lich an hound he scholde die.   (ii, 1858)

Thi deth was to the houndes like.   (ii, 3037)

Ther is a vice of Prides lore,
Which lich an hauk whan he wol sore,
Fleith upon heihte in his delices.   (i, 2671 ff.)

And thus he loketh on the fleissh,
Riht as an hauk which hath a sihte
Upon the foul, ther he schal lihte.   (v, 7070 ff.)

As povere as Job.   (v, 2505)

For certes ther was nevere keie
Ne frosen ys upon the wal
More inly cold than I am al.   (vi, 244 ff.)

Riht as a Leon in his rage.   (vii, 5240)

Thi regne also with pride on hih
Was lich the Leon in his rage.   (ii, 3034 f.)

Lich to the Leoun in his rage,
Fro whom that alle bestes fle,
Such was the knyht in his degre.   (ii, 2590 ff.)

          as it befalleth,
Of his knyhthode as a Leon
Be to the poeple a champioun.   (vii, 3536 ff.)

And he than as a Lyon wod
With hise unhappi handes stronge
Hire cauhte be the tresses longe.   (v, 5684 ff.)

And goth rampende as a leoun.   (vii, 2573)

This Tereüs be Progne his wif
A Sone hath, which as his lif
He loveth.   (v, 5885 ff.)

And seith, "So siker as the lif,
A god hath leie be thi wif.   (vi, 2163 f.)

That lich a Lomb whanne it is sesed
In wolves mouth, so was desesed
Lucrece.   (vii, 4983 ff.)

And lich unto the freisshe Maii,
Whan passed ben the colde schoures,
Riht so recovereth he his floures.   (v, 4172 ff.)

That lich unto the fresshe Maii,
Which othre monthes of the yeer
Surmonteth, so withoute pier
Was of this Maiden the feture.   (v, 6736 ff.)

For as the Netle which up renneth
The freisshe rede Roses brenneth
And makth hem fade and pale of hewe.   (ii, 401 ff.)

He stalketh as a Pocok doth.   (v, 6498)

With his brocours, that renne aboute
Lich unto racches in a route.   (v, 4387 f.)

A Peire of Bedes blak as Sable.   (viii, 2904)

          I sih also
The noble peple of Irahel
Dispers as Schep upon an hell.   (vii, 2656 ff.)

Whanne he is falle in such a drem,
Riht as a Schip ayein the Strem,
He routeth with a slepi noise.   (iv, 2729 ff.)

I wode as doth the wylde Se.   (iii, 86)

Sche passeth, as it were a Sky,
Al clene out of this ladi sihte.   (iv, 1436 f.)

Hire chekes ben with teres wet,
And rivelen as an emty skyn.   (i, 1680 f.)

That it (*Treason*) nys lich the Sparke fyred
Up in the Rof, which for a throwe
Lith hidd, til whan the wyndes blowe
It blaseth out on every side.   (ii, 2946 ff.)

That ther he was snow whyt tofore.   (iii, 807)

And as a bussh which is besnewed,
Here berdes weren hore and whyte.   (i, 2044 f.)

Or as a Stalon in the Fennes,
Which goth amonges al the Stod,
Riht so can he nomore good,
Bot takth what thing comth next to honde.   (viii, 160 ff.)

For thei were trewe as eny stiel.	(vi, 1814)
And he lay ded as eny ston.	(ii, 2741)
And he lay stille as eny ston.	(i, 1794)
The king stod stille as eny ston.	(i, 2104)
Wherof swounende ded for fere Sche was, and stille as eny Ston.	(ii, 846 f.)
Thus is he commun as the Strete.	(v, 2497)
Welmore whyt than eny Swan.	(iii, 797)
The servantz lich to drunke Swyn Begunne forto route faste.	(v, 6894 f.)
His frendly speches he affaiteth, And as the Tigre his time awaiteth In hope forto cacche his preie.	(vii, 4943 ff.)
For lich unto the greene tree, If that men toke his rote aweie, Riht so myn herte scholde deie, If that mi love be withdrawe.	(iv, 2680 ff.)
Which wepte as sche to water scholde.	(vii, 5018)
With teres, whiche, as of a welle The stremes, from hire yhen felle.	(iv, 839 f.)
Riht as men sen a welle springe, With yhen fulle of wofull teres, . . . Sche wepte.	(vii, 5004–5007)
And in a rage on hire he ran, Riht as a wolf which takth his preie.	(v, 5632 f.)
Bot lich to wolle is evele sponne, Who lest himself hath litel wonne.	(vi, 2381 f.)
Bot lich unto the wollesak Sche proferth hire unto this knyht.	(i, 1692 f.)

For as the wilde wode rage
Of wyndes makth the See salvage,
And that was calm bringth into wawe,
So for defalte of grace and lawe
This poeple is stered al at ones
And forth thei gon out of hise wones.   (vii, 4111 ff.)

OTHER PROVERBIAL PHRASES

And ek so lowde his belle is runge.   (iii, 452)

He wol ayeinward take a bene,
Ther he hath lent the smale pese.   (v, 4408 f.)

Prophetes false manye mo
To bere up oil, and alle tho
Affermen that which he hath told.   (vii, 2583 ff.)

Bot holden up his oil and sein
That al is wel, what evere he doth.   (vii, 2194 f.)

What he mai gete of his Michinge,
It is al bile under the winge.
          (v, 6525 f. [286] [cf. Notes, III, 508])

Of feigned wordes make him wene
That blak is whyt and blew is grene.   (vii, 2187 f.)

Therof the Jelous takth non hiede,
Bot as a man to love unkinde,
He cast his staf, as doth the blinde,
And fint defaulte where is non.   (v, 534 ff.)

Thanne was I furthest ate laste,
And as a foll my bowe unbende.   (i, 1966 f.)

And is that selve of whom men speke,
Which wol noght bowe er that he breke.   (i, 1247 f. [56a])

Bot he mai nevere longe laste,
Which wol noght bowe er that he breke.   (iii, 620 f. [56b])

And whan thei come were anon
Among thebreus, was non insihte,
Bot cacche who that cacche myhte.   (vii, 4420 ff.)

The chaf is take for the corn,
As forto speke of Romes myht.   (Pr 844 f.)

And bringe chaf and take corn.   (ii, 2127)

        It were a schort beyete
To winne chaf and lese whete.   (iv, 1709 f.)

Lo, how thei feignen chalk for chese.   (Pr 416 [282b])

And thus fulofte chalk for chese
He changeth with ful litel cost.   (ii, 2346 f. [282a])

Thus was the king withoute rodd
Chastised, and the queene excused
Of that sche hadde ben accused.   (vi, 2216 ff.)

And as who seith, upon the bridel
I chiewe.   (vi, 929 f.)

For al is bot a chirie feire
This worldes good, so as thei telle.   (Pr 454 f.)

And that endureth bot a throwe,
Riht as it were a cherie feste.   (vi, 890 f.)

For sparinge of a litel cost
Fulofte time a man hath lost
The large cote for the hod.   (v, 4785 ff. [68])

And thus the Cote for the hod
Largesse takth, and yit no Sinne
He doth, hou so that evere he winne.   (v, 7716 ff. [22])

   the tresor of Cresus
And al the gold Octovien.   (v, 4730 f. [264])

Now stant the crop under the rote.   (Pr 118)

Thus drinke I in myn oghne swot.   (i, 1390)

He takth, he kepth, he halt, he bint,
That lihtere is to fle the flint
Than gete of him in hard or neisshe
Only the value of a reysshe
Of good in helpinge of an other.   (v, 4691 ff. [100])

And thus the nyce reverence
Of foles, whan that he was ded,
The fot hath torned to the hed,
And clepen him god of nature.   (v, 1038 ff.)

And forth withal anon fot hot
He stal the Cow.   (iv, 3350 f.)

And so he wol his time borwe,
And wissheth after "God me sende."   (iv, 10 f.)

So was ther guile under the gore.   (v, 5730)

So that the heiere hond he hadde.   (vi, 404)

So what with hepe and what with crok
Thei make here maister ofte winne.   (v, 2872 f.)

So that I fiele and wel I wot,
Al is to hevy and to hot
To sette on hond withoute leve.   (v, 6599 ff.)

Upon the hond to were a Schoo
And sette upon the fot a Glove
Acordeth noght to the behove
Of resonable mannes us.   (Pr 356 ff.)

To sen a man fro his astat
Thurgh his sotie effeminat,
And leve that a man schal do,
It is as Hose above the Scho,
To man which oghte noght ben used.   (vii, 4303 ff.)

          for in an houre
He lest al that he mai laboure
The longe yer.   (iv, 969 ff.)

And so to me nys worth a kerse.   (iii, 588)

To hasten is noght worth a kerse.   (iii, 1652)

Bot Slowthe mai no profit winne,
Bot he mai singe in his karole
How Latewar cam to the Dole,
Wher he no good receive mihte.   (iv, 250 ff.)

The more I am redy to wraththe,
That for the touchinge of a laththe . . .
I wode.   (iii, 83–86)

So that myn happ and al myn hele
Me thenkth is ay the leng the ferre.   (iii, 70 f.)

And thus, as I have seid aforn,
I licke hony on the thorn.   (vi, 927 f.)

And I bod in the place stille,
And was there bot a litel while,
Noght full the montance of a Mile.   (viii, 2310 ff.)

And riht so ther ben manye of these
Lovers, that thogh thei love a lyte,
That scarsly wolde it weie a myte,
Yit wolde thei have a pound again,
As doth Usure in his bargain.   (v, 4410 ff.)

Riht so can he nomore good,
Bot takth what thing comth next to honde.   (viii, 162 f.)

Bot al nys worth a note schale.   (iv, 566)

For loves lust and lockes hore
In chambre acorden neveremore,
And thogh thou feigne a yong corage,
It scheweth wel be the visage
That olde grisel is no fole.   (viii, 2403 ff.)

Thus, for I stonde in such a wer,
I am, as who seith, out of herre.   (iii, 1148 f.)

Of yonge men the lusti route
Were of this tale glad ynowh,
Ther was no care for the plowh.   (iii, 1792 ff.)

I wot and have it wel conceived,
Hou that thi will is good ynowh;
Bot mor behoveth to the plowh,
Wherof the lacketh, as I trowe.   (viii, 2424 ff.)

And thus myn hand ayein the pricke
I hurte and have do many day.   (iii, 116 f. [62b])

Venus, which stant withoute lawe
In noncertein, bot as men drawe
Of Rageman upon the chance.   (viii, 2377 ff.)

Thogh it availe hem noght a reisshe.   (ii, 42)

I sette slep noght at a risshe.   (iv, 2853)

Than gete of him in hard or neisshe
Only the value of a reysshe.   (v, 4693 f.)

Bot Nestor, which was old and hor,
The salve sih tofore the sor,
As he that was of conseil wys.   (iii, 1801 ff.)

I am tormented in mi slep,
Bot that I dreme is noght of schep;
For I ne thenke noght on wulle.   (iv, 2893 ff.)

           sevene yer.   (i, 2922, 2991)

           sevene wynter age.   (ii, 3207)

           sevene yeres.   (iv, 239)

Tuo tonnes fulle of love drinke,
That maken many an herte sinke
And many an herte also to flete,
Or of the soure or of the swete.   (vi, 333 ff.)

Betre is to flete than to sincke.   (iii, 1628)

Now schalt thou singe an other song.   (ii, 3012)

He seide to me softe and faire.   (i, 232)

It takth ayein, bot softe and faire,
If eny thing stond in contraire.   (i, 3415 f.)

Bot he spak evere softe and faire.   (iii, 652)

      her flyht begonne
Out of the prison faire and softe.   (iv, 1058 f.)

      faire and softe
He goth now doun nou up fulofte.   (vi, 1195 f.)

To speke his wordes softe and faire.   (vii, 786)

Thus have I told thee softe and faire.   (vii, 3234*)

Thei setten upon thilke dede,
And spille more than thei spede.   (iv, 2585 f.)

I sette it at nomore acompte
Than wolde a bare straw amonte.   (v, 4735 f.)

For al ne sette I at a stre.   (iv, 1716)

And seith that such an Housebonde
Was to a wif noght worth a Stre.   (iii, 666 f.)

So is it all noght worth a Stree.   (iii, 2538)

      al nere it worth a stre.   (v, 997)

The more I am redy to wraththe,
That for . . .
. . . the torninge of a stree
I wode.   (iii, 83 ff.)

Delicacie his swete toth
Hath fostred.   (Pr 325 f.)

Full manye of suche nou aday
That taken wher thei take may.   (viii, 151 f.)

Hire thombe sche holt in hire fest
So clos withinne hire oghne hond,
That there winneth noman lond.   (ii, 468 ff.)

Thus he, whom gold hath overset,
Was trapped in his oghne net.   (v, 2707 f.)

And in a twinclinge of an yhe.   (v, 5935)

And in a twinklinge of a lok.   (i, 3033 f.)

That al nys worth an yvy lef.   (iv, 586)

He wolde make a womman wene
To gon upon the faire grene,
Whan that sche falleth in the Mir.   (i, 681 ff.)

And evere goth the whiel aboute.   (Pr 561 [207d])

Mi world stod on an other whiel.   (i, 178)

And make unto miself a whippe.   (iii, 120 [63])

Me were levere be fortrode
With wilde hors and be todrawe,
Er I ayein love and his lawe
Dede eny thing or loude or stille.   (v, 6054 ff.)

Al is peril that he schal seie,
Him thenkth the wolf is in the weie.   (iv, 327 f.)

Thanne is he wys after the hond.   (iv, 893)

And of an ynche a large spanne
Be colour of the pees thei made.   (i, 1112 f.)

SENTENTIOUS REMARKS

Thing that a man mai noght achieve,
That mai noght wel be don at Eve,
It mot abide til the morwe.   (iii, 1653 ff.)

          and thus I finde
That he that scholde go behinde,
Goth many a time ferr tofore.   (iv, 1737 ff.)

For who that loketh al tofore
And wol noght se what is behinde,
He mai fulofte hise harmes finde.   (v, 7350 ff.)

For every man hise oghne werkes
Schal bere.   (Pr 491 [191a])

Bot whanne he berth lowest the Seil,
Thanne is he swiftest to beguile
The womman, which that ilke while
Set upon him feith or credence. (i, 704 ff.)

These olde Philosophres wise
Thei writen upon thilke while,
That he mai best a man beguile
In whom the man hath most credence. (ii, 2674 ff.)

For who so wol an other blame,
He secheth ofte his oghne schame. (ii, 579 f. [108])

And as the blinde an other ledeth
And til thei falle nothing dredeth,
Riht so thei hadde non insihte;
Bot as the bridd which wol alihte
And seth the mete and noght the net,
Which in deceipte of him is set,
This yonge folk no peril sihe. (iii, 179 ff.)

That he wiste of himself no bote,
It halp him nothing forto mote
To gete ayein that he hath lore. (viii, 639 ff.)

For who is bounden, he mot bowe. (ii, 540)

And thus of that thei brewe soure
I drinke swete, and am wel esed
Of that I wot thei ben desesed. (ii, 246 ff.)

Men sein that trouthe hath broke his bond
And with brocage is goon aweie. (viii, 3032 f. [289])

To caste water in the fyr
Betre is than brenne up al the hous. (iii, 1632 f.)

Bot who that takth or gret or smal,
He takth a charge forth withal,
And stant noght fre til it be quit. (v, 7727 ff. [24])

Betre is upon the bridel chiewe
Thanne if he felle and overthrewe,
The hors and stikede in the Myr. (iii, 1629 ff.)

That every thing which he can telle,
It springeth up as doth a welle,
Which mai non of his stremes hyde,
Bot renneth out on every syde.
So buillen up the foule sawes
That Cheste wot of his felawes:
For as a Sive kepeth Ale,
Riht so can Cheste kepe a tale.   (iii, 427 ff.)

If so be that a king forsueie,
Fulofte er this it hath be sein,
The comun poeple is overlein
And hath the kinges Senne aboght.   (vii, 3928 ff. [242a])

For good consail is good to hiere.   (Pr 156)

For conseil passeth alle thing
To him which thenkth to ben a king.   (viii, 2109 f.)

For who that can no conseil hyde,
He mai noght faile of wo beside,
Which schal befalle er he it wite,
As I finde in the bokes write.   (iii, 727 ff.)

For if a man himself excite
To drenche, and wol it noght forbere,
The water schal no blame bere.
What mai the gold, thogh men coveite?   (vii, 4276 ff.)

Bot hou so that the dai be long,
The derke nyht comth ate laste.   (vi, 578 f.)

For al schal deie and al schal passe,
Als well a Leoun as an asse,
Als wel a beggere as a lord,
Towardes deth in on acord
Thei schullen stonde.   (i, 2247 ff. [154])

Althogh ther be diverse weie
To deth, yit is ther bot on ende,
To which that every man schal wende,
Als wel the beggere as the lord.   (iv, 2246 ff.)

For whan a thing is do for doute,
Fulofte it comth the worse aboute.   (vii, 3157 f.)

For lord and knave al is o weie,
Whan thei be bore and whan thei deie.   (v, 201 f.)

The povere is bore as is the riche
And deieth in the same wise,
Upon the fol, upon the wise
Siknesse and hele entrecomune.   (ii, 3246 ff. [153])

For ofte a man mai se this yit,
That who best doth, lest thonk schal have.   (v, 2264 f.)

And ek he tok a remembrance
How he that made lawe of kinde
Wolde every man to lawe binde,
And bad a man, such as he wolde
Toward himself, riht such he scholde
Toward an other don also.   (ii, 3274 ff.)

He drinkth the bitre with the swete,
He medleth sorwe with likynge,
And liveth, as who seith, deyinge.   (i, 1708 ff.)

Ther wol noman drinke of tho welles
Whiche as he wot is puyson inne.   (ii, 564 f.)

Men sein ther is non evidence,
Wherof to knowe a difference
Betwen the drunken and the wode,
For thei be nevere nouther goode;
For wher that wyn doth wit aweie,
Wisdom hath lost the rihte weie,
That he no maner vice dredeth;
Nomore than a blind man thredeth
His nedle by the Sonnes lyht.   (vi, 551 ff.)

He bad hem, if thei wolde winne,
They scholden se, er thei beginne,
Here ende, and sette here ferste entente,
That thei hem after ne repente.   (iii, 1811 ff.)

Senec witnesseth openly
How that Envie proprely
Is of the Court the comun wenche.

(ii, 3095 ff. [cf. Notes, II, 491])

And worldes ese, as it is told,
Be weie of kinde is the norrice
Of every lust which toucheth vice. (vii, 4384 ff. [74a])

Betwen the tuo extremites
Of vice stant the propretes
Of vertu. (v, 7641 ff. [90a])

Fair speche hath ofte brought above
Ful many a man, as it is knowe. (iii, 604 f.)

And fell so, as it scholde be. (iii, 1348 [133e])

All that schal be mot falle algate. (vi, 1613 [133b])

Al that schal falle, falle schal. (viii, 1172 [133a])

Thus fell the thing which falle scholde. (vi, 2093 [133c])

And as it scholde so betyde. (vi, 995 [133d])

Mai noman fle that schal betide. (ii, 2860 [205a])

So soffre thei that nedes mote. (Pr 698)

Bot whanne a man hath welthe at wille,
The fleissh is frele and falleth ofte. (viii, 288 f.)

Fortune stant no while stille. (Pr 563 [209a])

Bot fortune is of such a sleyhte,
That whan a man is most on heyhte,
Sche makth him rathest forto falle:
Ther wot noman what schal befalle. (vi, 1509 f. [210])

Bot al that myhte him noght availe,
For whom fortune wole assaile,
Ther mai be non such resistence,
Which mihte make a man defence. (vi, 1609 ff.)

Fortune mai noght stonde alway.   (vii, 2393 [209b])

The whiel per chance an other day
Mai torne.   (vii, 2394 f. [207e])

Fortune hath evere be muable
And mai no while stonde stable:
For now it hiheth, now it loweth,
Now stant upriht, now overthroweth,
Now full of blisse and now of bale.   (viii, 585 ff. [209c])

Fro this day forth fortune hath sworn
To sette him upward on the whiel;
So goth the world, now wo, now wel.   (viii, 1736 ff.)

That which was whilom grene gras,
Is welked hey at time now.   (viii, 2436 f.)

The corn is torned into gras,
That was a Rose is thanne a thorn,
And he that was a Lomb beforn
Is thanne a Wolf.   (i, 602 ff.)

Now hier now ther, now to now fro,
Now up now down, this world goth so.   (Pr 569 f.)

That erst was hete is thanne chele.   (viii, 2857)

For every joie bodily
Schal ende in wo.   (v, 193 f. [231a])

Which endeth al his joie in wo.   (vi, 1781)

It is a sori lust to lyke,
Whos ende makth a man to syke
And torneth joies into sorwe.   (vii, 4461 ff.)

Of every lust thende is a peine,
And every peine is good to fle.   (viii, 2096 f. [231b])

For men sen ofte time falle
Thing which men wende siker stonde.   (vii, 2390 f.)

So that al one he falleth ofte,
Whan he best weneth stonde alofte.   (v, 4705 f.)

The See now ebbeth, now it floweth,
The lond now welketh, now it groweth,
Now be the Trees with leves grene,
Now thei be bare and nothing sene,
Now be the lusti somer floures,
Now be the stormy wynter shoures,
Now be the daies, now the nyhtes,
So stant ther nothing al upryhtes,
Now it is lyht, now it is derk;
And thus stant al the worldes werk
After the disposicioun
Of man and his condicioun.   (Pr 933 ff.)

I se the world stonde evere upon eschange,
Nou wyndes loude, and nou the weder softe;
I mai sen ek the grete mone change,
And thing which nou is lowe is eft alofte;
The dredfull werres into pes fulofte
Thei torne.   (viii, 2259 ff.)

For what thing stant on aventure,
That can no worldes creature
Telle in certein hou it schal wende,
Til he therof mai sen an ende.   (v, 7817 ff.)

And natheles he that is riche
This dai, tomorwe he mai be povere;
And in contraire also recovere
A povere man to gret richesse
Men sen.   (iii, 2398 ff.)

Thus was he slain that whilom slowh,
And he which riche was ynowh
This dai, tomorwe he hadde noght.   (iii, 2461 ff.)

Fulofte and thus the swete soureth,
Whan it is knowe to the tast.   (i, 1190 f.)

That erst was swete is thanne sour.   (vi, 1127)

Right now the hyhe wyndes blowe,
And anon after thei ben lowe,
Now clowdy and now clier it is.   (Pr 923 ff.)

Bot wel is him whom god wol helpe.   (v, 2426 [197])

That god wol save mai noght spille.   (viii, 1160 [196b])

      He is riche and wel bego,
To whom that god wole sende wele.   (v, 2400 f. [193a])

Bot what the hihe god wol spare
It mai for no peril misfare.   (ii, 693 f. [196a])

For it is openliche schewed
That god to hem that ben wel thewed
Hath yove and granted the victoire.   (vii, 3787 ff.)

For Crist himself makth knowleching
That noman may togedre serve
God and the world.   (Pr 860 ff. [199a])

The vice of hem that ben ungoode
Is no reproef unto the goode.   (Pr 489 f.)

Senec conseileth in this wise,
And seith, "Bot if thi good suffise
Unto the liking of thi wille,
Withdrawh thi lust and hold the stille,
And be to thi good sufficant."   (v, 7735 ff.)

He is noght wys that fint him grieved,
And doth so that his grief be more.   (v, 7348 f.)

The happes over mannes hed
Ben honged with a tendre thred.   (vi, 1513 f. [214a])

In harde weies men gon softe,
And er thei clymbe avise hem ofte.   (iii, 1623 f.)

And therof, Sone, I wol thee rede,
Abyd, and haste noght to faste.   (iv, 1776 f. [5b])

To hasten is noght worth a kerse.   (iii, 1652)

I haste and evere I am behinde.   (iv, 290)

Folhaste is cause of mochel wo.   (iii, 1861 [9])

Folhaste doth non avantage,
Bot ofte it set a man behinde
In cause of love.   (iii, 1680 ff. [7b])

                for as men seith,
Whan that a man schal make his feith,
His herte and tunge moste acorde.   (v, 2923 ff.)

Ther sche is maister of the herte,
Sche mot be maister of the good.   (v, 4764 f.)

The fielinge of a mannes Hiele
Mai noght be likned to the Herte.   (viii, 2154 f.)

Fulofte it hath befalle or this
Thurgh hope that was noght certein,
Mi wenyinge hath be set in vein.   (i, 1944 ff. [141])

What man hath hors men yive him hors.   (v, 7719 [14])

Thogh it be noght the houndes kinde
To ete chaf, yit wol he werne
An Oxe which comth to the berne,
Therof to taken eny fode.   (ii, 84 ff. [105])

Thanne is he war, and seith at ende,
"Ha, wolde god I hadde knowe!"   (iv, 898 f.)

Bot know thiself, what so befalle.   (vii, 2389 [50])

Men sein, a man hath knowleching
Save of himself of alle thing.   (vi, 1567 f. [275])

The noble wise Salomon,
Which hadde of every thing insihte,
Seith, "As the briddes to the flihte
Ben made, so the man is bore
To labour."   (iv, 2340 ff. [76])

And yit unto this dai men seith,
A lappewincke hath lore his feith
And is the brid falseste of alle.   (v, 6045 ff.)

And thus betwen tomoche and lyte
Largesce, which is noght to wyte,
Halt evere forth the middel weie.   (v, 7689 ff. [91, 92])

Wher lawe lacketh, errour groweth,
He is noght wys who that ne troweth.   (Pr 511 f.)

Bot lich to wolle is evele sponne,
Who lest himself hath litel wonne.   (vi, 2381 f.)

Betre is to leve, than beginne
Thing which as mai noght ben achieved.   (v, 7346 f. [3])

To take where a man hath leve
Good is, and elles he mot leve.   (iii, 1725 f.)

For al is leveful that hem liketh,
To whom that elles it misliketh.   (v, 7053 f.)

And thus fulofte have I boght
The lie, and drank noght of the wyn.   (iii, 894 f.)

For who so wole his handes lime,
Thei mosten be the more unclene.   (ii, 574 f.)

For love is blind and may noght se.   (i, 47 [170a])

Bot sche which kepth the blinde whel,
Venus.   (i, 2490 f.)

As he (*Love*) is blind himself, riht so
He makth his client blind also.   (iii, 159 f. [172a])

I wot now wel that ye (*Love*) be blinde.   (iii, 1465)

The blinde god . . .
Cupido.   (iv, 1732 f.)

Thus was he (*Love*) blind.   (v, 1417)

                    this blinde Boteler.   (vi, 359)

The boteler which berth the keie
Is blind.   (vi, 453 f.)

Thus love is blind.   (viii, 2104 [170b])

For love, which that blind was evere,
Makth alle his servantz blinde also.   (viii, 2130 f. [172b])

            the blinde god Cupide.   (viii, 2268)

This blinde god.   (viii, 2794)

And seith love is a wofull blisse,
A wisdom which can noman wisse,
A lusti fievere, a wounde softe.   (v, 5993 ff.)

For al such time of love is lore,
And lich unto the bitterswete;
For thogh it thenke a man ferst swete,
He schal wel fielen ate laste
That it is sour and may noght laste.   (viii, 190 ff.)

Wher love is lord of the corage,
Him thenketh longe er that he spede.   (viii, 952 f.)

Who dar do thing which love ne dar?   (vi, 1261)

For love is he which nothing douteth.   (vi, 1266 [179])

For love is everemore in doute.   (v, 3850 [177b])

For evere yit it hath be so,
That love honeste in sondri weie
Profiteth, for it doth aweie
The vice, and as the bokes sein,
It makth curteis of the vilein,
And to the couard hardiesce
It yifth, so that verrai prouesse
Is caused upon loves reule
To him that can manhode reule.   (iv, 2296 ff.)

Bot forto loke of time go,
Hou lust of love excedeth lawe.   (viii, 262 f. [168a])

For Love put reson aweie
And can noght se the righte weie.   (i, 1051 f. [174])

For love, which is unbesein
Of alle reson, as men sein.   (viii, 153 f. [175])

Of love, which doth many a wonder
And many a wys man hath put under.   (Pr 75 f.)

Among the holi bokes wise,
I finde write in such a wise,
"Who loveth noght is hier as ded."   (iv, 2323 ff. [183a])

Who loveth wel, it mai noght misse,
And namely whan ther be tuo
Of on acord, how so it go,
Bot if that thei som weie finde;
For love is evere of such a kinde.   (iii, 1362 ff.)

          and thus this tirant there
Beraft hire such thing as men sein
Mai neveremor be yolde ayein,
And that was the virginite.   (v, 5646 ff.)

And seith, "Who that woll maister be,
He mot be servant to pite."   (ii, 3299 f.)

What man wol noght himself mesure,
Men sen fulofte that mesure
Him hath forsake.   (vii, 2159 ff. [284])

What helpeth it a man have mete,
Wher drinke lacketh on the bord?   (iv, 1718 f.)

Bot for o mis an other mys
Was yolde, and so fulofte it is.   (vi, 2359 f.)

What mai the Mous ayein the Cat?   (iii, 1643)

The more that the nede is hyh,
The more it nedeth to be slyh
To him which hath the nede on honde.   (viii, 2063 ff.)

He that noght hadde noght hath lore.   (iii, 2322)

Whil ther is oyle forto fyre,
The lampe is lyhtly set afyre.   (viii, 2775 f.)

If thou miht gete pacience,
Which is the leche of alle offence,
As tellen ous these olde wise.   (iii, 613 ff.)

Bot so wel halt noman the plowh
That he ne balketh otherwhile.   (iii, 514 f. [39])

       Prodegalite,
Which is the moder of poverte.   (vii, 2162 f. [102])

Forthi to thee nys bot o weie,
In which let reson be thi guide;
For he may sone himself misguide,
That seth noght the peril tofore.   (viii, 2918 ff.)

For al the world ne mai suffise
To will which is noght resonable.   (iii, 2436 f.)

Bot every riot ate laste
Mot nedes falle and mai noght laste.   (v, 7131* f.)

For often times of scarsnesse
It hath be sen, that for the lesse
Is lost the more.   (v, 4777 f.)

In Semblant, as men sein, is guile.   (iii, 1045 [113])

For every service axeth mede.   (vii, 2110 [84a])

Bot every labour axeth why
Of som reward.   (iv, 2023 f. [83])

The mede arist of the servise.   (viii, 2012 [84b])

And ek fulofte a litel Skar
Upon a Banke, er men be war,
Let in the Strem, which with gret peine,
If evere man it schal restreigne.   (Pr 507 ff.)

For Slowthe, which as Moder is
The forthdrawere and the Norrice
To man of many a dredful vice.   (iv, 3380 ff.)

Bot ofte is sen that mochel slowthe,
Whan men ben drunken of the cuppe,
Doth mochel harm, whan fyr is uppe,
Bot if somwho the flamme stanche.   (Pr 342 ff.)

And thus, how evere that thei tale,
The strokes falle upon the smale,
And upon othre that ben grete
Hem lacketh herte forto bete.   (Pr 425 ff.)

The brihte Sonne be the morwe
Beschyneth noght the derke nyht.   (vii, 4464 f.)

Suffrance hath evere be the beste
To wissen him that secheth reste.   (iii, 1639 f.)

Forthi betre is to soffre a throwe
Than be to wilde and overthrowe.   (iii, 1637 f.)

Whan thing is do, ther is no bote,
So suffren thei that suffre mote.   (viii, 339 f.)

A man mai finde of time ago
That many a swevene hath be certein,
Al be it so, that som men sein
That swevenes ben of no credence.   (iv, 2918 ff. [114a])

Bot what Maiden hire esposaile
Wol tarie, whan sche take mai,
Sche schall per chance an other dai
Be let, whan that hire lievest were.   (iv, 1498 ff.)

And everemore he seith, "Tomorwe."   (iv, 9 [75b])

Bot ther mai nothing stonde longe
Which is noght upon trowthe grounded.   (ii, 1752 f. [116])

For trowthe hise wordes wol noght peinte.   (i, 284 [118])

The trouthe, hou so it evere come,
Mai for nothing ben overcome;
It mai wel soffre for a throwe,
Bot ate laste it schal be knowe.   (vii, 1957 ff. [117])

A gentil herte his tunge stilleth,
That it malice non distilleth.   (Pr 61* f.)

Whan venym melleth with the Sucre
And mariage is mad for lucre.   (v, 2833 f.)

Thus hath he wel that wel deserveth.   (viii, 1962)

For ofte schal a womman have
Thing which a man mai noght areche.   (i, 3206 f.)

Word hath beguiled many a man.   (vii, 1564)

Betwen the word and that thei werche
Ther is a full gret difference.   (Pr 450 f.)

The word was lich to the conceite
Withoute semblant of deceite.   (Pr 113 f.)

For every worldes thing is vein.   (Pr 560 [150a])

For Wraththe seide nevere wel.   (iii, 835)

Bot thing which is with wrong begonne
Mai nevere stonde wel at ende;
Wher Pride schal the bowe bende,
He schet fulofte out of the weie.   (ii, 2954 ff.)

And upon this also men sein,
That fro the leese which is plein
Into the breres thei forcacche
Her Orf, for that thei wolden lacche   ·
With such duresce, and so bereve
That schal upon the thornes leve
Of wulle, which the brere hath tore.   (Pr 407 ff.)

For so wys man was nevere non,
Bot if he wel his yhe kepe
And take of fol delit no kepe,
That he with lust nys ofte nome,
Thurgh strengthe of love and overcome.   (i, 440 ff.)

Ther is yit on, which Ydelnesse
Is cleped, and is the Norrice
In mannes kinde of every vice,
Which secheth eases manyfold.   (iv, 1086 ff.)

So that an yhe is as a thief
To love, and doth ful gret meschief.   (i, 319 f.)

Betre is to yive than to take.   (v, 7725 [13a])

Bot as men sein that frele is youthe.   (viii, 834 [266])

II

PROVERBIAL MATERIAL IN GOWER'S FRENCH WORKS

1

MIROUR DE L'OMME

(29, 945 lines extant)

PROVERBS (51)

579 ff.	9307 f. (280)	17257 f. (129)
1725 ff. (64)	9445 ff. (138)	17449 (273)
1782 f. (270)	10427 f.	17555 f. (135)
2219 f. (200)	10959 f. (245)	18013 ff. (247)
4182 (233)	10961 (278)	18599 f.
5395 ff. (80)	11863 f.	18841 f.
5436	12397 ff.	19489 f. (98)
5521 (47)	12725 f. (201a)	20419 ff. (285)
5593 f. (145)	13116 (158)	20827 f. (255a)
5665 ff. (12)	13489 ff. (223)	20963 f.
6357 (128a)	14425 ff. (77b)	21085 f. (112)
6659 f. (122)	14440 ff. (79)	22927 f. (203)
7138 ff. (146)	15499 (16a)	23971 ff.
7969 (52a)	15817 (16b)	24265 (94)
8507 f. (162b)	16117 ff. (1b)	24962 f. (49a)
8836 ff. (288)	16511 f. (271)	25009 ff. (250)
8899 ff.	16532 (16c)	25015 (251)

PROVERBIAL PHRASES

Comparisons (101)

28	1112 ff.	1345 ff.
856 ff.	1132	1405 ff.
1101 ff.	1199	1459 ff.

1563 ff.	6142 f.	11705
1696	6253 ff.	12991 ff.
1981 ff.	6673 f.	13101
2054	6832 ff.	13213 ff.
2261	6842 f.	13428
2266	6886 ff.	13522 ff.
2500 ff.	6916 ff.	14929 ff.
2641 ff.	7057 ff.	15019 ff.
2833 ff.	7078 ff.	15104
2847	7671 ff.	15614 f.
2848	7719 f.	16760 f.
3178 ff.	7729 ff.	18073 ff.
3538 ff.	8158	18343 ff.
3631 ff.	8358 ff.	18346 ff.
3716 f.	8430 f.	18505 ff.
3721 ff.	8667 f.	18762 f.
3820 ff.	8696 ff.	19044
3875 f.	8848	20105 f.
3899 f.	8849	20119
3954	8882	20377 ff.
4147 ff.	8952	20516 f.
4209 f.	8971 ff.	20891 f.
4255 ff.	9253 ff.	21628 f.
4275 f.	9262 ff.	21709 ff.
4434 f.	9543	21725 f.
4784 ff.	9949 ff.	23698
4805 ff.	9955 f.	24153 ff.
4851	11034 f.	24507
5357 f.	11297 f.	25057 ff.
5380 f.	11440	28076 ff.
5502 f.	11528 f.	28478

Other Proverbial Phrases (27)

1944 (279)	4684 ff.	6648
2893 ff.	5605 f. (75a)	7054
3868 ff.	5811 (272)	7237 f. (66)
4162 ff.	6271	7319

8869 ff.	20886 ff.	25302 (282c)
10096 f.	21995	25442
17411 f.	23898	25629
17881 ff.	24632	25645 f.
20314 ff.	25039	27694

SENTENTIOUS REMARKS (123)

1618 ff. (60)	5266 ff. (74c)	12535 ff.
1808 (97)	5437 ff.	12721 ff.
2119 ff. (81)	5455 f. (77a)	12727 ff.
2182	6217 f. (123)	12733 ff.
2353 ff. (62a)	6601 ff.	12781 ff. (42a)
2785 ff. (33)	6757 ff. (96)	13177 ff.
2794 f.	6968 ff.	13485 ff.
3143 f.	7645 f. (274)	13657 ff.
3337 ff. (106a)	7835 f.	13669 ff.
3481 ff.	8029 ff.	13672 f. (38)
3495 ff.	8261 ff.	13684 ff. (110)
3631 ff.	8752 f.	13717 ff. (159)
3773 ff. (104)	8789 (134c)	13803 ff. (183b)
3893 ff.	8917 (134b)	14143 ff.
3913 ff.	9469 ff.	14341 ff. (90b)
4074 ff.	10400 ff.	14353 ff. (87)
4097 (134a)	10558 ff. (220)	14392 ff. (88)
4117 ff. (187)	10941 ff. (207b)	14395 ff.
4141 ff.	10948 ff. (214b)	15109 ff. (147a)
4153 ff. (41)	10969 ff.	15221 f.
4189 ff. (34)	11086 ff.	15277 ff. (51a)
4211 ff. (32a)	11257 ff.	15288 (51b)
4261 ff.	11305 ff.	15313
4366 ff.	11324 ff. (148)	15405 ff. (103a)
4369 ff.	11401 ff. (155)	15533 ff. (48)
4375 ff. (160)	11995 ff.	15656 ff. (157)
4702 ff.	12056 ff. (29)	16021 ff. (198a)
4748 ff.	12517 ff.	16051 f. (125)
4775 f.	12529 ff. (192)	16234 ff.

16315 f.	20125 ff. (216)	23387 f.
16645 ff. (32b)	20401 ff. (73)	23413 ff. (260a)
16669 ff. (42b)	20572 ff.	23450 ff.
16789 ff. (244b)	20626 ff.	23950 (150c)
16942 ff. (262)	20797 ff. (253)	23951 f. (217)
16952 ff.	20936 f.	24229 ff. (287)
17200 ff. (184)	21034 ff.	24260 ff.
17377 ff.	21097 f.	24994 f. (103b)
17394 ff. (186)	21105 ff.	25460 ff.
17617 ff.	22081 ff.	25490 f. (21)
17629 ff. (188)	22101 ff. (207c)	25741 ff.
17653 ff. (189)	22835 f. (241b)	25873 (121)
17941 ff.	22891 ff. (243)	27865 f.
18020 ff. (269)	23113 ff. (218)	27867 (181a)
18179 f.	23185 ff. (107)	28597 ff. (227)
18874 ff.	23338 ff. (120)	

2

BALADES

(1373 lines)

PROVERBS (6)

XVII, 14 (277)	XXIX, 8, 16, 24, 28
XXV, 8, 16, 24, 28 (181b)	XXXIIII, 8, 16, 24, 28
XXVIII, 7, 14, 21, 25 (16d)	XL, 1 (46)

PROVERBIAL PHRASES

Comparisons (12)

VII, 8	XXIII, 22 f.
VIII, 2 f.	XXX, 1 f.
X, 22 f.	XXX, 17
XV, 1 f.	XLIII, 14
XVIII, 11 f.	L, 6
XIX, 23	L, 19 f.

SENTENTIOUS REMARKS (15)

[I], 7, 14, 21, 25 (194)
II, 1 (226a)
II, 8, 16, 24, 28 (229)
XVI, 16
XVIII, 1 f. (86)
XX, 1 (207a)
XX, 9 (234)
XX, 10 (226b)

XXVIII, 20 (84c)
XXIX, 17 f. (11)
XXXV, 7, 14, 21, 25 (185)
XXXVI, 7, 14, 21, 25
XL, 8, 16, 24, 28 (163)
XLVIII, 3 ff.
L, 1 ff.

3

TRAITIÉ

(378 lines)

PROVERBS (2)

VI, 7, 14, 21 (4b)   XV, 7, 14, 21 (52b)

PROVERBIAL PHRASES

Comparisons (3)

IV, 6
V, 5 f.

XVII, 15 f.

SENTENTIOUS REMARKS (7)

III, 19 ff. (169a)
IV, 19 (290)
X, 7, 14, 21
XI, 7, 14, 21

XIV, 7, 14, 21
XIV, 12
XVII, 9 (169b)